THE VALUATION TREADMILL

Public companies now face constant pressure to meet investor expectations. A company must continually deliver strong short-term performance every quarter to maintain its stock price. This valuation treadmill creates incentives for corporations to deceive investors. Published more than twenty years after the passage of Sarbanes–Oxley, which requires all public companies to invest in measures to ensure the accuracy of their disclosures, *The Valuation Treadmill* shows how securities fraud became a major regulatory concern. Drawing on case studies of paradigmatic securities enforcement actions involving Xerox, Penn Central, Apple, Enron, Citigroup, and General Electric, the book argues that corporate securities fraud emerged as investors increasingly valued companies based on their future performance. Corporations now have an incentive to issue unrealistically optimistic disclosures to convince markets that their success will continue. Securities regulation must do more to protect the integrity of public companies from the pressure of the valuation treadmill.

James J. Park is Professor of Law at UCLA School of Law. He writes and teaches in the areas of securities regulation and corporate law. He was an editor of *Can Delaware Be Dethroned? Evaluating Delaware's Dominance of Corporate Law* (with Iman Anabtawi, Stephen Bainbridge, & Sung Hui Kim, 2018).

The Valuation Treadmill

HOW SECURITIES FRAUD THREATENS THE INTEGRITY OF PUBLIC COMPANIES

JAMES J. PARK

University of California, Los Angeles

CAMBRIDGE
UNIVERSITY PRESS

CAMBRIDGE
UNIVERSITY PRESS

University Printing House, Cambridge CB2 8BS, United Kingdom

One Liberty Plaza, 20th Floor, New York, NY 10006, USA

477 Williamstown Road, Port Melbourne, VIC 3207, Australia

314–321, 3rd Floor, Plot 3, Splendor Forum, Jasola District Centre, New Delhi – 110025, India

103 Penang Road, #05–06/07, Visioncrest Commercial, Singapore 238467

Cambridge University Press is part of the University of Cambridge.

It furthers the University's mission by disseminating knowledge in the pursuit of education, learning, and research at the highest international levels of excellence.

www.cambridge.org
Information on this title: www.cambridge.org/9781108837187
DOI: 10.1017/9781108938556

First published 2022

A catalogue record for this publication is available from the British Library.

Library of Congress Cataloging-in-Publication Data
NAMES: Park, James, 1975- author.
TITLE: The valuation treadmill : how securities fraud threatens the integrity of public companies / James J. Park, University of California, Los Angeles.
DESCRIPTION: Cambridge, United Kingdom ; New York, NY : Cambridge University Press, 2022. | Includes bibliographical references and index.
IDENTIFIERS: LCCN 2021053368 (print) | LCCN 2021053369 (ebook) | ISBN 9781108837187 (hardback) | ISBN 9781108940412 (paperback) | ISBN 9781108938556 (epub)
SUBJECTS: LCSH: Securities fraud. | Securities–Valuation. | Corporations.
CLASSIFICATION: LCC HV6765 .P37 2022 (print) | LCC HV6765 (ebook) | DDC 364.16/8–dc23/eng/20220105
LC record available at https://lccn.loc.gov/2021053368
LC ebook record available at https://lccn.loc.gov/2021053369

ISBN 978-1-108-83718-7 Hardback
ISBN 978-1-108-94041-2 Paperback

For Nellie, Josephine, and Lydia

Contents

Acknowledgments

This book reflects almost twenty years of work on the subject of securities fraud. I started as a practicing lawyer a few months after Congress passed the Sarbanes–Oxley Act. I worked on securities fraud cases in private practice and government and then had the opportunity to study securities fraud regulation more systematically when I became a law professor.

At an early stage of this project, I received excellent feedback and encouragement at a roundtable discussion held during a University of California, Los Angeles (UCLA) School of Law faculty retreat. Thank you to Iman Anabtawi, Stephen Bainbridge, Steve Bank, Dean Jennifer Mnookin, and Joanna Schwartz for that exchange.

Thank you to the many colleagues who provided feedback on parts of the book at various times. An incomplete list of this group includes Stuart Banner, Ilya Beylin, Brian Cheffins, Jessica Erickson, Robert Feldman, Joel Feuer, Brandon Garrett, Jonathan Glater, John Hueston, Arthur Laby, Donald Langevoort, Ann Lipton, Jon Michaels, Frank Partnoy, Michael Perino, Laura Posner, John Power, Joel Seligman, David Stuart, Randall Thomas, Andrew Tuch, Lynn Turner, Andy Vollmer, David Webber, Verity Winship, and David Zaring.

I benefited from the opportunity to present various chapters at several UCLA seminars; Brooklyn Law School; the 2021 Business Law Scholars Conference; the 2020 Corporate and Securities Litigation Workshop; the Southern California Business Law Workshop; Vanderbilt Law School; and Washington University School of Law.

Numerous research assistants at UCLA School of Law provided excellent assistance. Thank you to Matthew Brodsky, Alan Jiang, Vincent Liu, Jaime Maier, Flinn Milligan, Austin Reid, Kelvin Sun, and Chaliz Taghdis.

The UCLA School of Law library led by Kevin Gerson provided excellent research assistance. Thank you to Rachel Green, Caitlin Hunter, Jodi Kruger, Jenny Lentz, Lynn McClelland, and many others on the library staff.

My mentor, Judge Robert Katzmann, passed away suddenly about a week before I turned in this book's manuscript. Without his guidance and support, I would never have become a law professor. Thank you Judge.

Finally, this book would not have been possible without the support of my family. Thank you to my parents, who gave me the love, faith, and freedom that allowed me to pursue my dreams. Thank you to my wife, Nellie, who read every word of the manuscript and supports me in every way. Josephine and Lydia, you bring great joy to our lives and I hope that you will be interested in reading this book someday.

1

Introduction

At some point, it becomes almost impossible for management to deliver on accelerating expectations without faltering, just as anyone would eventually stumble on a treadmill that keeps moving faster.

McKinsey & Co., *Valuation: Measuring and Managing the Value of Companies*, 2020

The typical public corporation now runs on a *valuation treadmill*. If its stock is traded widely in public markets, it must take care to keep pace with market expectations. Whether it be through developing transformative new products or consistently meeting quarterly financial projections, a public company must continually convince investors that it will generate profits in future years just to maintain its stock price. If investors become concerned that a company's profitability is declining, they can drastically readjust its valuation.

Some companies respond to this *valuation pressure* by issuing misleading disclosures to obscure the reality that they cannot deliver the short-term results expected by investors. Consider the recent example of Under Armour, a company that makes apparel a runner might wear while on a treadmill.[1] For twenty-six consecutive quarters, the company met market expectations that its revenue would increase at an annual rate of more than 20 percent. Toward the end of that streak, the company's internal estimates made it clear that it could not continue this extraordinary rate of growth. Instead of acknowledging that it could not meet market revenue projections, the company pulled forward hundreds of millions of dollars in sales by asking its customers to accept early shipment of merchandise they had ordered for delivery the next quarter. The company feared that if the market perceived that its performance was slowing down, even by a little bit, its stock price would decline. Because Under Armour did not disclose its questionable tactics, investors who bought its stock paid too much for it, and the Securities and Exchange

Commission (SEC), the main government enforcer of the securities laws, sanctioned the company.

Federal law prohibits companies like Under Armour from issuing misleading disclosures to investors. To be fraudulent and actionable under Rule 10b-5,[2] the most widely cited prohibition of securities fraud, a misstatement must be motivated by an intent to deceive investors and cannot be just the result of a careless mistake.[3] The law regulating public company securities fraud is relatively new, emerging gradually over the last fifty years. For the first few decades after Congress passed statutes requiring public companies to issue truthful disclosure in the 1930s, securities fraud was viewed as mainly a risk for small companies, especially when they were selling stock to the public for the first time.[4] Such fledgling businesses did not have the resources to ensure that the information they reported was accurate. In contrast, the largest public companies were viewed as so dominant and profitable that they had little need to deceive investors and had the funds to minimize the risk of misstatements.

That is no longer the case. These days, investors bring a Rule 10b-5 lawsuit against a public corporation almost every week, claiming that they were damaged by a securities fraud. There is now an encyclopedic body of judicial decisions that regulates the truth of public company disclosures. Some of the most notorious corporate scandals over the last twenty-five years have involved the violent collapse of a significant public company in the wake of a securities fraud. Since 2002, every sizable public corporation must invest millions of dollars every year to assess whether its internal controls will effectively prevent it from issuing misleading financial statements.

This book explains how securities fraud became one of the main concerns of public company regulation.

One possibility is that as legal avenues for asserting securities fraud claims developed, investors and regulators increasingly filed cases for profit and glory. The federal rules of civil procedure were amended during the 1960s to permit the modern damages class action where every member of the class is part of the lawsuit, absent an affirmative decision to opt out. Plaintiffs took advantage of this new mechanism to aggregate the individual cases of thousands of investors damaged by a securities fraud into a single demand for millions of dollars. Courts developed doctrines under Rule 10b-5 that facilitated the filing of securities class actions against public corporations. The SEC formed a division devoted to enforcement in the early 1970s that began investigating public companies for securities law violations. In 1990, Congress gave the SEC the power to seek penalties for such violations, increasing its ability to punish and deter corporate securities fraud.

But the ability to sue public companies for their alleged misstatements does not completely explain the increasing regulation of public company securities fraud. Through the 1980s and much of the 1990s, the SEC rarely brought securities fraud cases against public companies, leaving enforcement to private plaintiffs. For a time, securities litigation was viewed by critics as advancing questionable theories of fraud and the courts and Congress thus narrowed the scope of securities fraud liability. It was not until relatively recently that securities fraud became viewed as enough of a threat to the integrity of public companies to justify a strong regulatory response.

Another theory is that changing executive compensation packages increased the incentive of corporate managers to commit securities fraud.[5] According to one leading scholar, "[t]he persons most responsible for the accounting irregularities at Enron, WorldCom, and a host of other companies were managers who, beginning in the 1990s, began to be primarily compensated with equity compensation and so had a strong incentive to recognize income prematurely in order to inflate reported income."[6] Under this view, securities fraud is most likely to be caused by rogue executives who act for selfish reasons.

But securities fraud started to emerge as a problem for public companies even before executives were paid mainly with stock. There were significant Rule 10b-5 cases brought against public companies during the 1970s, and by the 1980s, investors routinely filed securities fraud litigation against public companies. Many of the scandals of the late 1990s and early 2000s involved executives who were acting mainly for personal gain, but many involved groups of executives acting in the name of corporate goals. Indeed, during that period, the SEC shifted from mainly penalizing individuals to also penalizing corporate defendants for securities fraud.

This book develops a third explanation for the increasing regulation of public company securities fraud. It argues that securities fraud emerged as a significant risk for public companies as investors changed how they valued stocks. As investors adopted modern valuation models and attempted to develop projections of a corporation's ability to generate earnings into the future, it became more important for public companies to meet market expectations about their short-term performance. Public corporations now have a structural incentive to issue misleading disclosures to create the appearance that their economic prospects are brighter than they really are. Securities fraud regulation developed as valuation pressure incentivized public companies to deceive investors.

SECURITIES FRAUD OVER THE DECADES

The problem of securities fraud has evolved significantly over the decades. Prior to the 1970s, established public companies were unlikely to be viewed as the primary culprit of a securities fraud. Cases challenging the truth of public company disclosures emerged gradually during the 1970s and then became commonplace in the 1980s. Most of these actions were filed by private plaintiffs, but by the end of the 1990s, the SEC increasingly directed its securities fraud enforcement activity at public company defendants.

Some of the major securities frauds around the time of the passage of the securities laws in the 1930s involved corporate entities closely tied to their founders.

One such scandal involved Ivar Krueger, who raised funds from US investors to invest in foreign match monopolies. Law professor Frank Partnoy shows how Krueger relied on the opacity of a complicated corporate structure to mislead investors.[7] Another involved Samuel Insull, the former secretary of Thomas Edison, who was criminally tried for defrauding shareholders in his empire of electric utilities. Insull was accused of using misleading accounting to hide problems at his companies. While both scandals involved deception of public investors to inflate stock valuations, they occurred in a world where disclosure requirements and valuation methods were not as developed and standardized as they later became. Moreover, both frauds were mainly linked to these two individuals rather than to the corporate entities they controlled. Krueger had almost complete control over his companies and freely transferred funds between them. Insull won acquittal based on the argument that he did not personally profit from questionable accounting decisions.[8]

Such schemes were initially viewed as less of a risk in the corporate giants run by professional management teams that dominated the economic landscape after World War II. The corporate executive of the 1950s was an organization man who was part of a structured bureaucracy that relied on uniform processes and procedures to manage a complex organization. With their market power, large corporations generated massive profits on a consistent basis and could invest in research and development that would ensure their continuing dominance. Scholars describe this period of public trust in corporate management as the era of *managerialism*.

The collapse of the railroad conglomerate Penn Central in 1970 helped spark the beginning of a shift where public companies were viewed as responsible for securities fraud. The scandals at Penn Central and Equity Funding (the other major public company securities fraud of the 1970s) were not viewed as solely the responsibility of one or two individuals. In both cases, extensive reports investigated the corporate entity for the issuance of misleading statements that deceived investors.

By the 1980s, a new type of securities fraud allegation emerged. Relatively young companies quickly went public and achieved high market valuations by developing a transformative technology. These entrepreneurial companies did not always have the same structured bureaucracies as the managerialist corporation but could quickly achieve high market valuations based on their prospects for future profits. The fluctuation in the fortunes of these companies frequently prompted securities class actions by private investors. In 1988, the US Supreme Court facilitated the filing of securities class actions against public companies with stock trading in an efficient marketplace. In doing so, it essentially created a heightened duty for large public companies to issue truthful disclosures to public investors. The subsequent increase in securities litigation prompted Congress to pass the Private Securities Litigation Reform Act of 1995 (PSLRA),[9] which imposed procedural restrictions on class actions asserting securities fraud claims.

By the 1990s, large public companies had become nimbler and more bottom-line oriented as they faced foreign and domestic competition. They continually strove to meet market expectations by delivering reliable increases in profits. A significant number of companies violated accounting rules to meet financial projections set by market analysts. Less than a decade after the PSLRA, the securities frauds at major public companies like Enron and WorldCom prompted Congress to pass the Sarbanes–Oxley Act of 2002 (Sarbanes–Oxley), which significantly enhanced the obligation of public companies to invest in measures to prevent material financial misstatements.[10]

VALUATION AND SECURITIES FRAUD

The brief chronology of securities fraud just described ran parallel to significant changes to securities markets and public corporations.[11] During the managerialist period after World War II, the leadership of large companies did not face significant pressure to deliver increasing profits to maintain their stock price. Because of the size and complexity of their businesses, managers were given significant deference by investors who were mostly satisfied with passively owning a stable investment that paid dividends.

This comfortable state of affairs ended as investors increasingly determined the market value of a public company based on its potential for future earnings growth. The present value model that is now commonly used to value assets was known and applied to stocks by the late 1930s. Under this model, the value of any asset is equal to the present value of the cash flows it is expected to generate over time.[12] Assuming that such cash flows can be accurately predicted, calculating the price of an asset is as simple as summing the future cash flows after making appropriate adjustments for the time value of money. In the case of stocks, the cash flows can be dividends, earnings, or some other measure (to simplify matters, this book will focus on earnings). Put another way, the present value model recognizes that investors should value a company based not only on what it owns and earns today but also on what it will earn in the future.

Despite the intuitive appeal of the present value model, many experts were skeptical that markets could develop meaningful predictions of a company's profitability. There were too many uncertainties about corporate performance for investors to do more than guess about the future. The distinction between investment and speculation has always been difficult to define,[13] and extrapolating profits into the future inherently involves some degree of conjecture and guesswork. The experience of the 1920s showed how promises of future performance could drive stock prices up and create a bubble that could quickly collapse.

But as the managers of public companies became more sophisticated, they became better at predicting corporate costs, revenue, and earnings. As businesses grew larger and more complex, it was important to develop forecasts and budgets to monitor and manage the flow of resources within a firm. Corporations such as General Electric, IBM, and JCPenney began setting internal projections for their various divisions to better assess their performance.[14] A survey by the American Management Association found that while in 1951, only about half of its members had a central office that coordinated internal forecasting, in 1956 more than 80 percent had such an office.[15]

Investors also started developing methods to project corporate earnings. The number of research analysts who closely follow and analyze public company stocks increased to serve the growing number of institutions that were investing in stock markets. By the 1960s, the analysts began publishing their own projections of corporate profits for hundreds of public companies. These analyst projections were often informed by corporate forecasts, which were disseminated both publicly and in private meetings with analysts.

Such market projections could be inputted into present value models used by investors to determine how much they would pay for a stock. The actual financial results of a company could be compared to an earlier projection. If a company met the projection, it confirmed the predictions that were the basis for its valuation. If it exceeded the projection, there was an argument that its future performance would be greater than expected and its valuation should be higher. If it missed a projection, investors might reevaluate their predictions of the company's future and its stock price would go down.

As investors increasingly scrutinized the future performance of public companies, the pressure increased on corporate managers to continue delivering short-term results that met market projections. Companies that fell on hard times and could not generate profits had an incentive to hide that information from the market to maintain their stock price.

During the 1980s, many technology companies saw their valuations rise as the market anticipated the economic success of the promising new products they were developing. This optimism was based in part on past successes of companies that had created a new industry for personal computers. If the market learned that the product was a failure, that optimism could quickly reverse and a company's stock price would fall as investors reconsidered their predictions of profits. Companies thus had an incentive to be slow to acknowledge setbacks and difficulties with developing such products. Investors have always been willing to speculate on the prospects of emerging companies, but what was new was that such companies were increasingly judged based on their ability to show that they were on track to meet prior predictions of their performance.

By the 1990s, markets were systematically evaluating public company financial results on a quarterly basis. The projections of different research analysts were compiled, averaged, and published to reflect what the financial journalist Alex Berenson aptly called "the number."[16] It became increasingly important for a public company to meet this quarterly prediction of its revenue and earnings. The pressure to do so created incentives to violate accounting rules to deliver results that would meet market forecasts.

Securities fraud is the natural result of a world where public companies have been pushed to prioritize the maximization of shareholder wealth. Toward the middle of the 1980s, the business school professor Alfred Rappaport linked shareholder wealth maximization and corporate reporting in observing that "the principle that the fundamental objective of the business corporation is to increase the value of its shareholders' investment is widely accepted"; and that "[i]n both corporate reports and the financial press there is an obsessive fixation on earnings per share ... as the scorecard of corporate performance."[7] As investors became more assertive, they were more insistent that companies demonstrate that they were increasing profits. Over time, investors became more oriented on short-term performance in assessing the commitment and ability of public corporations to increase shareholder wealth.[8] As a result, it became important for corporate managers to continually meet market expectations.

In sum, as investors increasingly focused on developing concrete predictions of future performance in valuing stocks, the possibility of securities fraud threatened the integrity of public company valuations. Public companies faced pressure to generate results validating prior predictions of performance. A high valuation must be constantly earned. Any stumble can be magnified if it materially changes investor perceptions of the company's prospects. Some companies resort to securities fraud to manipulate investor perceptions of their earnings potential. If the integrity of public company valuations becomes significantly distorted, investors will no longer trust stock markets. Because stock prices rely so much on assessments of the future, a significant number of frauds can shake confidence in valuations of similar companies or even the entire market.

VALUATION AND SECURITIES FRAUD REGULATION

Because valuation models are what separate stock markets from casinos, it is important to police the integrity of the valuation process. Since valuation pressure affects most public companies, there is a case for structural measures that require them to invest resources to prevent securities fraud. Public company securities fraud is not solely caused by corrupt managers acting to enrich themselves but is often committed by generally ethical corporate managers who issue a misleading portrayal of the corporation as they pursue corporate goals.[19] Statutes such as Sarbanes–Oxley that require investment in ex ante measures to prevent securities fraud are best justified by the need to counteract the valuation pressure exerted by modern stock markets.[20]

Even though there is a case that all companies should be required to prevent securities fraud, it is more difficult to determine how extensive that obligation should be. The fact that there is a systemic risk of securities fraud for public companies does not mean that all or even most public companies will commit securities fraud. Many will resist and navigate the pressure with integrity. Securities regulation should be thoughtful in balancing the costs and benefits of measures to prevent securities fraud.

Moreover, current regulation may not be well-suited to address the pressure on public companies to commit securities fraud. Securities regulation predominantly regulates the accuracy of disclosures relating to the past rather than information that shapes investor perceptions of the future. This tendency was criticized by Homer Kripke as early as the 1970s but has never been completely addressed.[21] Roberta Romano has convincingly shown how Sarbanes–Oxley was passed in a frenzy and enacted recycled proposals raised by policy entrepreneurs.[22] There are thus serious questions about the effectiveness of the law and whether different reforms would have been more efficient.

Another issue is that securities enforcement imposes significant costs on public companies. Because perceptions of future performance can quickly change and affect a company's stock price, there are numerous opportunities to raise credible claims of securities fraud. It is difficult to distinguish cases where corporate managers make mistakes and are genuinely surprised about developments that undermine a rosy narrative and those instances where they actively manipulate perceptions of the future earnings power of a business. Determining whether a company has committed securities fraud often requires judges to make intensive, case-specific inquiries relating to complicated business developments.

The unclear boundaries of securities fraud liability thus generate significant litigation expense. Private enforcers have strong incentives to characterize any mistake by a company as fraudulent. While public enforcers are viewed as more measured and concerned about the public interest, they too have incentives to bring high-profile cases against large corporations. Because the costs of establishing fraudulent intent are so high, securities fraud cases against public companies almost always end in a dismissal or settlement rather than trial. The public is left to guess whether a large settlement reflected a severe fraud or whether the payment was motivated by the economic reality that the costs of litigating a case were too high.

Mindful of these challenges, this book concludes with proposals for improving securities fraud regulation in light of its thesis that valuation pressure is a significant driver of public company securities fraud. Securities law should do more to check the incentive of public companies to distort investor assessments of their future performance but should also take measures to reduce the costs of securities fraud enforcement.

- Public companies should be required to disclose projections of their financial performance as well as the basis for those projections, and an auditor should review the reasonableness of such projections.
- Public companies should have a stronger duty to update projections in light of significant new developments.
- The SEC should do more to preemptively address earnings management to meet market expectations.

- Securities fraud regulation should mainly focus on preventing and deterring misstatements that have a clear impact on the market's assessment of a public company's future performance.
- Courts should recognize that in some cases, the motive to meet market projections is sufficient to establish that a company acted with fraudulent intent.

SIX SECURITIES FRAUDS

Many books have examined individual cases and periods of securities fraud, but no book has looked at securities fraud in public companies from the 1970s through the present. By studying different eras, this book reveals how the problem of securities fraud has changed and how earlier frauds compare and contrast with more recent frauds. Each chapter is anchored by a securities fraud case that is representative of a period. Each chapter also discusses other significant cases and developments during that time. The book begins with the SEC's case against Xerox, which provides a general introduction to the modern valuation treadmill and the basic issues raised by public company securities fraud. The next five chapters proceed chronologically from the 1970s to the present in tracing the evolution of valuation and public company securities fraud.

Xerox: Xerox was the target of one of dozens of accounting fraud investigations brought by the SEC around the early 2000s and was the first public company to pay a substantial SEC penalty for misstating its earnings and allegedly committing securities fraud. By the late 1990s, companies were increasingly under pressure to deliver results that met analyst forecasts of their quarterly earnings. As its core business declined, Xerox violated accounting rules to create the appearance that it was meeting ambitious earnings projections that predicted double digit growth. The Xerox case established that securities fraud was a risk not only for less reputable companies, but for companies with a storied past that previously did not have the need to misrepresent their performance. By penalizing Xerox rather than just its individual executives, the SEC signaled it believed that there was a corporate incentive to commit securities fraud.

Penn Central: The next chapter goes back to the 1970s to examine the early emergence of securities fraud as an issue in public companies. A little more than two years after it was formed through a merger in 1968, the Penn Central railroad filed for bankruptcy. In prior decades, shareholders placed great trust in professional corporate managers to make decisions for large companies. Penn Central shook this faith by showing how the businesses of even the largest conglomerates run by expert managers could fail without warning. Penn Central faced pressure to deliver financial results that showed it could survive the declining profitability of its core railroad business. It used a number of improper measures such as manipulating its accounting through an improper asset sale so that it could report a small profit rather than a loss for a quarter where it had promised significant improvement in its financial performance. While the public was unaware of the extent of Penn Central's problems, insiders and banks exited their shares before the company collapsed, showing how securities fraud can enrich those with privileged access to information. In investigating Penn Central, the SEC for the first time set forth a detailed theory of public company securities fraud. Penn Central was the largest of several accounting frauds uncovered during the 1970s that were motivated by a desire to manipulate market expectations.

Apple: During the 1980s, the technology industry became the primary setting where the issue of corporate securities fraud was debated. Computer companies developed new products with volatile prospects. Investors increasingly valued such companies based on their ability to meet projections. If a company missed market expectations and its stock price fell, private plaintiffs would often accuse it of securities fraud. Courts struggled with the question of when the failure to fulfill optimistic predictions would trigger securities fraud liability. In the mid-1980s, Apple's stock fell by 25 percent upon the announcement that it would discontinue the defective disk drive of its Lisa computer. Investors brought a Rule 10b-5 suit alleging that Apple knew of problems with the drive that made its optimistic predictions of success for the Lisa misleading. In May 1991, a jury found two executives of Apple Computer liable for $100 million in losses suffered by purchasers of Apple stock. As securities class actions were increasingly filed against companies that failed to meet a projection, critics argued that such suits were meritless. In 1995, Congress responded by passing the PSLRA, which limited the liability of public companies for issuing a false projection.

Enron: Less than a decade after the enactment of the PSLRA, the shock of the collapse of Enron helped spur Congress to pass Sarbanes–Oxley, which requires all public companies to take substantial measures to reduce the risk of securities fraud. Enron encouraged the view that it could create extraordinary revenue growth through innovation. As its projects failed, it used improper accounting techniques to create the appearance that its success was continuing. When it became clear that the trajectory that provided the basis for its valuation was false, the company's stock price quickly collapsed. Enron's executives argued that they did not know the company's accounting was improper because it was approved by its auditors. But even if they did not know every detail of its accounting transgressions, they knew that the company was using questionable means to hide losses and inflate revenue to meet quarterly earnings projections. Sarbanes–Oxley recognized the development of fundamental incentives to mislead the market about the prospects of a public company. The securities frauds at Enron and WorldCom also prompted criminal prosecutions that resulted in the conviction of their CEOs based on specific evidence that linked them to efforts to meet financial projections.

Citigroup: The relative lack of serious government sanction of the banks that were almost swept away by the collapse of the housing market and resulting financial crisis of 2008 helps illustrate the limits of securities fraud liability. For example, the massive financial conglomerate Citigroup clearly misrepresented its exposure to subprime mortgage assets by billions of dollars. Though it was required to make civil payments, it was not penalized as harshly as companies like Enron and WorldCom. Even if the company had not misled investors about its subprime exposure, it likely would have been pushed to the brink of failure by an unprecedent financial crisis. Citigroup argued it was just as surprised by the extent of the financial turmoil as the public. There were few major government enforcement actions against public companies arising out of the 2008 financial crisis because a compelling theory of securities fraud never emerged. Unlike the cases arising from the Enron era, courts and regulators viewed many of the misstatements of the financial crisis defendants as mistakes made in managing unprecedented turmoil in the markets rather than securities fraud.

GE: The final case study looks at how the concept of securities fraud may continue to evolve. The clearest cases of securities fraud involve a violation of accounting rules to meet an earnings projection. There is an open question as to when real earnings management, where companies make economically questionable decisions that generate revenue to meet earnings projections, can be considered to be fraudulent. Consider the case of General Electric (GE). For more than a decade, GE never missed a quarterly earnings projection. It was able to do so because it was a conglomerate with superior managers who were able to effectively allocate resources among its various businesses. If performance in one business lagged in a quarter, GE might sell an asset in another division to generate revenue to offset the shortfall. For years, GE's use of real earnings management was an open secret to investors, yet it was rewarded for delivering smooth earnings with a high stock price. By the 2010s, GE's tactics pushed losses into the future periods until they grew so large that they could not be denied. In the investigation arising out of GE's problems, the SEC required the company to pay a major penalty for conduct that included real earnings management practices.

The final chapter of the book concludes by discussing the future of securities fraud regulation and offering some proposals for reform.

* * *

It is important to note that this book does not cover all frauds or even all types of securities fraud. Its scope is limited to companies with stock that is frequently traded in public markets. It focuses mostly on corporate misstatements that are meant to artificially inflate the trading price of a company's stock. Securities frauds such as Ponzi schemes, market manipulation, and aggressive sales tactics by brokers have been covered in some excellent books and are topics to be left for another day.[23]

This is a book that looks at securities fraud from the perspective of a law professor. Understanding such fraud requires not only deciphering a complex statutory and regulatory scheme but also understanding thousands of court decisions and SEC administrative materials arising out of securities fraud enforcement cases. This body of law is so difficult to decipher that it led one law professor to write an article asking, "What Is Securities Fraud?"[24] This internal perspective on the law is supplemented by history, economics, finance theory, accounting studies, and empirical analysis of data on securities enforcement cases.

In telling the story of securities fraud in public companies, the book draws upon an extensive secondary literature. Much of this scholarship has focused on studying enforcement mechanisms, particularly class actions brought by defrauded investors;[25] this book takes a somewhat different approach in examining the causes, evolution, and consequences of public company securities fraud.

The Valuation Treadmill tells the story of how securities fraud came to threaten one of the most important institutions in our society, the public corporation.[26] While it is human nature to lie, the problem of fraud is especially complicated within large organizations with valuations that are constantly scrutinized by investors. It is only by understanding the history of public company securities fraud that we can better address the problem in the future.

Xerox and the Pressure to Meet Projections

Had Xerox reported its revenues and earnings consistent with its accounting in earlier years, Xerox would have failed to meet Wall Street earnings-per-share expectations in 11 of 12 quarters in 1997–1999.

Securities and Exchange Commission, 2002

While it did not receive the same attention as the cases arising out of the Enron and WorldCom frauds, the Securities and Exchange Commission's (SEC) enforcement action against Xerox was significant because it was the first where the agency imposed a significant penalty on a corporate defendant for misleading investors about its financial results. The case was part of a concerted effort beginning in the latter half of the 1990s to address misstatements by public companies to meet market projections of quarterly earnings. Because many of the issues raised in public company securities fraud cases were present in the Xerox case, it provides an ideal introduction to the subject of securities fraud.

Allegations of securities fraud by public companies were common by the late 1980s but were predominantly made in class actions filed by private parties. These lawsuits were often brought without concrete evidence that a misstatement was made with fraudulent intent. Because of the frequency that plaintiffs cried fraud, many courts and policymakers believed that most of these lawsuits were strike suits meant to extract a settlement from a deep-pocketed defendant. Through much of the 1980s and 1990s, the SEC, which is viewed by many commentators as a more measured enforcer than private parties, did not bring many significant securities fraud actions against public corporations. The agency did not have power to impose penalties for general violations of the securities laws until 1990, and for the next decade preferred to penalize individual executives rather than companies.

The SEC's imposition of a $10 million penalty on Xerox was especially meaningful because of the company's storied past. The corporation that became Xerox spent years developing a copier that used plain rather than chemically treated paper based on patents developed by a lone inventor whose work was motivated in part by the experience of copying legal texts by hand while studying to become a patent attorney.[1] Its copiers substantially reduced the cost of reproducing documents, exponentially increasing business efficiency. Xerox reached $1 billion in revenue faster than any other company at the time and increased its annual earnings by double digits for years.[2] Investors bid up the company's stock to reflect the expectation that the company's monopoly power would enable it to continue increasing its profits over time. Xerox faced significant competition after antitrust regulators forced it to license its technology in the 1970s, but the company survived and prospered because it systematically improved its efficiency during the 1980s by adopting quality control methods. By the 1990s it appeared that Xerox's success had continued in a new world where documents were increasingly stored digitally, reducing the need for paper copies.

In reality, there was evidence that the company violated accounting rules to create the appearance that its financial results were meeting market expectations. The SEC viewed Xerox as part of an epidemic of companies that committed securities fraud in response to valuation pressure. The blame for these securities frauds was not isolated to individual executives but was also the responsibility of the corporate defendant. The SEC penalty on Xerox was an important acknowledgment that securities fraud had become a serious threat to the integrity of public companies. The SEC's efforts in cases like Xerox helped establish the foundation for the important securities enforcement actions arising out of the collapse of Enron and WorldCom and the subsequent passage of Sarbanes–Oxley.

XEROX'S ACCOUNTING MISSTATEMENTS

Public company securities fraud manipulates the market's valuation of a stock by conveying misleading facts to investors. In Xerox's case the misrepresentation at issue involved the company's financial statements, which include quantitative measures of its performance for a period. A corporation with publicly traded stock is required to release financial reports that are prepared pursuant to generally accepted accounting principles (GAAP), which consist of "a body of accounting and reporting customs, conventions, and procedures."[3] Because every company represents that its financial statements comply with GAAP, its financial results are misrepresented if they are inconsistent with GAAP. If a financial misstatement reflects a large enough error that overstates the company's performance, it can distort the decisions of investors who may value a stock more highly than without the error.

Though aspects of it were complex, the effect of Xerox's accounting violations can be described in a few sentences. The company moved revenue that its business would earn in later quarters to earlier quarters. By doing so, it reported higher earnings than warranted to create the appearance that its profits were growing from quarter to quarter. The stock market trusted these numbers, and Xerox's stock price rose to reflect the expectation that the company would continue to increase its earnings. A problem with such a manipulation is that revenue cannot be counted twice. At some later point, Xerox would have to make up for the revenue that it had moved up from later to earlier quarters. Unless its performance dramatically improved, it would have to continue misrepresenting its financial results to avoid reporting a decline in revenue. As the SEC declared in its complaint against the company, "by accelerating future revenues and profits into the present, Xerox made the prospect of achieving future expectations even more difficult and increased the company's vulnerability to future business downturns."[4]

The most significant of Xerox's tactics related to the way that it accounted for what it earned by leasing its copiers to business customers. Leasing had played an important role in Xerox's business model for decades. One of the problems the company initially faced was the expense of its machines. Its copiers cost more to purchase than existing copiers that used chemically coated paper. Over the long run, because they used plain paper that was cheaper than treated paper, Xerox machines had a cost advantage. As explained by Judge Jon Newman, the judge who presided over an antitrust trial against the company in the 1970s, "customers pay more for making a single copy on plain paper than on coated paper, but the plain paper process becomes cheaper than coated paper when large quantities of copies are made."[5] At a critical time in Xerox's history, IBM turned down the opportunity to purchase Xerox's unique technology because a management consultant advised that given the high cost of a plain paper copier, there would only be demand for about 5,000 units. Xerox solved this problem by leasing its copiers rather than selling them. A customer could rent a unit for $95 a month and would pay Xerox 5 cents per copy over a threshold of 2,000 copies.[6] This business model worked in part because the convenience of making copies was said to have a "narcotic effect" on employees who made many more copies than expected.[7]

By the 1990s, in addition to leasing copiers, Xerox would offer customers financing and servicing for a single bundled payment. Accounting rules treated the revenue earned from leasing the copier differently from the revenue earned from financing and servicing the copier. Because Xerox leased the copiers for essentially their entire working life, the transaction could be treated under accounting rules as a sale of the copier. The total of all the lease payments to be made over the full term of the lease could thus be recognized as revenue immediately (discounted to present value) rather than waiting for the payments to come in over the course of the lease. In contrast, Xerox was required to record the revenue it earned from financing and servicing over time rather than at the start of the lease. These were continuing services that earned revenue over multiple periods rather than in a single sales-like transaction. Xerox's SEC filings disclosed its commitment to an accounting policy where it would recognize leasing revenue immediately, while waiting to recognize financing and service revenue.[8]

In order to boost its revenue, Xerox used several methods that arbitrarily increased the portion of the bundled payment that reflected payment for leasing the copier. If it collected more for the lease and less for financing and servicing, Xerox could recognize a higher percentage of the bundled payment immediately rather than recording the payment over time. The impact of this move on the company's financial statements was significant. Xerox was able to move more than $3 billion of revenue to earlier reporting periods during the mid-1990s.[9] Because it had been recognized early, this revenue would not be available for the later periods when it had actually been earned. The SEC took the position that these practices violated GAAP and were misleading because they were a significant change in Xerox's revenue reporting that was not disclosed to investors.

While accounting rules are sometimes vague and can make arbitrary distinctions, they are important because they provide a basic framework for reporting. So long as all companies act in good faith to apply GAAP, their earnings will be roughly comparable. When a company misapplies the rules to boost its revenue, it can create the appearance that it is doing better than its competitors. Moreover, consistent application of accounting rules ensures that a company's current results are comparable to its past results. When a company like Xerox significantly changes its practices without informing investors, it disrupts the expectation that its present reports are prepared on the same basis as its past reports.

THE PRESSURE ON XEROX TO MEET QUARTERLY PROJECTIONS

Why did Xerox risk its reputation and credibility by overstating its revenue and earnings? It did so to counter the perception that its business was in decline. Xerox was faced with the challenge that its traditional copier business was becoming outdated as technological advances allowed documents to be easily reproduced, sent, and managed digitally. The management of Xerox had long anticipated that its copiers could be made obsolete through computer technology, and the company had invested in research relating to computers.[10] Years before, it formed the Palo Alto Research Center (PARC), which resulted in inventions such as the laser printer, Ethernet, and the basic model for the personal computer (which was plagiarized by Apple Computer, the company discussed in Chapter 4). However, Xerox's efforts to find the next blockbuster product did not reproduce its past success with its plain-paper copier, and it was struggling to produce growth in its earnings.

Like other companies at the time, Xerox sought to convey that its future was bright by consistently meeting earnings projections. Recall that in modern stock markets, research analysts develop and publish predictions of the quarterly financial performance of many public companies. By the 1990s, there was a belief that better managers should be able to produce consistent financial performance. As one study reported, "[t]he common belief is that a well-run and stable firm should be able to 'produce the dollars' necessary to hit the earnings target, even in a year that is otherwise somewhat down."[11] The fact that a company did not deliver what was expected of it could prompt the market to conclude that its managers were not competent and could not be trusted to create shareholder value.

Xerox, along with other public companies, thus spent considerable effort to ensure that its earnings would not fall short of market projections. By meeting projections, Xerox could confirm that it had become a company that was meeting new challenges raised by technological change. While striving to meet a performance metric is not inherently problematic, difficulties can arise when a company's business is failing and the company is unwilling to acknowledge that it cannot manage its way out of its problems.

The SEC argued that Xerox's effort to move earnings to earlier periods was best understood as part of a larger scheme to meet its quarterly earnings projections. Its complaint specifically noted that the "investment climate of the 1990s," which emphasized meeting projections, created pressure on Xerox.[12] Without the company's misstatements, the company would not have met its projections in eleven of twelve quarters from 1997 through 1999 and instead would have shown no growth in its earnings. By meeting projections forecasting growth, Xerox created the impression that it would continue to grow in the future, justifying a higher stock price than if its growth prospects were dim. In a front page 1999 *Wall Street Journal* article titled "Xerox Recasts Itself as Formidable Force in Digital Revolution," the company's CEO pointed to the company's "double-digit U.S. revenue growth, soaring profits, and its array of new digital devices" as evidence that it was beating its many competitors.[13] Xerox did not seek to change its accounting on a whim, it did so to support a particular narrative it was conveying to the stock market.

Establishing a motive for Xerox's accounting misstatements was important, as a company is not liable for securities fraud simply because it makes a mistake in its accounting. The primary rule that prohibits securities fraud, Rule 10b-5, requires the plaintiff to show that the defendant's misrepresentation was not just an accident, but was made with the intent to deceive investors. In some cases, it is clear that the company deliberately lied to the market. If a company simply makes up sales that never happened, it is not difficult to conclude that its intent was fraudulent. In other cases, it is less clear that a company meant to deceive investors. When the issue is whether the timing of the reporting of sales complies with accounting standards, the company can claim it simply made an incorrect judgment that was not part of a concerted plan to defraud the market. As one court explained, "[a]llegations of a violation of GAAP provisions ... without corresponding fraudulent intent, are not sufficient to state a securities fraud claim."[14] The securities laws do not severely punish companies for errors in their public statements. The misrepresentation must be accompanied by what courts refer to as *scienter*, an intent to deceive investors.

Courts have described two main ways to establish scienter, or fraudulent intent, in a case brought under Rule 10b-5. The first focuses on the motivation of individual managers to mislead investors. For example, if corporate executives sold an unusual amount of their personal stock holdings while issuing a misstatement that inflated the company's stock, a fact finder might reasonably conclude that the misstatement was not just an accident but meant to deceive investors for the enrichment of the executives.[15] The second relates to the company's knowledge that a statement is false. If a corporation and its employees issue misstatements with a reckless disregard for the truth, an inference could be drawn that the misstatement was meant to deceive investors. As one federal appellate court explained, *recklessness*, which requires more than a simple lack of care, can be established with evidence of "defendants' knowledge of facts or access to information contradicting their public statements" or evidence that "defendants failed to review or check information that they had a duty to monitor, or ignored obvious signs of fraud."[16]

The SEC's case against Xerox was based primarily on a theory of recklessness. There was a divergence in Xerox's internal knowledge and its public statements. A narrow way of formulating the argument would be that the company knew that its accounting was not in good faith compliance with GAAP despite its public commitment to such compliance. A broader argument could also be made that the company knew that its reported financial results did not reflect the true state of the company's business.

In a common move, Xerox contended that it did not fabricate the revenue it reported; it simply reported it earlier with the consent of its accountants. Because of the complexity of GAAP, there is often an argument that an aggressive accounting move that increases revenue is justified. There may not be an objectively correct answer with respect to whether a vague accounting rule has been properly applied. In Xerox's case, its allocation of customer payments between financing and services (which were recognized over time) and the use of the copier (which could be recognized immediately) was based on a range of assumptions about prevailing interest rates and sales margins in foreign markets. Xerox could claim that its assumptions were reasonable and reflected managerial judgment. Moreover, Xerox argued (as did companies like Enron) that it did not act with fraudulent intent because its accounting had been approved by its outside auditor, KPMG (KPMG later argued that it too had been deceived by Xerox).[17] Corporate managers are not necessarily experts in all aspects of accounting and thus must rely on their external auditors.

It is clear, though, that Xerox was not applying accounting principles in good faith. While GAAP inherently requires companies to exercise their judgment, GAAP also requires that companies use their discretion in good faith to inform investors of their true financial condition. There was evidence that Xerox changed the assumptions behind its revenue calculations mainly to meet earnings projections rather than using assumptions that would most accurately reflect its business operations. It had internal targets that it wished to meet and altered its reporting practices to bridge the gap between its desired and real results. As the SEC alleged in its complaint, Xerox believed that "the accounting function was just another revenue source and profit opportunity." When a KPMG partner objected to its practices, Xerox pressured KPMG to reassign the partner. Rather than simply accept the judgment of its experts, Xerox actively shaped its own audit and arguably hid behind their stamp of approval. In doing so, the company evidenced an intent to manipulate the process and deceive investors.[18]

There was evidence that Xerox knew that its financial statements did not accurately reflect its true condition. Indeed, it separately tracked the impact of its accounting manipulations in a separate internal document. This additional set of books indicated that Xerox had knowledge that its true financial performance diverged from its public financial reports. Even while knowing that its operations had shown "no growth," Xerox continued to issue optimistic statements about its growth and the trajectory of such growth. Its financial statements provided quantitative support for this false narrative. It is reasonable to conclude that Xerox did not inform investors when it made significant changes to its reporting because it knew that its stock price would plummet if the market knew the truth.

The SEC essentially concluded that Xerox's public disclosures lacked integrity. There was a significant divergence between what the company knew about its performance and the story it told to the public. This inconsistency supported a finding of recklessness necessary to satisfy the scienter requirement of Rule 10b-5.

Had Xerox simply become a corrupt company? There is not a simple answer to this question. Xerox's employees may have justified pushing its auditor to allow questionable accounting because the company's history of overcoming adversity led them to genuinely believe that no matter what the challenge, the business would eventually get back on track. Xerox could have thought that over time, it would find a way to generate enough revenue to make up for the revenue it had improperly accelerated. Xerox might have viewed its accounting moves as part of a legitimate set of options used by managers to manage a complex business and the expectations of investors who might overreact to temporary shortfalls in performance.

Xerox was not the only public company that used accounting misstatements to meet its quarterly projections toward the end of the 1990s. Driven in part by the pressure to meet projections, major public companies violated GAAP at an alarming rate. Just in the first half of 1998, Cendant, Sunbeam, and Waste Management admitted that they needed to correct significant errors in their financial statements. All three companies had pursued aggressive growth strategies and had seemingly met their quarterly earnings projections with regularity. The revelation that their income was hundreds of millions of dollars less than reported resulted in substantial declines in their stock prices, which led to bankruptcy for Sunbeam; restructuring for Cendant; and the sale of Waste Management to another company.

In the wake of these initial scandals that hinted at deeper problems, the SEC began acting more aggressively to target accounting misstatements. The SEC chairman at the time, Arthur Levitt, highlighted the practice of misapplying accounting standards to meet earnings projections, famously calling it a "Numbers

Game."[19] He observed that the problem was not limited to companies of questionable reputation but "companies whose products we know and admire." The SEC
staff issued a bulletin clarifying that even a small error in a company's accounting
would be considered material, or important, to investors if it "hides a failure to
meet analysts' consensus expectations" or was motivated to "'manage' reported
earnings."[20]

Xerox was accompanied and followed by a significant number of SEC cases
targeting corporate misstatements to meet projections. In 2004 the SEC sued an
Alabama company that operated rehabilitation centers, HealthSouth, for inflating its
earnings by more than $2.5 billion starting in 1999. HealthSouth systematically
overstated the revenue it expected to receive as reimbursement from private and
government insurance providers for the health care services it provided. It did so
allegedly to "meet or exceed 'Wall Street' expectations" represented by "projections
disseminated by HealthSouth and the investment banks and analysts that were
involved in the scheme."[21] It thus reported revenue in the short term that eventually
would have to be adjusted downward, sacrificing future earnings.[22] The SEC
investigated the accounting of the software company, Computer Associates, which
helped spur a restatement of more than $2 billion in 2004. The SEC brought suit,
alleging that the company's "reported revenue and earnings per share appeared to
meet or exceed Wall Street analysts' expectations, when – in truth and fact – those
results were based in part on revenue that [Computer Associates] recognized
prematurely and in violation of GAAP."[23] The SEC relied on a projections theory
in numerous securities fraud cases as summarized in the following chart.

SEC cases alleging securities fraud by public company to meet projections

Company	Period of Fraud	Motive to Meet Projections	SEC Corporate Penalty
Cendant	1988–2000	"The scheme was driven by senior management's determination that CUC would always meet the earnings expectations of Wall Street analysts and fueled by disregard for an obligation that the earnings reported needed to be 'real.'"	None
Informix	1994–1996	"The fraudulent content described herein was driven by some former managers' need to meet or exceed the Company's internal and financial revenue goals, which were based, in part, on financial analysts' expectations."	None
HealthSouth	1996–2003	"When [HealthSouth] earnings fell short of such estimates, [the CEO] directed [HealthSouth] accounting personnel to 'fix it' by artificially inflating the company's earnings to meet Wall Street expectations."	$100 million

Xerox	1997–2000	Accounting fraud "allowed Xerox to meet or exceed Wall Street expectations in virtually every reporting period from 1997 through 1999."	$10 million
Raytheon	1997–2001	Accounting errors "enabled . . . Raytheon . . . to meet certain internal and external earnings targets."	$12 million
Tyco	1997–2002	Tyco inflated income "to enhance and smooth its reported financial results and to meet earnings projections."	$50 million
Computer Associates	1998–2001	When accounting fraud ended, Computer Associates "[m]issed its [q]uarterly [e]stimates."	$225 million
Symbol Technologies	1998–2003	The company and top management "fostered an aggressive 'numbers driven' corporate culture obsessed with meeting financial projections."	$37 million
Federal National Mortgage Association	1998–2004	Alleging "violations had the effect, among other things, of falsely portraying stable earnings growth and reduced income statement volatility and . . . achieving forecasted earnings."	$400 million
Qwest	1999–2002	"Qwest senior management exerted extreme pressure upon other officers and managers and demanded that, through the use of one-time sales or other means, they meet earnings projections in order to prevent any further drop in the price of Qwest stock."	$250 million
Global Crossing	1999–2002	Without questionable transactions, Global Crossing "would not have met securities analysts' estimates for its first and second quarter 2001 pro forma results."	None
Enron	1999–2001	One objective of Enron fraud was "to meet or exceed the published expectations of industry analysts forecasting Enron's reported earnings-per-share and other results."	None
WorldCom	1999–2002	"[A] decline in income created a substantial risk that WorldCom's publicly reported income would fail to meet the expectations of Wall Street analysts and that the market price of WorldCom's securities would therefore decline."	$2.25 billion
Bristol-Myers Squibb	2000–2001	The company used accounting manipulation when its "results still fell short of the Company's targets and analysts' consensus earnings estimates."	$100 million

United Rentals	2000–2002	Senior officers "engaged in a series of fraudulent accounting schemes in order to meet the Company's earnings forecasts and analyst expectations."	$14 million
Nortel Networks Corp.	2000–2003	Alleging the company "engaged in two fraudulent accounting schemes ... to meet ... unrealistic revenue and earnings guidance."	$35 million
Cardinal Health	2000–2004	Claiming that company "engaged in a fraudulent earnings and revenue management scheme" to "present a false picture of its results of operations to the financial community and the investing public – one that matched Cardinal's publicly disseminated earnings guidance and analysts' expectations, rather than its true economic performance."	$2.5 million

In this climate, Xerox's efforts to meet its earnings projections were viewed as reflecting a broader problem. The SEC believed that the problem of accounting fraud was closely linked to a corporate motivation to meet earnings projections. Public companies were violating GAAP to meet forecasts of their performance and validate the narrative that their profits would continually grow. The SEC conveyed through enforcement its belief that there was a systemic incentive for public corporations to misrepresent their financial performance.

XEROX'S PAST

Public companies did not always face relentless pressure to meet projections. For decades, Xerox had no need to deceive investors about its prospects. The copier company was part of the Nifty Fifty stocks that institutional investors were willing to pay a premium to own. Many of these companies had significant market power so that investors had confidence that they would continue to grow over the years. As *Forbes* noted at the time, their high "multiple discounted not only the future but also the hereafter."[24]

Xerox was able to provide reliable information about its growth to the market. As the biography of its revered CEO, Joe Wilson, described the company in the 1960s,

> Xerox was in a remarkable position for a company whose earnings were growing so very rapidly: Xerox actually *knew* its future. It knew what its future earnings were going to be for several years out because with a meter reading the month-by-month usage of each and every 914 [copy machine], the patterns of usage – particularly the rate of increasing usage – could easily be analyzed and projected out into the future.

The usage of each particular 914 could be compared with the past patterns of increasing usage of all existing 914s, sorted into comparable groups by size of company, by number of employees, by industry and adjusted for by such macro factors as changes in GNP or inflation. With increasing accuracy in estimates for each machine, the actual volume of usage for the whole population of 914s could be forecast with remarkable accuracy.[25]

The company had come a long way from its earlier years, when there was uncertainty about the demand for its product. As it was preparing to launch its first copier, after some debate Xerox budgeted for the production of 15,000 units when sales forecasts had predicted demand for 7,500 units.[26] After its initial success, Xerox made aggressive forecasts about its future performance. In 1961, its CEO correctly predicted in a speech to research analysts that the company would exceed $1 billion in revenue by the end of the decade at a time when it had only $100 million in sales.[27]

Profits came so easily to companies like Xerox that managers were not as compelled to maximize shareholder wealth. A *New Yorker* profile from 1967 described an interview where its CEO was more interested in discussing "non-profit activities and his theories of corporate responsibility" than the business itself.[28] The article noted that the "Xerox spirit" encouraged "emphasizing 'human values' for their own sake."[29] Xerox not only spent corporate funds on donations to institutions such as the University of Rochester, which benefited its local community, but spent $4 million to support a film series about the United Nations.[30] Such an emphasis on improving societal well-being is less common for companies trading on US stock markets today (although that could be changing), where companies must focus on increasing profits for shareholders.

The private company that initially developed Xerox's technology also was not pressured to generate immediate profits. For several years, the venture lost money as it invested in commercializing basic technology that had been developed and patented by a lone entrepreneur. It raised funds from private investors who were willing to make a long-term investment. The University of Rochester's early investment of $200,000 in Xerox stock made it one of the nation's wealthiest universities after the company went public and the value of the shares grew to $120 million by the early 1970s.[31] A significant difference between private and public companies that extends to the present day is that private companies do not have to contend with constant stock market scrutiny.

Over time, investors came to put more pressure on public companies to demonstrate that their earnings were growing. They knew that corporate managers had developed internal projections that would be useful in predicting a company's earnings stream. Public companies began to share these forecasts with research analysts who used them in setting their own projections for company performance. By the 1960s, projections for many public companies were compiled, published, and widely disseminated. Meeting projections became a mechanism for assessing managerial competence and testing the validity of earnings trajectories that were used in valuation models.[32]

For various reasons, it became more difficult for Xerox to maintain its consistent growth. Xerox's market dominance eroded in the 1970s after the Federal Trade Commission brought a suit alleging antitrust violations that was settled with Xerox agreeing to license its technology to competitors. New entrants, such as Canon from Japan, aggressively grew their businesses by developing new products directed at small customers Xerox had ignored.[33] Because it could no longer rely on the comfort of its monopoly position, Xerox sought to beat its competitors by improving its management. It brought in consultants and adopted efforts to improve the efficiency of the company. Over the 1980s, Xerox became known for its efforts to implement cutting-edge management techniques. It systematically implemented quality controls and changed a culture that had become complacent with success. Rather than monopoly power, Xerox's competitive edge became superior management, and it experienced a revival in its fortunes. While it was not completely clear that these managerial techniques were the reason for its success in recapturing market share from competitors,[34] the company received several management awards that it made sure to highlight in its SEC filings for decades. For example, its 1997 10-K (which the company filed around the beginning of its alleged fraud) noted that in 1980, its Japanese subsidiary had won the Deming Prize, which is awarded for companies that exhibit the management philosophy of Total Quality Management.

Part of Xerox's management prowess during the 1980s included making ambitious forecasts to the market and then meeting them. Two journalists described the efforts to meet a revenue forecast in 1985. The copier group "continued to lag well behind schedule and a big bubble remained in the final quarter of the year. Then they pulled out every trick in the bag – special pricing, added incentives for the sales force – and barely managed to hit the big forecast."[35] While nothing in this account indicated that the company violated accounting standards to meet its forecast, such practices can still be problematic. For example, special pricing involves selling products at a substantial discount. Simply waiting might mean that the company could sell the same product at full price and earn more from the sale. Just as misapplying accounting rules essentially sacrifices the future for the present, aggressive price cutting compromises the future to meet an earnings projection. Yet courts are reluctant to find that such earnings management without a clear accounting violation is securities fraud. Prominent companies like General Electric used such methods for years to consistently meet its projections. As will be discussed later in this book, there is a case that securities fraud liability should be triggered in some cases of earnings management even in the absence of a clear violation of GAAP.

The pressure to meet forecasts became even greater over time. When they first became widespread over the 1960s and 1970s, projections mainly forecast performance for annual periods but by the 1980s, quarterly projections became more common. Toward the start of the 1990s, financial data services began to disseminate more widely a consensus number that reflected the average of analyst estimates to investors. This provided a single number that could be used to assess a company's quarterly financial results. Numerous studies have documented that companies increasingly focused on meeting such projections. For example, one study of more than 5,000 public firms covering the 1990s found an unusually high number of instances where companies just met or slightly exceeded earnings projections.[36] The importance of projections was widely noted by the press. As a *Fortune* magazine article reported in 1997, while "[e]xecutives of public companies have always strived to live up to investors' expectations ... it's only in the past decade that ... those expectations have become so explicit."[37]

DISCOVERING AND MANAGING SECURITIES FRAUD

Because the entire point of a securities fraud is to withhold information from public investors, most securities frauds remain hidden. As one study reports, corporate frauds are rarely found by government agencies and are usually first reported by private parties.[38] The SEC is respected and feared, but it has limited resources and often reacts to events rather than proactively finding violations. Corporations themselves often are the first to find an initial problem and disclose it to the public. Other times, a whistleblower within the company will directly alert the press and regulators to an issue. The story of how the Xerox fraud was gradually revealed shows how evidence of securities fraud can come to light.

In June 2000, Xerox announced the discovery of accounting issues in its Mexico business and that it would be firing the responsible managers. The problem was that the division significantly underreported the number of customers who were delinquent in their copier lease payments. As a result, it overstated its earnings, which would be reduced by such delinquencies. The acknowledgment prompted both internal and SEC investigations.

The accounting problem in Mexico by itself was enough to cause a substantial decline in Xerox's stock and prompt a downgrade in its credit rating. Using a standard public relations tactic, Xerox sought to create the impression that the problem was isolated to one country. It hoped to convince regulators that the fraud resulted from rogue actors acting on their own without its knowledge. Though an initial inquiry by a law firm confirmed this story of isolated fraud, that narrative was contradicted by an employee in Xerox's treasury department. A few weeks after the Mexico issue was announced, he wrote an extensive memo to the company's senior management outlining his concerns with Xerox's aggressive accounting throughout the company. The company's treasurer allegedly instructed him not to distribute the memo unless he "wanted people to go to jail." The whistleblower was fired and then took his story to the *Wall Street Journal*.

In February 2001, the *Journal* published an article based on the whistleblower's account that thwarted Xerox's efforts to minimize the significance of its accounting errors.[39] It described a "corporate culture that cut bookkeeping corners to make up for deteriorating business fundamentals and maximize short-term results." The accounting issues did not originate in Mexico but came from the "developing-markets corporate group" at company headquarters. According to the article, the problems were especially shocking because "[l]ess than two years ago, Xerox was widely hailed as a symbol of American corporate reinvention, lauded for having beaten back a stiff challenge from Japanese rivals."[40]

In April 2001, Xerox delayed the filing of its Form 10-K because of a dispute with its auditors. The next month, it announced a restatement of its earnings, which was initially viewed as revealing isolated problems at the company.[41] In a restatement, a public company acknowledges and corrects a material error in its financial reports. Prior to the mid-1990s, very few public companies restated their financial statements. A survey of 277 audit partners published in 1989 revealed that they believed that finding a material accounting irregularity was a rare event.[42] One study looked for such restatements during the 1977–1988 period and only found a total of forty-one firms that restated their earnings to correct for an overstatement.[43] Another article described several studies on company restatements from 1976 to 1994 as "document [ing] that restatement companies tend to be smaller, less profitable, slower growing, and less likely to have audit committees than their industry or control counter-parts."[44] They were not multinational public companies that won international awards for their superior management.

By the early 2000s, it became more common for large public companies to restate their financial statements. In 1997, ninety-two public companies issued restatements. In 2001, the year of Xerox's restatement, 225 public companies acknowledged material mistakes.[45] The increase in restatements reflected both the pressure to meet earnings projections as well as the SEC's more aggressive stance on accounting issues. The SEC steadily increased its enforcement activity during this period. It reported ninety-one actions directed against financial reporting violations in 1997 and 149 actions in 2002.[46] The SEC's cases not only reacted to company restatements, they prompted companies to issue restatements preemptively. Public companies understood that they might avoid SEC sanction by acting on their own to address a past error. If they found and addressed an accounting problem before it was discovered by regulators, they could bolster their argument that the problem was limited to individuals rather than reflecting fraudulent intent by the company. As they cleaned house internally, public corporations acknowledged the extent to which their managers had engaged in questionable practices.

About a year after the restatement, the SEC concluded that Xerox's accounting issues were much broader than the company had acknowledged. In April 2002, the SEC filed a complaint alleging that the company had committed securities fraud at the same time it announced that Xerox had agreed to a $10 million penalty to resolve the case. The SEC later brought an enforcement action against the company's management team that was also resolved through the payment of penalties.

As Xerox's accounting became subject to suspicion and then additional problems came to light, Xerox's stock price steadily fell from approximately $50 a share to around $10 a share. Much of the decline happened at a time when the stock market was generally increasing. Xerox had lost credibility with investors. The Value Line Investment Survey, which provides research summaries of public companies for investors, includes a metric called Earnings Predictability, which measures the reliability of a company's forecasts. In 1997, Xerox had an Earnings Predictability score of seventy-five. By 2002, its score had fallen to fifteen. As investors became less confident in Xerox's projections, they were not willing to pay as much for its stock.

PUNISHING SECURITIES FRAUD

Who should be punished for a securities fraud involving a public company? In the Xerox case, the corporation itself paid a civil penalty. While such SEC corporate penalties have become common, they were not an option for most securities fraud violations prior to 1990 when Congress gave the SEC the general power to penalize violations of the securities laws. Even with the authority to levy a penalty, the SEC did not extensively use its power against companies, preferring to bring cases against individuals. Because corporations can only act through people, there is an argument that the SEC should identify and punish only those individuals responsible for the securities fraud. But as securities fraud became seen as a product of corporate culture, it became more difficult to let companies go without punishment.

The SEC's effort against public companies like Xerox was not the first time it had addressed fraud in public company financial statements. At the start of the Reagan administration, the SEC announced that it would look closely at the problem of accounting fraud.[47] A congressional report noted that in the wake of the poor economy of the 1970s, the SEC had "reported increasing incidences of companies inflating their profits, overstating inventories, issuing false financial statements and making false and misleading statements regarding their financial condition in communications sent to public shareholders."[48] An influential 1987 report by the National Commission on Fraudulent Financial Reporting noted that "[a] frequent incentive for fraudulent financial reporting that improves the company's financial appearance is the desire to obtain a higher price from a stock or debt offering or to meet the expectations of investors."[49]

But without the power to seek civil penalties, SEC enforcement had a limited ability to deter securities law violations. One study examined 188 accounting enforcement cases brought by the SEC from 1982 to 1989. It found that the typical action was settled with the sole sanction of an injunction prohibiting additional violations of the law.[50] The SEC had the power to award disgorgement, but the remedy was rarely used,[51] and did not provide much deterrence because the defendant would only have to refund gains from the misconduct.[52] Some of the SEC's cases were followed by criminal prosecution, and many resulted in the resignation of top managers and private litigation by shareholders. Though there is some shame in admitting to a violation and promising not to engage in the same conduct, without penalty power the SEC could not issue sanctions that adequately reflected the severity of a violation.

The National Commission on Fraudulent Financial Reporting made the case for expanding the range of sanctions available to the SEC. It explained that "[e]xpress fining authority also would enable the SEC to distinguish better among perpetrators of fraudulent financial reporting, imposing heavy fines, in addition to other sanctions, at one end of the spectrum, and imposing smaller fines in lieu of excessively harsh sanctions at the other end of the spectrum."[53] Influenced by this report, Congress passed the Securities Enforcement Remedies and Penny Stock Act of 1990,[54] which gave "the SEC authority to seek civil money penalties for violations of any provision of the four major federal securities statutes."[55] Support for the SEC's new power was not uniform. An op-ed in the *New York Times* raised the possibility that the SEC could seek penalties against corporate executives for minor violations such as failing to file "stock ownership reports."[56] While these fears were not realized, the statute did give the SEC wide discretion to impose penalties for securities law violations.

At least initially, the SEC tended to penalize individuals rather than companies. The SEC reported that from 1997 to 2002, "the majority of the persons held responsible for the accounting violations were members of issuer senior management."[57] Prior to the Xerox case, the SEC "sparingly ... obtained civil penalties in substantial amounts ($1 million and $3.5 million) from public companies."[58] The initial wave of public company accounting frauds that emerged by the late 1990s did not trigger penalties for the violating corporations. For example, Cendant, which was formed through the merger of two companies, discovered that one of those companies, CUC International (CUC), had overstated its revenue over three years by about $500 million.[59] A report by the company's audit committee found that its accounting manipulations "closely mirrored the amount needed to bring CUC's results in line with Wall Street earnings expectations."[60] The revelation of the fraud resulted in a loss of more than $20 billion in Cendant's market capitalization,[61] but the company was not required to pay an SEC penalty (though some of its executives did and CUC's CEO was convicted of criminal securities fraud). In the Waste Management case, the SEC imposed a penalty on various company's executives as "a lesson to him and to others,"[62] but not on the corporation.

While corporate penalties for securities fraud can convey the view that misconduct originated from a problematic corporate culture, the cost of such penalties is borne by corporate shareholders. One long-standing view is that such stockholders are innocent of wrongdoing and that they should not bear the cost of corporate misconduct.[63] As Woodrow Wilson noted in a speech to the American Bar Association in 1910, corporate fines "fall upon the wrong persons; more heavily upon the innocent than upon the guilty; as much upon those who know nothing whatsoever of the transactions for which the fine is imposed as upon those who originated and carried them through – upon the stockholders and the customers rather than upon the men who direct the policy of the business."[64] Indeed, many shareholders can be victims of the fraud because they purchased stock at inflated prices and the value of their holdings often decline after the revelation of the fraud.

On the other hand, shareholders can also reap the gains of a fraudulent scheme. If the fraud is not discovered, the corporation can use an inflated stock price to make acquisitions or raise funds that can increase the company's value for shareholders. As Louis Brandeis, who was famous as a reformer of corporations before becoming a Supreme Court Justice, once wrote: "There is no such thing to my mind . . . as an *innocent* shareholder. He may be innocent in fact, but socially he cannot be held innocent. He accepts the benefits of the system. It is his business and his obligation to see that those who represent him carry out a policy which is consistent with the public welfare."[65]

In the Xerox case, it was difficult to limit blame to just a few of its executives who acted solely to enrich themselves. The SEC's theory was that the fraud was part of a systematic effort by the company to meet its earnings projections. An internal witness had testified that the company was "falling apart at the seams," and that these manipulations were a way of hiding that fact from the public.[66] The company's board was slow in acknowledging the problem, characterizing the accounting problem as "minor" in initial press reports. In bringing an enforcement case against a group of the company's executives, the SEC faulted the "tone at the top" that they set for the company. Some of the misleading statements could be traced to individual executives, but the most important misrepresentation, the company's incorrect income statement, was issued under the company's name. As securities fraud became a problem linked to corporate culture, the case for penalizing the corporation became stronger.

As is common in securities fraud cases involving accounting fraud, Xerox's auditor, KPMG, was also held responsible for the fraud. How could Xerox have committed fraud if its auditors had signed off on its accounting decisions? Xerox contended in defending litigation brought by its investors that it was "a business that sought, received and followed the advice of a professional accounting firm (KPMG) until the government agency charged with interpreting and enforcing the applicable accounting guidelines announced its disagreement with the accounting firm."[67] KPMG did not support this position and claimed that Xerox had withheld information from it. The auditor argued that it had confronted Xerox about its accounting and required it to restate its earnings. The SEC assigned blame to both parties, requiring KPMG to also pay a $10 million penalty (equal to what Xerox paid) and disgorge its audit fees.[68] Xerox pushed KPMG to sign off on questionable decisions, but KPMG failed to bring its concerns to Xerox's board of directors.

The decision to impose a substantial penalty on Xerox reflected broader concerns at the time about the state of public company accounting. The sheer number of scandals raised questions about the integrity of stock market valuations. As the SEC was negotiating with Xerox, Enron filed for bankruptcy, thrusting the problem of securities fraud into the national spotlight. The speed and severity of the SEC's response likely reflected political pressure to show that it was treating the problem seriously. A skeptic could argue that rather than a thoughtful shift, the SEC's turn to larger penalties was spurred by the need to do something different to demonstrate it was effectively responding to a crisis.

The SEC's civil penalty against Xerox was supplemented by a much larger payment to resolve litigation by Xerox's shareholders who purchased stock during the period of the fraud. About seven years after it settled the SEC's case, a federal judge approved private class action settlements of $670 million for Xerox and $80 million for KPMG. These cases were brought by Xerox investors who claimed they paid too much for the stock, which was inflated by the company's fraud. The lead plaintiff was a state public pension fund, what law professor David Webber calls a Working-Class Shareholder, who could argue that the fraud reduced the value of retirement funds meant to benefit state workers.[69]

This settlement was remarkable because less than a decade before Xerox revealed its problems, Congress had passed a law that made it more difficult for investors to sue for securities fraud. As will be discussed more extensively later in this book, around the mid-1990s, the common perception was that most securities class actions were frivolous suits designed to harass companies for stock price drops they could not control. The SEC's pathbreaking enforcement actions against Xerox and other companies made it difficult to argue that private suits alleging securities fraud were almost always meritless. Indeed, the complaint against Xerox cited the SEC's investigation as well as the SEC chairman's speech highlighting the problem of earnings misstatements to support its case.[70] The class action did more than simply repeat the evidence found in the SEC's investigation. Just two months after the SEC settled with Xerox, the company announced an additional restatement of almost $2 billion in earnings. The private class action thus litigated a larger set of misstatements than was addressed by the SEC action.

THE LEGACY OF XEROX

For much of the 1990s, Xerox was a juggernaut with a peak market capitalization of over $50 billion. More than twenty years later, it is now a much smaller company, worth less than $5 billion. The securities fraud delayed the inevitable realization by investors that Xerox's status as one of the nation's most dominant companies had come to an end.

By misrepresenting its financial results, Xerox sought to recapture its past when it dominated its market. However, it did not have to go the route of misstating its earnings. The company could have reported lower earnings numbers that missed analyst forecasts but accurately reflected its performance. It could also have communicated to investors that expectations for its growth were too high.[71] Xerox instead publicly committed to aggressive revenue targets that called for double digit growth that it could not deliver. If it had conveyed more realistic assumptions, it would have avoided a cloud of corporate scandal and perhaps would have been able to gradually strengthen its business.

After cases like Xerox, it became clear that securities fraud was not just a danger for subpar companies with few prospects. It had also become an issue for the largest, most prestigious public companies. Even the most successful companies must continue to demonstrate that they will generate earnings into the future. The pressure to continually perform and deliver results has become a structural part of public securities markets. Such pressure can create or amplify a problematic corporate culture. When such a culture emerges, it is not enough to single out a few individuals for sanction.

If securities fraud has systemic causes, there is a stronger case that robust corporate governance measures are necessary to address the issue. While the SEC does not have direct authority to regulate the way public companies are managed, it could highlight the link between securities fraud and corporate governance. SEC Chairman Levitt made it a point to opine on the issue of corporate audit committees. He drew a distinction between a bad audit committee, which "convenes only twice a year before the regular board meeting for 15 minutes," and a good audit committee that "meets twelve times a year before each board meeting; where every member has a financial background; where there are no personal ties to the chairman or the company; where they have their own advisers; where they ask tough questions of management and outside auditors; and where, ultimately, the investor interest is being served."[72]

For better or worse, the Xerox case was the start of a more punitive approach to enforcing the prohibition of securities fraud against public companies. The size of SEC penalties increased to the point where a $10 million corporate penalty was viewed as a slap on the wrist.[73] The escalating size and routine use of civil fines to punish corporate securities fraud raised a number of issues.[74] First, the subjectivity of determining the amount of a penalty resulted in concerns about leaving too much discretion to the SEC. Without a clear set of rules for calculating penalties, some offenders will be punished too much while others will not be punished enough. Because of their deep pockets, corporations are able to pay higher penalties than individuals, creating a temptation for regulators to signal vigorous enforcement by extracting record-breaking payments. The SEC attempted to set forth guidance about the numerous factors it would consider in deciding whether a penalty was warranted,[75] but the process is still far from a science. Second, as it became routine for public companies to settle an enforcement case by paying a penalty, the expressive value of such penalties has become diluted. Instead of attempting to identify individuals responsible for the fraud and developing cases against them (as it did in the Xerox case where six executives paid $22 million in fines and penalties),[76] the SEC could quickly negotiate a civil penalty with a corporation that was eager to put the case behind it. This practice was criticized by a federal judge, Jed Rakoff, who famously refused to approve an SEC settlement in 2007 with Bank of America because it did not identify those responsible for securities law violations.[77] Another problem with SEC settlements is that public companies can take the position that the payment of a settlement reflected nothing more than the cost of doing business, especially because SEC settlements typically specify that the settlement is not an admission of wrongdoing. Indeed, Xerox stated in its annual report that it settled the SEC's enforcement matter to enable the company "to focus on continuing to improve our operations and restore the Company's financial health." Judge Rakoff also drew attention to this policy in 2011 by refusing to approve an SEC settlement with Citigroup because it did not contain an admission of wrongdoing. While the decision was later overturned on appeal,[78] the case highlighted questions about the effectiveness of corporate penalties.

The Xerox case provides a sweeping overview of the emergence of public company securities fraud as a significant regulatory issue. Such fraud was initially seen as a problem for smaller companies with uncertain prospects. As larger companies became subject to market scrutiny of their financial results, they also had an incentive to misrepresent their performance. As will be discussed more extensively later in this book, because the SEC came to view securities fraud as a systemic problem, the solution was to not only punish such fraud, but increase regulation of public companies.

3

Penn Central and the Decline of Managerialism

[B]ig corporations do not lose money.

John Kenneth Galbraith, 1967

Publicly held companies do not lose money.

Stanley Goldblum, President of Equity Funding Corporation of America, 1969

Between the end of World War II and the start of the 1970s, regulators did not view securities fraud as a significant risk for large public companies. Major corporations often had market power in their industries and could be counted on to generate profits. They reinvested these profits in research and development and managerial training to perpetuate their advantage. They could acquire competitors or companies in unrelated industries to create new revenue streams. Investors trusted the competence of professional managers who would make wise decisions that avoided major disaster.[1] Under this paradigm of *managerialism*, corporate managers were not as pressured by stock markets. There was thus little reason for an established public corporation to misstate its financial results. Even if it did, such a misrepresentation would be unlikely to hide serious problems that threatened a company's solvency.

The perception during this period was that securities fraud was isolated to smaller companies with stock that did not trade on exchanges. Until 1964, such companies were not required to file periodic disclosure with the Securities and Exchange Commission (SEC). A Special Study of Securities Markets conducted by the SEC during the early 1960s found that 93 percent of securities fraud violations involved such unlisted companies.[2] Based on this report, Congress passed legislation imposing periodic disclosure requirements on companies that were not listed on exchanges but had a substantial number of shareholders.

The sudden collapse in 1970 of Penn Central, the nation's largest railroad and sixth largest company in terms of assets, shook investor confidence in the competence of corporate managers and is viewed by many legal scholars as helping spur the demise of managerialism.[3] Penn Central was the product of a merger of the country's largest and third-largest railroads, the Pennsylvania and New York Central. The two companies built the major interstate railroad routes in the middle of the nineteenth century and had competed since then.[4] Both of the companies paid regular dividends and were viewed as safe investments for decades (as was General Electric, the subject of Chapter 7). Only two years after the merger closed in 1968, the newly formed conglomerate was unable to complete a bond offering it needed to continue operating after its railroad operations lost $100 million in the first quarter of 1970, double the predicted loss of about $50 million.[5] Unlike Citigroup during the financial crisis of 2008 (the subject of Chapter 6), which was saved by a government bailout, Penn Central was unable to persuade the government to intervene. Penn Central's board was criticized for its failure to prevent the crisis and for devoting the first part of its final meeting to discussing and approving executive salaries before turning to the issue of saving the company.[6]

The Penn Central scandal was not only a case of corporate mismanagement but was also the first time the SEC developed an extensive theory of public company securities fraud. Like Xerox, Penn Central was a company with a proud past that used extraordinary measures to maintain the illusion that its economic prospects were bright. The company was not forthright about its ability to overcome the decline of its core railroad business. Penn Central was one of the first large public company failures that was extensively investigated by the SEC, which concluded in a 392-page report that the company maintained earnings projections that were "consistently overoptimistic" even though its internal numbers documented that the company's operating performance was declining.[7] The SEC explained how the railroad used a variety of questionable accounting tactics to hide the deterioration of its core business from investors. By conveying undue optimism about its prospects after the merger that created it, Penn Central justified a higher stock price than warranted by the reality of its situation. Company insiders and Wall Street institutional investors knew before the public that Penn Central was likely to fail. There were allegations that they took advantage of their access to information about the company's true condition to sell their shares to avoid losses.

The Penn Central case shows how investors by the late 1960s were beginning to place pressure on public companies to demonstrate that their financial performance was on an upward trajectory. It was the largest and most infamous of a string of securities frauds in publicly traded corporations that were uncovered during the late 1960s and 1970s. Many of these frauds were motivated by a desire to grow earnings and meet market projections. Investors had increasingly shifted to using valuation methods that emphasized future performance. Penn Central showed how even a large public company could respond to valuation pressure by misstating its financial performance.

THE SEEMING INVULNERABILITY OF CONGLOMERATES

Penn Central was a conglomerate that included not only two railroads but a diverse array of assets that the Pennsylvania and New York Central had accumulated over the years, in better times when they were among the most prominent corporations with stock of secure value.[8] It owned both Grand Central Terminal and Penn Station as well as nearby properties. The merger combined "five New York hotels, huge chunks of real estate in California and Florida, pipeline and trucking companies, amusement parks, and interests in Madison Square Garden, the New York Knickerbockers basketball team and the New York Rangers ice hockey team."[9] As the company's core railroad business struggled, Penn Central hoped that it could generate earnings from its diversified assets to offset any losses.

The announcement of the largest merger ever attempted sparked concerns that the combined entity would be too powerful. Antitrust review of the combination required more than half a decade and a trip to the US Supreme Court to resolve. Opponents argued that the merger would mean fewer rail options for consumers in the economically important east coast. They feared that prices would rise and the quality of service would decline as competition lessened.[10] There was suspicion that the two railroads had hidden profits to avoid antitrust scrutiny and that their extensive nonrailroad assets would help them expand into and dominate other areas of transportation.[11]

On the other hand, the merger was also a sign of weakness. With the construction of interstate highways and increasing availability of affordable air travel, demand for railroads to transport goods and passengers had steadily weakened. Several railroads had recently filed for bankruptcy, and others were seeking to merge as the industry faced overcapacity.[12] One commentator asserted around this time that "[o]nly a fool would project railroad earnings for the full year at this time."[13] Even with their storied past, the two iconic railroads recognized that they were no longer dominant. Indeed, the poor performance of the New York Central, which had been close to collapse, prompted it to seek a partner.[14] Several years before the merger, its chairman took his own life, reportedly because of dismay at the company's poor prospects.[15] A pessimistic view that proved prophetic was that the combination was "a breathing spell in an otherwise headlong dive into bankruptcy and possible government ownership."[16]

One hope for the merger was that creating an entity of great size would provide protection from broader economic trends that threatened the railroads. There was a general belief during the age of managerialism that large companies were more stable and unlikely to fail. As the economist Joseph Schumpeter observed, big businesses have the resources to invest in planning that will give them an advantage over smaller firms in navigating the waves of creative destruction inherent to capitalism.[17] The management expert Peter Drucker observed that the monopoly power of large businesses allowed them to provide more "social stability" than smaller companies.[18] Rather than competing, the New York Central and Pennsylvania would consolidate resources and create efficiencies. The companies predicted that the merger would generate $75 million a year in cost savings.[19] With these additional resources, the new railroad would have the money to turn its core business around.[20] As the US Supreme Court observed in adjudicating the antitrust challenge to the merger, the two companies did not have "profits . . . sufficient to put the roads in a position to make improvements important to the national interest" and "the merger would enable the unified company to accelerate investments in transportation property[,] . . . continually modernize plant equipment[,] . . . and provide more and better service."[21]

Though it was not an explicit motivation for the union of the companies, there may have been an unspoken hope that a railroad as large as the Penn Central would not be permitted to fail. Some commentators believed that the government would intervene to support essential industries that fell on troubled times.[22] Indeed, as noted earlier, on the eve of its bankruptcy, the company lobbied the federal government for a loan that would allow it to continue to operate.

For a time, investors were persuaded that the plan to create a new conglomerate would succeed. From the time the merger was announced to its closing, the combined market capitalization of the companies quadrupled, approaching $2 billion at its peak (about $28 billion in 2021 dollars).[23] The market bought into the idea that the future of the companies would be more promising if they were combined rather than if they remained competitors. As two commentators who wrote about the scandal soon after the bankruptcy observed, "[b]igness has always been admired in this big country, and for quite a while investors put great store in Penn Central's sheer size."[24] Its prominence for a time helped ensure that the company had access to capital markets. In selling Penn Central's commercial paper, Goldman Sachs reportedly overcame the hesitation of one investor by explaining that "there was no reason for concern" because the company had $6.5 billion dollars in assets.[25]

In addition to the advantage of bigness, the merger was based on the belief that diversified conglomerates were inherently safer than more specialized companies. The Penn Central merger was seen as the "beginning of a profitable conglomerate growth."[26] Rather than put all of a company's eggs in one basket, owning a wide range of businesses would provide protection against temporary industry downturns. Even if the railroad business was in a slump, the amusement park business might be on a roll. Conglomeration also relied on the view that expert managers could create value. With a wide range of assets at their disposal, executives would generate a reliable stream of earnings. Some economists believed that managers were better than markets at allocating assets because of their superior access to corporate information.[27] They were in the best position to allocate resources from less promising projects to more promising projects. An example of such a capital allocation decision was Penn Central's effort to invest in new businesses, such as air freight, that were growing more than its railroad business.[28] The company highlighted its diversification strategy in its annual reports to shareholders.

The success of conglomerates like International Telephone & Telegraph (ITT) provided evidence that large, diversified businesses could deliver growing earnings for shareholders. ITT started as an international manufacturer of telecommunications equipment and improved its ranking on the Fortune 500 list from number 52 in 1959 to number 9 in 1970 by acquiring hundreds of companies, including Sheraton Hotels, Avis Rent-a-Car, and Continental Baking (the maker of Wonder Bread).[29] Instead of passively collecting profits, conglomerates like ITT were motivated to increase them. Its CEO, Harold Geneen, "was determined that ITT should present a record of steadily increasing earnings, growing every quarter, to reassure the most skeptical investor that this company, like a liner with stabilizers, was invulnerable to economic storms."[30] Acquisitions allowed ITT to show increasing earnings as new businesses were added to its portfolio.[31]

Even as Penn Central touted its transformation into a conglomerate, there were signs that the strategy was no guarantee of success. Just a few months after the railroad merger closed, the conglomerate Litton Industries reported quarterly earnings that were lower than the previous year's comparable period.[32] The resulting fall in the company's stock price was widely noted by the media. The failure to deliver growth in earnings shook confidence that conglomerate managers would invariably produce profits.

The sharp market reaction to Litton's earnings decline was a sign that managers were facing more pressure from investors. In an earlier time, as the business historian Robert Sobel noted, "The Pennsylvania was not to seek maximization of profits but rather minimization of complaints – especially from influential shippers and travelers."[33] Companies were more likely to look after the interests of workers. Indeed, the merger agreement had provisions protecting against job reductions.[34] Investors were generally passive and did not pressure managers to maximize shareholder wealth. The Harvard economist John Kenneth Galbraith explained, "[s]o long as earnings are above a certain minimum it would also be widely agreed that the management has little to fear from the stockholders."[35] According to Brian Cheffins, the lack of pressure to maximize shareholder wealth during this period "helped to temper corporate wrongdoing."[36]

By the late 1960s, institutional investors such as mutual funds had become more common and paid close attention to earnings. A 1965 *Forbes* article observed that the "whole railroad industry has been guilty of not being profit-conscious," but that approach was changing.[37] A financial analyst in 1967 described the new era of "instant performance" where valuation methods had shifted from "income return, dividends and yield" to "instant earnings growth."[38] A 1969 article in *Forbes* observed that conglomerates "were ideal vehicles for a stock market that had become increasingly performance-minded."[39] A 1972 article in the *Harvard Business Review* noted that investors were increasingly valuing companies based on their future earnings. It observed that there was an "increasing sensitivity of the market to relatively small changes in the company results" and that "a rather small change in expectations may cause a disproportionate stock price movement."[40]

Penn Central thus faced pressure to deliver reports that did not fully reflect its massive losses to investors. Markets no longer deferred to managerial expertise but instead demanded performance. To survive, it would have to create the impression that the merger was succeeding.

PENN CENTRAL'S HIDDEN LOSSES

By the late 1960s, Penn Central was faced with the steady decline of its core railroad operations, which were not profitable. The question was whether this reflected a permanent trend that could not be reversed, or whether measures could be taken to reinvigorate the business. Research analysts were generally aware that the company's railroad business was operating at a loss, but they still believed that the company could recover. Just a few months before the bankruptcy filing, one report predicted that Penn Central's stock had significant appreciation potential despite its poor performance, which created room for improvement. It explained that "the huge railroad deficits incurred over the past year . . . allow for the possibility of a turn-around of magnitude."[41] Penn Central actively promoted the narrative that the worst was behind it. In an interview with *BusinessWeek* about six months before the bankruptcy, Penn Central's CEO cited the possibility of new revenue sources and merger savings that had been greater than expected in concluding that "the tide in the road's fortunes had turned."[42]

To support the turnaround story, the company created the appearance of profits. A report by the Interstate Commerce Commission documented that Penn Central's CEO "issued a mandate to maximize earnings immediately upon assuming control."[43] Part of this strategy included efforts to hide the company's problems from investors. As the SEC later described: "Penn Central management was engaged in an attempt to conceal the extent of the deterioration of the company. One of the elements in this program was the presentation of financial statements which did not reflect the adverse results of railroad operations and which minimized adverse trends in the total business."[44] The company used a variety of questionable accounting decisions that recorded transactions in a way that did not reflect their economic substance.

One of Penn Central's tactics was to monetize its real estate assets to improve its reported operating results.[45] The company did not maintain a clear distinction between revenue it earned from asset sales and revenue it earned from its railroad business. After the company filed for bankruptcy in 1970, *Fortune* magazine criticized Penn Central for recording real estate revenue as part of its operating income.[46] In 1969, Penn Central reported $4.4 million in operating earnings, but $82 million of its operating revenue came from real estate sales. In response to the article, Penn Central's auditors asserted that "Penn Central is one of the largest real estate companies in the world and has substantial real estate transactions every year."[47] Viewed as a conglomerate, Penn Central's operations could be viewed more broadly than its railroad business.

The use of well–timed real estate sales to boost earnings would not normally be viewed as misstating financial results, but there were details about some Penn Central transactions that raised questions about whether they involved valid sales. For example, Penn Central recognized income from the sale of two Six Flags amusement parks to a limited partnership consisting of investors seeking tax losses. Penn Central retained control over the parks as well as the risk of loss if the limited partnership was not able to pay off the substantial debt it took on to purchase the parks. The accounting professor Abraham Briloff, who was developing a reputation for pointing out questionable accounting by companies, argued that this was not a sale and thus about $25 million was improperly included in Penn Central's 1969 10-K.[48] A similar argument was raised decades later with respect to the energy company Enron, which inflated its earnings through transactions with special purpose entities that appeared legitimate on their face but were flawed because they did not represent true sales to third parties. Penn Central's auditor filed an ethics complaint against Briloff arguing he was making unfounded allegations against it and questioned whether "one ordinary transaction netting $25 million or $30 million to Penn Central [was] material?"[49]

The Six Flags transaction could only be material in the context of a system where investors focused on periodic reports of company earnings. While it represented less than half of the revenue generated from Penn Central's real estate transactions for the year, without it, the company would have reported an annual loss in 1969 of $20 million, rather than a profit of $4.4 million.[50] It also would have reported a loss for the second quarter of 1969, for which it had predicted "a favorable showing," rather than earnings of $21.9 million.[51] Briloff noted that there was evidence that the company went to great lengths to execute this transaction before the end of the quarter.[52] Ultimately, the SEC agreed with Briloff's analysis that the amusement parks had not been sold and were an attempt by Penn Central's management to generate the appearance of income.[53] It noted that the transactions "played an important role in management's attempts to control quarterly earnings."[54] In doing so, the SEC acknowledged that even a relatively modest accounting misstatement could be significant given the importance of interim results to the valuation process. The problem was that the company was manipulating perceptions of its earnings trend: "the earnings figures being given to the public were not an accurate picture of the earning power of the corporation."[55]

Penn Central could argue that while some of its transactions misapplied accounting rules, such rules were more ambiguous during the 1970s than they later became. As one proponent of reform wrote in the early 1970s, "a large number of choices do exist as to reporting the amount of net income of a corporation."[56] Another wrote that there was a "cornucopia of [accounting] practices from which to choose."[57] Two accounting professors described net income (earnings) as "a 'meaningless' figure, not unlike the difference between twenty-seven tables and eight chairs."[58] Indeed, Penn Central's auditor stood by its accounting decisions with respect to Penn Central, though it later agreed to an SEC review of its auditing practices.

AN EXPANSIVE THEORY OF SECURITIES FRAUD

In its report of investigation, the SEC asserted a new and expansive theory of securities fraud against Penn Central. It argued that the company's focus on maximizing shareholder wealth motivated it to create a misleading impression of its financial condition. Rather than emphasizing specific violations of accounting rules, the SEC's report took a holistic approach in explaining how the company deceived investors.

The SEC pointed to not only Penn Central's misrepresentation of its past results but its efforts to manipulate perceptions of its future performance. Even as it acknowledged struggles with its business, the company "took pains to suggest that future results would be better" and claimed the "railroad as the asset which has the greatest potential."[59] The company's chairman pushed the company to explore "all possible avenues of increasing reporting income or avoiding actions which would reduce reported income."[60] Penn Central's efforts reduced reported losses from its railroad business in 1968 and 1969 by more than $100 million in each year.[61] As a result, the company created the impression that its problems were manageable and it had time to fix any problems as the integration of the two businesses progressed.

Penn Central and its managers argued that they did not intend to deceive investors. They claimed that they genuinely believed that the company would recover. An article in *Fortune* magazine described Penn Central's CEO as having an "incurable optimism" that led him to believe "that if he kept saying he could do something he would inevitably succeed at it."[62] Just as Xerox's executives claimed they relied on the company's auditors, the CEO "sought to create the impression that he was not an accountant and would almost blindly and without question accept anything accounting personnel proposed."[63]

Penn Central's securities fraud was not as egregious as the other major public company securities fraud of the 1970s, which was committed by Equity Funding, a Los Angeles insurer. That company inflated its earnings by fabricating insurance policies that had never been issued. It then transferred the fake policies to unwitting reinsurers for cash payments that Equity Funding misreported as revenue. The scheme was unsustainable because Equity Funding was then obligated in future years to pass on premiums to the reinsurer that it had supposedly earned from the nonexistent insurance policies. The company thus had to issue even more bogus policies to meet these obligations.[64] By the end of the scheme, more than 50,000 fake insurance policies had been issued, representing about $2 billion in insurance coverage.[65] The company went to extraordinary lengths to hide the fraud. A group headed by a young manager in his twenties and support staff working from the company's Beverly Hills office quickly created fake insurance files in response to requests by auditors who had randomly selected policies to verify.[66]

Equity Funding was not the first public company to make up financial results. In 1938, the New York Stock Exchange suspended trading of the pharmaceuticals company McKesson & Robbins after the revelation that it had forged parts of its inventory. The fraud was undetected by company auditors, prompting an SEC investigation and calls for reform.[67] But Equity Funding's fabrication was distinctive because it happened in the context of new market pressure to increase earnings. The report by the bankruptcy trustee observed that the Equity Funding scandal was "essentially a securities fraud" in that it was "initially motivated and then sustained throughout the decade of its existence by an obsessive desire on the part of its participants to inflate and keep aloft the market price of [the company's] common stock."[68] Equity Funding was viewed by the market as "a financial services conglomerate with a fabulous growth record that apparently was immune from the economic ups and downs that affect the stock market and most other corporations."[69] In fact, the amount of fake revenue reported from 1964 through 1972 was equal to almost twice the profits the company reported during that timeframe.[70] As concerns grew about the extent of the fraud, Equity Funding's president flatly rejected the possibility of stopping it because it would have required reporting flat earnings to the stock market.[71] After the fraud was revealed and the company collapsed, he pleaded guilty to criminal felony charges and was sentenced to eight years in prison.[72] Hundreds of the company's employees were tarnished by association and could not find employment within the insurance industry.[73] Investors recovered about $60 million in settlements through securities litigation.[74]

Penn Central was not as mendacious as Equity Funding. It did not blatantly create false revenue. Its concern was with buying time to turn around a struggling business rather than boosting its stock price to higher levels. But it engaged in enough questionable reporting to support a significant claim for securities fraud. The SEC sued Penn Central and its high-level officers for violations of Rule 10b-5 and other securities law provisions about four years after its bankruptcy filing.[75] The core of the complaint was a basic accounting fraud claim. The SEC alleged that Penn Central's financial statements were "materially false and misleading in that . . . they reflected the results of programs and practices designed to improperly record revenue items . . . while not recording appropriately expenses."[76] These errors were "designed . . . to conceal the adverse operational performance and critical financial condition" of Penn Central.[77] Notably, the complaint also asserted a broader theory that might not be viable under current Rule 10b-5 doctrine faulting Penn Central's statements of optimism about the merger, its use of dividends to "create a false impression of financial soundness," and the deceptive assertion that the company's "diversification program" was "highly successful."[78] The suit was described by the

SEC, which had recently formed a separate enforcement division in 1972, as "one of the most important ever brought by the agency."[79]

The SEC only sought injunctive relief in its case against Penn Central as it did not have the power to seek penalties at the time. The SEC's case was supplemented by class actions filed by investors against Penn Central's officers and other parties alleging claims under Rule 10b-5. As described by a federal district court, their claim was that "various reports, statements, documents and press releases were intended to and did inflate the market price of Penn Central Co. stock and affect plaintiffs and the investing public in their decisions to purchase, sell and hold Penn Central Co. stock."[80] The complaint noted that insiders who knew about the company's true condition sold a substantial amount of their stock before the truth became known. The private litigation settled in 1976 for about $10 million,[81] a modest amount given the size of the losses suffered by investors. On the other hand, given that only a portion of the alleged misstatements involved accounting violations, there was an argument that only part of the investor losses could be linked to fraudulent misrepresentations.

The SEC also brought claims against a number of capital markets gatekeepers who failed to prevent the fraud. The SEC sued Peat Marwick, Penn Central's auditor, for signing off on its financial statements even though they "were not presented in conformity with generally accepted accounting principles."[82] It also sued Goldman Sachs, which underwrote Penn Central's commercial paper.

Goldman knew that the company was having cash flow problems but did not further investigate the situation. Instead, it represented to investors that the company was a high-quality issuer that was being closely monitored. Even as it was selling the railroad's commercial paper to investors, Goldman was reducing its own holdings in Penn Central.[83] Under one account, the bank finally stopped selling Penn Central commercial paper after the law firm Sullivan & Cromwell alerted it to problems in Penn Central's financial statements.[84] In defending itself, Goldman argued that it was just as surprised as investors by this unprecedented failure of a leading public company.[85] It also noted that the commercial paper was sold to sophisticated investors who did not need protection. In addition to facing SEC charges, a jury ordered Goldman to pay several Penn Central commercial paper investors $3 million plus interest (covering 100 percent of their losses), and the investment bank paid millions to settle other investor litigation.[86]

By the time of Penn Central's bankruptcy, markets were scrutinizing corporate performance. The nation's largest railroad could not escape the pressure of demonstrating to capital markets that its turnaround plan was succeeding. The company used a wide range of measures, some of which were questionable, to deceive investors. When investors no longer trusted its financial statements, the company could not access the funds it needed to survive. Investors who were unaware of the precarious state of the company were shocked as their stock proved to be worth a fraction of what it had been trading for.

INSIDER TRADING

Penn Central's efforts to avoid reporting the full extent of its losses can be viewed in light of a theory developed by Jennifer Arlen and William Carney. They contend that securities fraud is typically committed by managers who act in their own selfish interests when they believe that their company is in its last period and likely to fail.[87] They explain that securities fraud "generally will be committed by officers and directors seeking to conceal from the market, and from the firm's shareholders, that the firm is ailing in an attempt to save their jobs and their investments in the firm."[88] While such conduct may be irrational in that the chance of a successful turnaround is very low and may not be the course of action preferred by the shareholders, the manager hopes that "by committing fraud he is able to buy sufficient time to turn the ailing firm around."[89]

One selfish reason executives hide the failing condition of a firm is to provide themselves with an opportunity to sell their shares in the company before the stock price collapses. Some of Penn Central's officers, particularly its chief financial officer (CFO), sold a substantial percentage of their shares before Penn Central's problems were fully disclosed to the public. Collectively, Penn Central's executives sold 70 percent of the shares they owned between the closing of the merger and the bankruptcy filing.[90] On the other hand, Penn Central's CEO, who was an important driver of the effort to maximize reported earnings, did not sell any shares during this period.[91]

The financial institutions who learned of Penn Central's problems as it was attempting to raise new funds systematically exited their positions. During the two and a half months before the bankruptcy filing, nine institutional investors sold more than 1.8 million shares, representing a third of all the shares traded over that period.[92] Penn Central's collapse thus raised questions about whether its securities fraud gave insiders and privileged investors time to profit at the expense of the public.

The securities laws seek to equalize access to the most important information about a public company and its prospects.[93] They mandate truthful disclosure of a company's financial results and other information to encourage such parity. Securities fraud, which avoids such disclosure, undermines that policy and creates significant asymmetry between the public and insiders. Individuals who know the truth have an unfair advantage relative to public investors. There is thus a close relationship between securities fraud and insider trading.

As noted earlier, insider trading is now commonly cited as a motivation for public company executives to commit securities fraud. A misstatement is more likely to be viewed as part of a scheme to deceive investors rather than an innocent mistake when a company's managers take advantage of the situation to convert their shares into cash. It is more difficult for executives to argue that they believed the condition of the company was sound when they dramatically reduce their personal investment in its equity. When insiders systematically sell their shares, questionable accounting decisions look more like a concerted effort to defraud markets rather than good faith judgments made under pressure.

At the time of Penn Central's collapse, the law of insider trading was just emerging. Just a few years earlier in the important *Texas Gulf Sulphur* decision,[94] the influential US Court of Appeals for the Second Circuit set forth a broad rule prohibiting trading by anyone in possession of material information about a company. The federal appellate court held that any individual, not just insiders, was required to disclose that information before trading on it. Such insider trading would be fraudulent conduct that would violate Rule 10b-5. Though this equal access rule would later be limited by the US Supreme Court (one of the cases where it did so involved trading in Equity Funding stock),[95] the selling by banks that possessed information about Penn Central's condition would have potentially run afoul of *Texas Gulf Sulphur*.

The SEC filed an insider trading claim against Penn Central's CFO but not against other executives who also sold stock.[96] Asserting a defense that is common even today, the Penn Central managers argued that their sales were part of routine efforts to diversify their holdings. Banks denied that they traded on insider information because the divisions that knew of Penn Central's troubles were separated from the divisions that made investment decisions. Given the uncertain state of the law and the presence of factual uncertainty, the SEC may have believed that winning insider trading cases against most of the potential defendants would be too challenging.

The sales by Penn Central insiders were disturbing and problematic, but it was not clear that the primary motivation for the company's fraud was to enrich individual executives. There were also corporate incentives to commit securities fraud. As one court noted in another case, securities fraud often involves "a frenzied effort by a troubled company to conceal its difficulties for as long as possible."[97] Penn Central knew that if it did not hide the true state of its business, it could fail, causing turmoil not only for shareholders but the company's many workers and consumers. It is possible that the company's shareholders would have preferred that the managers simply throw in the towel, but it is also possible that the shareholders would have preferred that the managers try to turn the company around. It is important to recognize that corporate securities fraud is often motivated by more than the enrichment of company executives.

The reports of insider trading in Penn Central stock reduced confidence that managers were public trustees who acted selflessly. As stock awards became a more important way of compensating executives, the enrichment of executives continued to be cited as a motivation for securities fraud. Decades later, much was made of the fact that Enron executives sold millions of dollars in stock before their questionable accounting decisions were discovered. Fairly or not, unusual sales of stock before a stock price decline can be a powerful factor supporting a finding of securities fraud.

CORPORATE GOVERNANCE

An extensive portion of the SEC's report on Penn Central discussed its corporate governance. It especially criticized the company's board for remaining passive while its management misrepresented the prospects of its core business. As managers became more important to large corporations, shareholders relied on boards to represent their interests and prevent managerial misconduct. Unlike a smaller company, Penn Central had the resources to assemble a reputable board of directors. The question was why the board did not do more to address Penn Central's problems before they became too large to handle. The collapse of Penn Central prompted some of the first attempts to link corporate governance and securities fraud in public companies.

Penn Central was clearly mismanaged. The company paid $100 million in dividends even as its operating cash flow was declining, an amount that might have provided it with sufficient liquidity to survive (the company's failed bond offering that prompted its bankruptcy filing attempted to raise $100 million). Moreover, there were allegations of self-dealing within the company. For example, in addition to selling enough stock to prompt a charge of insider trading, the company's CFO was a shareholder of an investment fund while also controlling Penn Central's pension fund. The two funds made several investments in the same companies, raising the possibility that Penn Central's pension fund investments were being directed in such a way to increase the value of the shares owned by the CFO's fund.[98] Years later, Enron was viewed as corrupt partly because of self-dealing by its CFO who profited from an entity that entered into questionable transactions with Enron.

But not all mismanagement of a company will support an allegation of securities fraud. A company must deceive investors to be liable under Rule 10b-5. Simple incompetence is not enough. Even self-dealing may be insufficient to establish a securities fraud claim if it does not involve transactions large enough to significantly affect the company's market value. The securities laws do not give the SEC the general power to require that public companies adhere to high standards of corporate governance. Securities regulation primarily addresses fraud with some connection to the purchase or sale of securities.[99] Shareholders have other remedies provided by corporate law rather than securities law that permits them to sue boards or managers for their general misconduct.

At the same time, it is difficult to completely separate the issues of securities fraud and corporate governance. Investors often view securities fraud as a sign that a company's corporate governance is inadequate. If a company with a nine-figure market valuation suddenly files for bankruptcy, there will be questions about why its board failed to ensure that the company's problems were disclosed earlier to the market. As public corporations grew larger and more complex, and investors came to realize that they could not always trust management, it became more important for corporate boards to monitor managers for fraud.

At the time of the Penn Central scandal, the norm was that boards of public companies deferred to corporate managers. The SEC's report concluded that the railroad's directors "were accustomed to a generally inactive role" in the company and "never changed the view of their role."[100] This criticism may not have been entirely fair. Prior to the bankruptcy, several board members wrote letters to the CEO complaining that they had not been provided with sufficient information to evaluate Penn Central's performance.[101] The board claimed to be just as surprised as outside investors by the poor state of the company. Once it became clear that it was close to bankruptcy, the directors leapt to action in seeking a government bailout and dismissing the company's CEO and CFO.

The stunning collapse of Penn Central helped support efforts to improve the performance of boards. Several years after the scandal, Melvin Eisenberg argued that one of the primary functions of the board is to monitor management. In his important book, *The Structure of the Corporation*,[102] Eisenberg argued that such monitoring is difficult when the board is dominated by members who are also managers. He thus proposed that companies should increase the number of directors who are independent of managers. Reformers such as Ralph Nader argued for more significant change through measures including the federal regulation of corporate law.[103] The SEC increased its efforts to change the corporate governance of public companies in the 1970s. Through its enforcement powers, the SEC required some companies that violated the securities laws to implement various reforms such as adding independent directors to their boards. Not all experts believed that corporate governance reform was warranted and would be effective. A former SEC commissioner, Roberta Karmel, later described this period of SEC activism as "an effort to blame business for the prevailing climate of corruption, a stagflation economy and a long bear market."[104] A new Republican administration in the 1980s shifted the administrative agency away from corporate governance regulation. It was not until the late 1990s that securities fraud was again seen as a problem of public company governance.

THE AFTERMATH OF PENN CENTRAL

The failure of Penn Central generated a significant amount of media coverage and attention from regulators and Congress. Along with some other corporate scandals that occurred during the 1970s, Penn Central helped spur federal efforts to improve the disclosure, accounting, and internal controls of public companies. The need for these reforms reflected a new recognition that securities fraud was not just a problem for small companies. These efforts also reflected the evolution away from the managerialist paradigm that had largely deferred to corporate managers.

The immediate economic impact of Penn Central's bankruptcy was limited. There was some concern that the commercial paper market would be affected by the company's default. If investors believed that other public companies had similar problems, they might be unwilling to invest in their short-term debt. The Federal Reserve quickly intervened with a $2 billion program to support the market, and there were no other significant defaults. Railroad stocks generally fell by an average of 20 percent but recovered as it became clear that Penn Central's tactics were not widespread in the industry.

Penn Central was not the only accounting fraud by a public company during the 1970s that generated investor lawsuits and SEC enforcement. The sudden collapse of the Four Seasons Nursing Centers corporation resulted in a securities class action alleging that from 1968 to 1970, the company "made many optimistic statements with respect [to its] projected earnings ... which were not realized."[105] In addition to a private settlement of $8 million, a number of the company's executives and its auditors were criminally prosecuted and pleaded guilty to criminal securities fraud for improperly inflating the company's profits.[106] Investors won a $50 million settlement in a securities class action against US Financial, filed after the SEC questioned its accounting and its trading was suspended by the New York Stock Exchange in 1972.[107] The SEC later brought suit against US Financial (which filed for bankruptcy) and its auditor, alleging that it inflated its revenue by selling assets to parties controlled by its insiders.[108] A number of US Financial's executives were indicted and its chairman received a three-year prison term.[109] The fabrication of revenue at National Student Marketing, a company that sold products to college students, resulted in class actions that recovered $35 million through settlements;[110] criminal convictions of some of the company's auditors;[111] and a controversial SEC enforcement case against its law firm.[112] While the profile of these companies and others was not as significant as Penn Central, these cases are evidence that by the 1970s public companies had an incentive to inflate their earnings and revenue to meet market expectations.

In the wake of the increasing scrutiny of public company financial reporting, the SEC pushed for better accounting standards. The SEC Chair, William J. Casey, who later headed the CIA, gave a 1972 speech in which he argued for a shift where "making earnings statements as comparable and as uniform as possible will gain priority over the frequently conflicting objective of affording management choice and flexibility in the way it keeps score."[113] An extensive study by a Congressional subcommittee observed that "[c]ontinued revelations of wrongdoing by publicly owned corporations have caused a new awareness of the importance of accounting practices in permitting such abuses to occur."[114] Various reforms such as the creation of the Financial Accounting Standards Board, an independent body that would develop uniform accounting standards with less industry influence, followed.[115]

By the mid-1970s, another set of scandals involving public companies emerged. After the Watergate scandal, investigations that initially focused on scrutinizing questionable political contributions found that a significant number of corporations were paying bribes in connection with their overseas businesses.[116] The regulation of corporate bribes did not fall within the original reach of the securities laws, but the

SEC took the position that its periodic disclosure requirements had been violated because the corporations had not disclosed the bribes.

Congress responded by passing the Foreign Corrupt Practices Act of 1977 (FCPA), which amended the securities laws to prohibit bribery by public companies. In addition, the FCPA enacted some important provisions relating to corporate disclosure. The statute amended section 13 of the Securities Exchange Act of 1934 to add two requirements. First, public companies are required to keep books and records that in "reasonable detail, accurately and fairly reflect the transactions and dispositions of the assets of the issuer."[117] Second, the FCPA requires public companies to "devise and maintain a system of internal accounting controls sufficient to provide reasonable assurance" that the company's accounting complies with GAAP.[118] The legislative history set forth an expectation that "[t]he establishment and maintenance of a system of internal controls and accurate books and records are fundamental responsibilities of management."[119]

Initially, public corporations were concerned about the internal controls requirement because its general wording seemed to give the SEC substantial power to reshape their reporting processes.[120] However, the SEC signaled a few years later (at the start of the Reagan administration) that the law would not be aggressively enforced. The SEC released a policy statement in 1981 addressing the "spectre which some commentators have raised of exposure to Commission enforcement action, and perhaps criminal liability, as a result of technical and insignificant errors in corporate records or weaknesses in corporate internal accounting controls."[121] The SEC reassured public companies that internal controls should mainly be shaped by the "judgment of company management."[122] It explained that given the "almost infinite variety of control devices which could be utilized in a particular business environment," it believed that "considerable deference properly should be afforded to the company's reasonable business judgments in this area."[123] In addition to a lenient substantive interpretation of the requirement, the SEC suggested that it would not enforce it. The release observed that "we have not chosen to bring a single case under these [accounting] provisions that did not also involve other violations of law."[124] The power of the internal controls mandate thus became largely dormant for more than two decades until it was resurrected by Sarbanes–Oxley.

* * *

A skeptic might look at Penn Central and argue that even without the fraud, the company would have likely failed. Better management could not have avoided the reality that the railroad industry was in fundamental decline. The company was arguably pushed into bankruptcy through losses caused by events out of its control – the poor economy in the late 1960s and higher operating costs from an unusually harsh winter that exacerbated its cash flow problems.[125] Many other railroads went bankrupt during the 1970s.[126] Penn Central's railroad assets were eventually consolidated with other failed railroad assets and transferred to an entity owned by the US government.[127]

But Penn Central did more than make a series of unwise corporate decisions. Its financial statements did not reflect reality, and it was the realization that the railroad's reporting was false that prevented it from accessing the capital markets. As the SEC viewed the case, "[p]erhaps management had hopes of some future improvement, but the shareholders and the public were entitled to be provided with the picture as it existed at the time, minus the impact of the temporary expedients being utilized to provide the illusion that the company was on the road to recovery when it was not."[128] Only a privileged few truly understood the depths of the company's problems.

The Penn Central scandal showed how even a large corporation with billions of dollars in assets, a storied past, and professional managers could deceive investors. Its earlier successes did not immunize it from the emerging pressure to show investors earnings growth. The managerialist paradigm was no longer dominant, and public corporations had to continually deliver evidence that supported their market valuations. Penn Central was an example of how this valuation pressure could result in conduct that threatened the integrity of a corporate giant's disclosure. While those concerns faded for a time in the absence of a securities fraud of similar magnitude as the Penn Central and Equity Funding cases, for various reasons,[129] they reemerged in a similar form decades later.

4

Apple and the Controversy of Projections Litigation

This case presents the grimly familiar picture of disappointed investors crying fraud after fortunes were lost when a promising corporation stumbled.

US District Court for the District of Massachusetts, 1993

In the Xerox and Penn Central cases, public companies misstated their financial statements to support false narratives of their ability to continue generating profits. Companies also shape investor perceptions of their future performance through disclosures about their businesses, particularly with respect to important products. Just as the conglomerates of the 1970s sought to satisfy market expectations by reporting earnings increases, the computer companies of the 1980s faced pressure to successfully complete the development of new technologies. Investors were willing to pay more for a stock to take into account the possibility that a promising product would be widely embraced by consumers. However, if there was a significant setback, they could lose faith and flee the stock. Computer company stocks were thus more volatile than the stocks of companies in traditional industries.[1]

By the end of the 1980s, the increasing use of forecasts by investors to value companies and the changing fortunes of technology companies helped spur an explosion of what has been described as projections litigation. If a company introduced a product that was not as successful as predicted, or had some other problem with its business, its stock price would decline as it missed prior projections that turned out to be too ambitious. The failure would provide investors with a basis for arguing that a company's management had been aware of business problems, did not acknowledge them, and instead issued overoptimistic disclosures to maintain the company's stock price.

The securities class action filed in the mid-1980s against Apple Computer (Apple) and some of its executives for the failure of the Lisa computer involved the typical arguments raised in cases alleging that a company deceived investors about the prospects of an important product. On the one hand, investors should understand that companies have an incentive to portray their future optimistically and know that not every prediction comes to fruition. Apple argued that it believed in good faith that the product would be a success and should not be punished for its failure. On the other hand, companies have an incentive to hide setbacks that might adversely affect their valuation. The plaintiffs argued that Apple's failure to acknowledge known problems with an important product was deceptive.

The Apple case went to trial in 1991, and a jury found that two of Apple's executives were liable under Rule 10b-5 and awarded the plaintiffs $100 million in damages. Before the trial, a federal appellate court had narrowed the scope of the case by ruling that the stock market was well aware that the Lisa computer had problems and that Apple's generally optimistic statements about the new desktop did not affect the valuation of its stock. However, the appellate court found that Apple's failure to disclose problems with the disk drive it was developing for the Lisa could support a claim for securities fraud. Specific statements concerning the potential of the drive at some point were arguably false, unknown to the market, and if they were made with fraudulent intent, would support liability under Rule 10b-5. The jury's verdict was overturned by the trial court, which ordered a retrial against just Apple, and the parties settled the case for a fraction of the original award of $100 million rather than try the case again.

The Apple securities litigation highlighted some of the problems with the private litigation that was the primary mechanism by which securities fraud cases were brought during the 1980s. Because of the difficulty of writing clear rules identifying when knowledge of a potential business failure supports an allegation of securities fraud, it was challenging for courts to screen out bad cases from good cases. When the stock price decline that spurred a case against a public company was significant, the potential damages that could result from a class action brought under Rule 10b-5 were high enough so that there was a significant incentive for the defendant to settle the case rather than risk a large jury verdict.

To address this problem, in 1995, Congress acted to provide stronger protections from meritless securities fraud litigation for public companies. Many of the provisions in this law, the Private Securities Litigation Reform Act (PSLRA),[2] made it more difficult for projections litigation to succeed when it is based solely on vague allegations that corporate managers knew that their predictions would not come to fruition. The Securities and Exchange Commission (SEC) supported this law because it had adopted a policy of encouraging public companies to issue projections and believed that litigation would discourage such voluntary disclosure. Even with the PSLRA, allegations of a fraudulent misstatement that fails to acknowledge problems with a product or business that would affect the company's prospects are still commonly filed. However, for these cases to proceed, plaintiffs must describe specific evidence that a corporation had contemporaneous knowledge of substantial problems when it made an optimistic statement.

THE APPLE SECURITIES CLASS ACTION

The Promise of the Lisa

At the start of the 1980s, Apple faced an uncertain future. It needed a new product to build on the success of its iconic personal computer, the Apple II. Sales of that computer had grown from 2,500 units in 1977 to more than 200,000 units in 1981, providing the foundation for its record–breaking initial public offering. A company that had started just a few years earlier in a garage had become a corporation worth more than a billion dollars. Its transition to an established public technology company had not been completely smooth. The immediate sequel to the Apple II, the Apple III, had a design defect that tended to make its computer chip overheat. IBM entered the personal computer market toward the end of 1981 with the introduction of its IBM PC. Apple thus faced a formidable competitor and needed to innovate to keep its share of the market. Rather than rely on the genius of its cofounders, Apple had to show that it had created an organization that could continue to develop successful new computers.

Part of the inspiration for Apple's next project came from Xerox. As it dominated the plain-paper copier market, Xerox had enough resources to invest in research unrelated to its core business. It devoted its Palo Alto Research Center (PARC), which was located across the country from its east coast headquarters, to developing computer technology. When Apple was a promising start-up, Xerox made an investment in the company. In return for the right to buy 100,000 shares in Apple for $10.50 a share,[3] Xerox granted the cofounder of Apple, Steve Jobs, the right to visit PARC twice. During that visit, Jobs famously took note of the graphical interface and mouse that the PARC researchers had developed.

These features were incorporated into the Lisa, which specifically targeted business customers rather than individuals who wanted a computer for personal use. Simultaneously, Apple developed a smaller version of the Lisa for the home market called the Macintosh. While Jobs initially worked on the Lisa, he later lost control of that project and instead took over the effort to develop the Macintosh. The two products competed internally within Apple for resources and prominence.

While the plan was to develop a computer that would sell for about $2,000, the Lisa initially retailed for $9,995. Though this was cheaper than the $16,000 cost of the personal computer that Xerox unsuccessfully introduced to the market, the price of the Lisa was too high given its capabilities. The computer was slow and could not handle graphics. Apple projected it would sell 59,000 Lisa computers in the first year but only sold about 20,000. The high-performance disk drive Apple had developed for the Lisa, the Twiggy, was so problematic that it had to be discontinued. The day after the announcement that the Twiggy would be replaced, Apple's stock price fell by 25 percent.

As the problems with the Lisa became evident, Apple's stock price fell from $63 in November 1982 to $17 in September 1983. While at least part of the decline reflected the flood of new competitors introducing their own computers, the resulting investor losses spurred a lawsuit alleging securities fraud.

The Rise of Securities Class Actions

When Penn Central collapsed during the early 1970s, securities class actions were in their infancy. A class action, where a group of plaintiffs brings one suit making the same allegations against a defendant, only became a potent way of recovering securities fraud damages in 1966. That year, the Federal Rules of Civil Procedure were amended to permit the filing of a class action that presumed that all members of the class were included in the action unless they chose to opt out.[4] Any investor that purchased stock at a price inflated by fraud would automatically be part of the ensuing securities class action, increasing the potential damages in such a case. Private class actions offered a way of supplementing enforcement by government agencies. The SEC at the time did not have the power to impose penalties, and thus the private actions filed against companies like Penn Central and Equity Funding were the main avenue for stock purchasers to win a monetary recovery.

In bringing a private suit, investors can invoke broad legal prohibitions of securities fraud. Section 10(b) of the Securities Exchange Act of 1934 generally prohibits "manipulative or deceptive" practices "in connection with the purchase or sale of any security" and authorizes the SEC to pass rules regulating such practices. The SEC used this power to pass Rule 10b-5, which plaintiffs commonly invoke against corporations that issue material misrepresentations with the fraudulent intent to inflate the price of their stock.

For some time, there were questions about whether Rule 10b-5 could be used to sue public companies for securities fraud. Unlike a typical fraud case where a misstatement is made directly by the seller to a buyer, a public company's misrepresentation is not typically aimed at a single purchaser. The SEC in its 1963 Special Study of Securities Markets was unsure about the "usefulness" of Rule 10b-5 in addressing misleading company statements.[5] As late as 1967, a prominent securities lawyer noted that the legal theory "that a corporation may be liable for damages if it issues a misleading [earnings] statement and investors, relying on that statement buy or sell the company's securities" was "not settled."[6] Adam Pritchard and Robert Thompson found a 1968 memo by Judge Henry Friendly, who sat on the US Court of Appeals for the Second Circuit, expressing concern about the costs that would be incurred by corporations if they were liable under Rule 10b-5 for misleading press releases.[7] The Second Circuit pushed past this concern and dropped the requirement that a statement be directed at a particular investor.[8] Toward the end of the 1960s and early 1970s, investors started bringing Rule 10b-5 claims against public companies for losses caused by fraudulent misstatements.[9]

Another question was whether a Rule 10b-5 claim arising out of a corporate misstatement could be brought as a class action. When a corporation speaks, not all stock purchasers listen. Many investors who suffered losses and could be part of a class were unaware of the allegedly fraudulent corporate statement when they bought the stock. Such potential plaintiffs cannot claim that they relied on the misstatement at issue in deciding to buy the corporation's stock. Because reliance is an element of any fraud claim, their case would be much weaker than the case of a plaintiff who could show reliance on the misstatement. Because class action procedural rules only permit parties in similar situations to be part of the same class, there was an obstacle to bringing a class action on behalf of all those who purchased the stock while it was inflated by a fraud.

Even if not every investor is aware of information the corporation releases to the public, the stock market is always paying attention. Some sophisticated investor or research analyst will understand the significance of the new information. Under what financial economists call the efficient markets hypothesis, transactions by informed investors in a stock frequently traded in a public market will move the stock's price to a level that reflects all publicly available information. In such an efficient market, if a false corporate statement is believed and inflates the market price, investors will have paid too much and are damaged regardless of whether they were aware of that particular statement.

Public company securities fraud has thus been described by courts as a fraud on the market. In a Rule 10b-5 case involving an accounting fraud in the late 1960s, the court explained, "the predominant issue in this case is the alleged fraudulent nature of [the defendant's] financial statements and representations and their effect on the market price of [the defendant's] securities."[10] If the price of a stock trading in an efficient market is inflated by a false statement, investors who relied on the integrity of that market price are all similarly affected. Courts thus presumed that such investors met the reliance requirement of Rule 10b-5 and had enough in common to join together in a class action. Notably, many of the pioneering courts that adopted this theory did so in cases involving allegations of misstated earnings.[11] These decisions reflected the reality that investors were increasingly assessing earnings in valuing companies and that the dissemination of incorrect financial statements could distort stock prices. In 1988, the US Supreme Court drew on the efficient markets hypothesis in adopting a fraud-on-the-market presumption for Rule 10b-5 class actions in its *Basic v. Levinson* decision.[12]

This presumption mainly enabled the filing of securities class actions against larger public companies with stock that traded frequently in markets such as the New York Stock Exchange that could be considered efficient. Such stocks are more likely to be monitored closely by investors who will trade quickly on new information. In contrast, the presumption is not available when a company's stock only trades infrequently in an inefficient market. It is often not possible to bring a securities class action against a small public company that is not listed on a national stock exchange. Securities fraud litigation thus imposes greater obligations on large public companies to speak truthfully to the marketplace. With *Basic*, securities fraud regulation decisively shifted away from its original focus on emerging companies selling securities to the public for the first time to policing the integrity of the markets where the stock of significant public companies trade.[13]

Apple's Projections and Rule 10b-5

After the Lisa failed, the question was whether Apple had misled the stock market about its prospects. Apple had been confident and upbeat about the new computer, declaring that "Lisa is going to be phenomenally successful." The plaintiffs who sued Apple for securities fraud alleged that the market price was inflated by positive predictions about the product's impact on Apple's profitability. They claimed that Apple knew about problems with the Lisa that should have been shared with investors.

There was legal support for the argument that Apple could be liable under Rule 10b-5 for a false prediction. In its 1974 decision in *Marx* v. *Computer Sciences Corporation*,[14] the US Court of Appeals for the Ninth Circuit, which covers Apple's home state of California, extensively analyzed the ways in which a financial projection can be false. The case involved a forecast issued by a vice president of a computer company. While addressing a group of stock analysts, he predicted that the company would earn about $1.00 per share for the fiscal year. Copies of the speech were printed, and the forecast was disseminated to a broader set of investors. The plaintiff bought the company's stock at a price of $30 a share. At the end of the year, the company missed the forecast and announced earnings of only 41 cents per share, and its stock price fell to $10 a share.[15] The plaintiff sued under Rule 10b-5.

The Ninth Circuit began its decision in *Marx* by establishing that a projection is more than just an opinion. It wrote that "a forecast, essentially a prediction, may be regarded as a 'fact.'"[16] When a corporation makes a projection, at the very least it represents that the projection is more than a wild guess. The court explained that "because such a statement implies a reasonable method of preparation and a valid basis . . . it would be 'untrue' absent such preparation or basis."[17] *Marx* implied that investors could challenge a prediction as false on the ground that the corporation did not have an adequate basis for the prediction.

In *Apple*, the district court initially dismissed the complaint, which alleged that the company violated Rule 10b-5. On appeal, the Ninth Circuit considered whether the case could proceed. The appellate court cited *Marx* in acknowledging that "projections and general expressions of optimism may be actionable under the federal securities laws." It observed that every projection makes "at least three implicit factual assertions: (1) that the statement is genuinely believed, (2) that there is a reasonable basis for that belief, and (3) that the speaker is not aware of any undisclosed facts tending to seriously undermine the accuracy of the statement."[18]

Under *Marx*, Apple's optimistic statements about the Lisa could be misstatements if Apple did not have a reasonable basis for those statements or knew of facts that undermined their accuracy. However, both the district and appellate courts were unwilling to conclude that investors naively believed optimistic projections made with respect to the computer. They recognized that markets do not take every statement at face value. The industry would not have blindly accepted Apple's prediction that the Lisa would be a success. Indeed, many computer magazines and newspaper articles had expressed skepticism about the Lisa's prospects. Because Apple was a public company, its stock traded in markets where sophisticated investors would be aware of these expert views and the real risk that the project would fail. It would be unfair to presume that efficient markets are affected by misleading information (which would permit the lawsuit to go forward as a class action under *Basic* v. *Levinson*) but are not affected by other publicly available information. Both district and appellate courts thus concluded under what is commonly called the truth-on-the-market doctrine that Apple's optimistic statements about the Lisa and its prospects could not support a claim for securities fraud.

In contrast, this defense did not protect Apple when it had specific information unknown to the market about a problem that would prevent it from fulfilling its optimistic goals. Part of the promise of the Lisa was that it would include a high-performance disk drive called the Twiggy. Apple conveyed the impression that the drive was a finished product and would give the Lisa an advantage over its competitors. It thus stated in a press release that the disk drive "ensures greater integrity of data than the other high density drives by way of a unique, double-sided mechanism designed and manufactured by Apple."[19] It also stated that the Twiggy had been developed over three years and subject to extensive testing for the last year. These statements essentially represented that Apple had a basis for predicting that the Twiggy would make the Lisa a more attractive product for customers. But before these statements were released, Apple's internal testing had found significant problems with the speed and reliability of the drive that would delay its successful completion by many months. Thus, the company may not have had a genuine belief or reasonable basis in the truth of its prediction that the disk drive would make the Lisa a better product. As the Ninth Circuit explained, there was an "issue of whether Twiggy's technical problems were material facts tending to undermine the unqualified optimism" of Apple's statements.[20] Because outsiders did not know of these problems until Apple abandoned the Twiggy, the statement that the Lisa would have a high-performance disk drive could have distorted Apple's stock price.

The Trial

After the appeal, the case was remanded for trial on the deceptiveness of Apple's statements about the Twiggy's promise. Apple and the plaintiffs debated whether the failure to disclose the Twiggy's problems was a scheme to deceive investors or reflected challenges typical of developing new technology. Did Apple know at some point that the product had problems that made failure likely? Or did it believe in good faith that the problems could be resolved? These were questions that arose not only with respect to the Lisa, but other innovative products developed by technology companies.

Apple first argued that its statements relating to the Twiggy would not have been taken literally by the industry. It asserted that companies commonly announced the introduction of products that had not been completely developed. Some of this technology would never actually become commercially viable. One *Forbes* magazine article famously referred to such products as vaporware that were marketed with "a grandiose promise delivered late or never."[21] Apple thus contended that "computer industry preannouncements are understood to mean that the product is not ready."[22] A company might widely publicize a product before it was completed to guide other companies interested in developing related products. For example, it would be useful for software companies to know about the Twiggy so they could begin developing programs compatible with the disk drive. If the stock market was aware of this norm, the truth-on-the-market defense might also protect Apple's statements about the Twiggy.

One response to this argument is that such a practice, even though accepted by the computer industry, can go too far. A preannouncement that simply describes a product under development is different from a preannouncement that portrays a product as essentially complete. If a disk drive was described as basically finished, it would be a surprise to investors to later learn that there were specific problems that threatened its viability.

In addition to claiming it had not issued a misleading statement, Apple asserted that it had acted in good faith rather than with fraudulent intent. Unlike some examples of vaporware, it was not guilty of promising a product that it never intended to develop. It made a significant investment in the disk drive and actually delivered it (though consumers were not pleased with its performance and it had to be discontinued). Moreover, it argued that the problems that emerged were typical of the development cycle for a groundbreaking technology. There are almost always challenges that must be overcome under time pressure, and there will be differences in opinion between experts as to whether those challenges can be successfully resolved. It contended that it should not be held liable for "strong language written by frustrated engineers working under intense pressure for long hours."[23]

The plaintiffs' response was that specific aspects of Apple's statements were misleading, raising questions about whether the company acted in bad faith. Internal testing established that the product was unreliable at the time Apple announced that the drive "ensures greater integrity of data" and "has undergone extensive testing and design verification during the past year." By highlighting that the Twiggy had been subject to testing, Apple implied that Twiggy had passed such tests when in fact it had not. There was thus a question of fact as to whether Apple had a good faith basis for claiming that the Twiggy was a feature of the Lisa that would contribute to its success.

A jury resolved these contested factual issues at trial. In May of 1991, it found two high-level Apple executives liable (Jobs was found not liable) for securities fraud. It awarded the plaintiffs compensation equal to the amount Apple's stock was inflated by its fraud, a total of $2.90 per share. This translated into $100 million in damages. The *San Francisco Chronicle* reported that the verdict "prompted legal experts to predict a flood of new litigation."[24]

The impact of the verdict was somewhat muted when several months later, the judge in the case overturned it on the basis that the company rather than its executives was the only party that could be liable for the fraud. The court found persuasive the argument that the individual defendants did not author the press release on the Twiggy and thus any securities fraud was the responsibility of Apple rather than its executives. Put another way, this was a securities fraud by a corporation rather than its individual managers.

Toward the end of 1991, the parties settled the case for $16 million. While a fraction of the alleged losses, the settlement may have been reasonable given that the problem with the Twiggy was only one of many reasons that the Lisa had failed. Approximately half of the settlement was allocated to pay the attorneys who represented the class.[25] Around the same time, Apple settled a separate securities class action for $3.8 million claiming that Apple's profit projections had been too optimistic given its shift to selling low-cost Macintosh computers.[26] Such multimillion-dollar paydays were understandably viewed as incentivizing attorneys to influence investors to continue to aggressively file securities class actions.

The Aftermath of the Apple Verdict

Even though Apple ultimately paid only a fraction of the $100 million verdict, the jury's initial award raised concerns about leaving the determination of whether a company committed securities fraud to a group of lay persons. There was a risk that a jury would impose catastrophic damages for the failure to comply with vaguely defined law. The precedent of the Apple verdict was leveraged by plaintiffs' attorneys to argue for larger settlements from defendants who now had a greater reason to fear that taking the case to trial would bet the company.[27]

Apple was also significant because it confirmed in a high-profile case that companies could be liable under Rule 10b-5 for failing to meet a projection relating to its future performance. John Coffee, a leading securities law expert, noted the importance of the decision, writing: "Few experienced corporate lawyers need to be reminded of the conclusion by the [Ninth] U.S. Circuit Court of Appeals in the *Apple Computer Securities Litigation* in 1989 that projections and general expressions of optimism may be actionable under the federal securities laws."[28] The fact that the Ninth Circuit covers Silicon Valley, the home of the computer industry, made the legal doctrine established by the decision even more significant. While the Ninth Circuit had affirmed the dismissal of some of the claims against Apple under the truth-on-the-market doctrine, it had also made it clear that the defense would not apply if the market was unaware of problems with a product. Just a few years after it issued its opinion in *Apple*, the Ninth Circuit cited the case in finding that the failure of a company to disclose technical problems with a computer printer was misleading in light of its earlier optimistic statements.[29]

The securities class action against Apple was one of many filed against public companies after they missed a projection. By the start of the 1990s, a substantial number of securities class actions were triggered by the failure of a company to meet a projection, though the majority of cases did not involve such an allegation. One study found that from January 1990 through December 1993, 40 percent of securities litigation complaints involved an allegation of a missed projection.[30] Another study looking at securities class actions settled between 1989 and 1994 found that 25 percent alleged dissemination of a misleading projection.[31] A different study observed that while a decline in stock price by itself was not enough to trigger a securities fraud suit, such suits were often prompted by a decline linked to the failure of the company to meet an earnings forecast.[32]

Data on a sample of securities class actions filed in 1994 and 1995 that I independently examined shows that securities class actions were filed and settled frequently by the mid-1990s (Table 4.1).[33] While about 30 percent of these lawsuits involved a misstatement about the company's future prospects, a similar percentage involved an allegation that the company's financial statements violated GAAP. It was thus unclear that the typical securities class action solely alleged that a company missed a projection. A high percentage of the cases, almost 80 percent, ended in a settlement. The average settlement was almost $8 million, but the median settlement was around $3 million. The typical settlement was thus much lower than the $60 million settlement of the Equity Funding case in the 1970s, which remained the largest settlement of a Rule 10b-5 class action involving a public company's inflated stock price until the mid-1990s. It is fair to say that while securities class actions were filed frequently over the 1980s and early 1990s, they did not target misconduct of the same magnitude seen at Equity Funding.

TABLE 4.1. *Securities class actions filed in 1994 and 1995*

	1994	1995	Total	% of Total
Securities Class Actions Filed	147	143	290	100.0
Accounting Violation Alleged	48	41	89	30.7
False Forward-Looking Statement Alleged	42	48	90	31.0
Bankruptcy	3	7	10	3.4
Dismissed	37	29	66	22.8
Settled	110	114	224	77.2
Average Settlement	8,314,765	7,491,831	7,889,776	
Median Settlement	3,750,000	3,025,000	3,250,000	

Securities class actions alleging that a projection was misleading often argued that there was a divergence between the projection and internal information known to a public company's management.[34] For example, the briefly popular Atari game system spurred a lawsuit claiming that Atari's statements that its success would continue were misleading in light of information it had about new competitors.[35] Despite the argument that Atari did not appreciate the impact of the competition and revised its projections for the product's performance downward,[36] the case resulted in a $17.54 million settlement (slightly more than the Apple settlement).[37] In other cases, public companies successfully defended themselves by pointing to internal budgets that were consistent with market projections.[38]

Litigation directed at projections often raised the question of whether a company should have updated the projection. Investors surprised by a missed projection often argue that the company knew the projection was unrealistic and should have informed the public. Courts have acknowledged such a duty to update, though courts differ about the extent of the duty. For example, one appellate court explained that "a duty to update opinions and projections may arise if the original opinions or projections have become misleading as the result of intervening events."[39] If a company learns facts that make a prior prediction misleading, it could have a duty to inform the public.

At the same time, courts have been cautious about defining the duty to update too broadly. Not every piece of potentially negative information about a company's prospects must be immediately released to the public. The challenge of applying a duty to update is that a company's fortunes can fluctuate on a day-to-day basis. A product's development may face challenges one day that are resolved the next. The US Court of Appeals for the First Circuit thus reversed a jury verdict against the instant camera company Polaroid that found the company liable under Rule 10b-5 for failing to disclose that its new instant movie camera was a "commercial failure."[40] The appellate court held that the company did not have to make such an updated disclosure because it was unclear that the company believed that the product was a failure at the time the disclosure allegedly should have been made. Companies should have some leeway to use their judgment in deciding when to inform markets about adverse developments.

The frequency of private litigation alleging securities fraud for the failure to meet a projection was not only an issue for the defendant companies but also the SEC. Though it had originally discouraged projections on the ground that they were too unreliable, the SEC changed its approach toward the end of the 1970s as it became clear that forward-looking information was essential to valuing companies. It adopted the recommendation of an Advisory Committee on Disclosure, that "the Commission actively and generally encourage the publication of forward-looking and analytical information in company reports to shareholders and in Commission filings."[41]

To the extent that the fear of securities fraud litigation discouraged companies from issuing projections, such cases undermined this SEC policy. Surveys of corporate executives reported that securities litigation was a substantial deterrent for companies wishing to issue projections. As one study reported, during the early 1990s only half of exchange-traded companies issued projections in any year. The reason was that "managers believe the law imposes a type of 'strict liability' for forecasts; that is, they face stockholder lawsuits if their forecasts turn out to be wrong, even when those forecasts are made in an unbiased way with the best information available."[42] A *Wall Street Journal* article declared – "Now It's SEC vs. the Lawyers" – and highlighted the way in which private securities fraud suits had undermined the SEC's policy. It observed that "plaintiffs' attorneys have used class-action lawsuits as a means of making companies guarantors of any and all forward-looking statements."[43]

Years earlier, the SEC had considered whether it should protect companies from projections litigation. It wanted to shield companies from frivolous litigation, but tellingly was not willing to completely shield companies from Rule 10b-5 liability for their forecasts. It thus passed a safe harbor that protected company statements such as "a projection of revenues, income (loss), earnings (loss) per share" from being considered a "fraudulent statement."[44] If the rule had stopped there, it may have essentially eliminated projections litigation. However, the SEC attached a condition to this protection. The safe harbor would not protect a public company if its projection "was made or reaffirmed without a reasonable basis or was disclosed other than in good faith."

Because of this exception, the safe harbor was not much help to defendants because of the reality that very few corporate defendants were willing to risk a trial on a securities class action. If the defendant cannot win dismissal of a Rule 10b-5 claim at an early stage, it will likely make a payment to the plaintiffs. The exception to the safe harbor raised factual issues that a judge typically cannot decide. Resolving whether a projection was made in good faith and had a reasonable basis requires weighing evidence, a task that should usually be performed by a jury.[45] Plaintiffs learned that they could often avoid dismissal by arguing that the projection was issued in bad faith.

Federal courts attempted to manage the flood of projections litigation. Some openly expressed skepticism about the merits of these cases. As one federal appellate court lectured plaintiffs, "[t]he market has risks: the securities laws do not serve as investment insurance. Every prediction of success that fails to materialize cannot create on that account an action for securities fraud."[46] Another federal appellate court described class actions as following a familiar pattern where "[a]t one time the firm bathes itself in a favorable light. Later the firm discloses that things are less rosy. The plaintiff contends that the difference must be attributable to fraud."[47]

Other courts created legal doctrines to facilitate the dismissal of securities class actions. In an appeal involving the future president, Donald Trump, the US Court of Appeals for the Third Circuit described a way that companies could avoid liability for a failed projection.[48] They could include cautionary statements in their disclosure documents warning investors of risks to the company. Trump's Taj Mahal casino in Atlantic City filed for bankruptcy after selling $675 million in bonds to investors. The bondholders sued, alleging that the casino had falsely predicted it would generate sufficient cash flow to cover its interest payments. However, the casino had also disclosed the risks of its business such as the seasonal nature of its cash flow that might not correspond to scheduled interest payments. The Third Circuit found that the disclosure had been sufficiently specific to warn investors that the casino might default on the bonds. Put another way, if the company's disclosure adequately "bespeaks caution" about a potential failure, the warning can offset the impact of a misleading statement about its prospects. As one court observed, the emergence of the bespeaks caution doctrine reflected "a relatively recent, ongoing, and somewhat uncertain evolution in securities law, an evolution driven by an increase in and the unique nature of fraud actions based on predictive statements."[49] Though it offered public companies some comfort, the application of the doctrine was far from certain. Donald Langevoort observed in 1994 that "the bespeaks caution doctrine is still in its infancy" and "its future evolution is uncertain." [50]

THE PRIVATE SECURITIES LITIGATION REFORM ACT

Partly because of its concerns about projections litigation, the SEC supported the PSRLA, which placed significant limitations on securities class actions. The PSLRA did not eliminate the ability of investors to bring a class action under Rule 10b-5. Rather, it used procedural requirements, as well as a stronger safe harbor for projections, to make it more difficult to bring suits of questionable merit. The law created significant protections for public corporations when they communicate with the market. It recognized that as companies were increasingly valued based on their potential to develop future profits, it would be counterproductive to require them to extensively defend every failure to fulfill prior predictions.

The legislative history of the PSLRA focused on lawsuits against computer companies such as Apple. One Senate report cited a "rising tide of frivolous securities litigation" that targeted "American business, particularly younger companies in the high-tech area."[51] Other congressional reports observed that these class actions were often spurred by the failure to meet earnings projections. The House of Representatives reported that a "typical case involves a stock, usually of a high-growth, high-tech company, that has performed well for many quarters, but ultimately misses analysts' expectations."[52] The Conference Report similarly noted: "Technology companies – because of the volatility of their stock prices – are particularly vulnerable to securities fraud lawsuits when projections do not materialize. If a company fails to satisfy its announced earnings projections – perhaps because of changes in the economy or the timing of an order or new product – the company is likely to face a lawsuit."[53] The emphasis on projections illustrated how public companies and their valuation shifted during the 1980s. The stock market now relied heavily on projections in setting the stock prices of public companies. Investors were willing to assign high values to entrepreneurial companies with strong prospects. While there had previously been speculative booms triggered by new technologies, this particular boom intersected with a more sophisticated valuation infrastructure that systematically scrutinized whether public companies were meeting market expectations.

As an institution, the SEC put its stamp of approval on the increasing importance of projections in valuing public corporations. It maintained its position that companies should be encouraged to issue projections and that securities litigation deterred projections. An SEC proposal for a stronger projections safe harbor noted that "companies that [made] voluntary disclosure of forward-looking information subject[ed] themselves to a significantly increased risk of securities antifraud class actions."[54] It also noted the deficiency of its existing safe harbor, which was "infrequently raised by defendants, perhaps because it compels judicial examination of reasonableness and good faith, which raise factual issues that often preclude early, prediscovery dismissal."[55]

SEC Chairman Arthur Levitt, who later initiated a crusade against accounting misstatements to meet projections (as discussed in Chapter 2), supported much but not all of the PSLRA (as did his predecessor as chairman, Richard Breeden). In doing so, he often referenced public company projections. In testimony before the House of Representatives, he explained that "[t]he threat of misdirected litigation also tends to impede beneficial corporate disclosure practices, such as the dissemination of forward-looking information, that the Commission encourages."[56] This argument proved to be influential. Congress essentially accepted this argument, concluding in its conference report: "[f]ear that inaccurate projections will trigger the filing of [a] securities class action lawsuit has muzzled corporate management."[57] As a leading practitioner explained, "[t]he single greatest impetus to passage of the Reform Act was the perception – amply supported by the evidence – that issuers had been deterred from making projections and from disseminating soft information because of a fear of liability if their public statements failed accurately to predict the future."[58]

The legislative history of the PSLRA was littered with references to the SEC's support for the statute. Its position provided credible support for reform, especially because the SEC has usually supported the right of private investors to bring a securities fraud suit. Indeed, some of the SEC staff was opposed to the PSLRA.[59] The director of the SEC's Division of Enforcement defended securities litigation in testimony before Congress as not being excessive in nature and providing compensation to investors in light of the tendency of the SEC not to seek a full recovery covering all losses.[60]

The PSLRA's goal of protecting companies from projections litigation was reinforced by the passage of the State Law Uniform Standards Act (SLUSA), which extended the requirements of the PSLRA to class actions alleging securities fraud claims under state law in state court. There was evidence that cases were being filed in state court to avoid the restrictions of the PSLRA.[61] The SEC again took sides with corporations against private litigation and attributed the failure of companies to issue more projections after the passage of the PSLRA in part to "fear of state court liability, where forward looking statements may not be protected by the Federal safe harbor."[62] In signing the law, President Clinton, who had unsuccessfully vetoed the PSLRA, noted that SLUSA was based on the idea that markets "function best when corporations can raise capital by providing investors with their best, good-faith future projections."[63] The rhetoric supporting SLUSA confirmed that the reform of securities litigation was closely tied to the policy goal of encouraging public companies to issue projections to the public.

A New Safe Harbor

The PSLRA directly addressed the problem of projections litigation by providing defendants with a broader safe harbor for forward-looking statements by public companies. As one commentator noted, the safe harbor was the "most hotly contested provision" of the PSLRA.[64] There was concern that any safe harbor would go too far in shielding companies that tried to mislead the market through unrealistic projections.

The PSLRA safe harbor covers any statement by a public company that is forward looking. It offers two types of protections. First, it extended the bespeaks caution doctrine discussed by the Third Circuit in the *Trump* case so that it applied nationwide. Any projection "accompanied by meaningful cautionary language" is shielded from securities fraud liability. A public company could now protect itself from securities fraud liability through extensive disclosure about the risks of its business. Second, it replaced the prior SEC safe harbor's reasonable basis and good faith standard with an actual knowledge test. A company can only be liable under Rule 10b-5 for missing a projection if it knew that the projection was wrong. Importantly, because of the difficulty of establishing knowledge, courts are often willing to find that there is insufficient evidence of knowledge at an early stage of the case.[65]

By reformulating the legal standard to require knowledge, the PSLRA safe harbor implied that only a small percentage of missed projections could be considered fraudulent. It is not enough for a shareholder to point to a stumble in the company's performance. To punish companies for simply failing to predict the future would mean that only public companies that never surprise investors will be free from securities litigation. The PSLRA gave public companies more freedom to issue aggressive projections they might not meet.

For some skeptics, the safe harbor provided too much protection for forecasts. Joel Seligman, who had testified before Congress on the PSLRA, declared that the provision "was not so much a safe harbor as a safe ocean."[66] The main concern was that even a knowingly false projection would be shielded if it was accompanied by cautionary language. While plaintiffs could always argue that such "cautionary language" was not "meaningful," there was concern that without a clear standard, courts would not require strong warnings to investors. President Clinton vetoed the PSLRA partly on the ground that its legislative history supported a standard permitting a cursory cautionary statement to be "meaningful."[67]

In retrospect, the safe harbor did not completely stop private litigation directed at projections. While after the passage of the PSLRA, courts often dismissed projections cases for insufficient evidence of knowledge,[68] there have also been cases where the plaintiff was able to sufficiently describe facts supporting the allegation that the defendant knew a projection was false.[69] Moreover, courts have not uniformly shielded knowingly wrong projections based on weak cautionary language.[70]

The evidence on whether the PSLRA and its safe harbor were successful in influencing public corporations to issue projections is mixed. A number of studies have found evidence that more companies issued financial forecasts after the PSLRA.[71] For example, a study that looked at the issuance of earnings projections by public companies from 1994 through 2003 found that "the proportion of firms issuing guidance" went "from less than 10% in the mid-1990s to around 25% in 2001–2003."[72] More companies issued projections after the PSLRA, but even after the passage of the law, most companies did not.

Pleading Fraudulent Intent

The PSLRA also imposed obligations on plaintiffs to describe evidence of securities fraud at an early stage of the case. It was not enough for investors to point to a substantial investor loss after the company missed a projection. The new law required plaintiffs to provide concrete allegations that an inaccurate disclosure was part of a scheme to mislead investors. If they did not, the case would be dismissed. Because it did not exactly specify what is required to sufficiently allege fraud, the PSLRA gave judges substantial power to shape the boundaries of Rule 10b-5.

Prior to the PSLRA, in many jurisdictions, a securities class action would go through the same process as any other case filed in federal court. The plaintiff could file a complaint with general allegations that a public company may have committed securities fraud. The plaintiff would not be required to spell out the details establishing that the corporation acted with fraudulent intent. Instead, the litigation process permitted the plaintiff to seek evidence through the discovery process that could support the allegations in the complaint.

This standard litigation process proved unworkable for securities class actions. The triggering event for a securities fraud claim, the significant decline in a company's stock, happens virtually every day to some public company. There are hundreds of opportunities each year for investors to bring a securities lawsuit claiming they were misled and paid too much for a stock. In other areas of the law, claims for substantial damages are less frequent. Consider products liability litigation. It is not common for a product to be so dangerous that it causes substantial harm to thousands of individuals. In some years, there may only be a handful of mass torts generating lawsuits, making the overall costs of such litigation more manageable. Because of the sheer number of securities class actions that were being filed by the late 1980s, permitting them all to proceed on the hope that they might find some evidence of fraud would impose substantial costs on public companies.

Courts were thus careful not to blindly credit all cries that a stock price decline reflected fraudulent conduct. Even before the PSLRA, federal courts were dismissing private claims of securities fraud for failing to meet the requirements of Federal Rule of Civil Procedure 9(b) (Rule 9(b)), which requires a plaintiff to "state with particularity the circumstances constituting fraud or mistake."[73] Under this standard, rather than simply claim that there was a fraud, the plaintiff must describe the details of the fraud to give the defendant more notice of the conduct that is being challenged. The US Court of Appeals for the Second Circuit cited this rule in requiring plaintiffs in Rule 10b-5 cases to describe the alleged securities fraud with specificity.[74]

The Second Circuit read Rule 9(b) as requiring the plaintiff to describe allegations supporting a "strong inference of fraudulent intent."[75] An investor cannot bring a suit after a loss with the vague hope that evidence of fraud will be found later. There must be good reason to believe that the loss was caused by a fraudulent scheme rather than because of an accident or misfortune. The Second Circuit thus required more than general allegations that a corporation missed a projection and its stock fell in price. In one early case, it noted that a particular Rule 10b-5 claim directed at a projection could go forward only because the complaint specifically described that defendants had information that optimistic statements were untrue and sold large blocks of stock before the truth was revealed to the public.[76]

The PSLRA extended nationwide the Second Circuit's requirement that a plaintiff describe facts supporting a "strong inference" of securities fraud. This increased the standard for proving the defendant's wrongful state of mind, or scienter, in the jurisdictions that had not read Rule 9(b) as requiring the plaintiff to describe securities fraud with specificity.[77] After the passage of the PSLRA, the Ninth Circuit, which decided the *Apple* appeal, clarified in its *Silicon Graphics* decision that to survive a motion to dismiss, a complaint must describe "in great detail, facts that constitute strong circumstantial evidence of deliberately reckless or conscious misbehavior."[78] In applying that standard, the court appeared to break with past decisions finding that evidence of divergence between internal and external forecasts was enough to support a finding of fraudulent intent. It observed that any "sophisticated corporation uses some kind of internal reporting system" and that permitting cases "to go forward with a case based on general allegations of 'negative internal reports' would expose all those companies to securities litigation whenever their stock prices dropped."[79] There is evidence that the market viewed *Silicon Graphics* as having the potential to reduce the costs of securities litigation. A study found a statistically significant increase in stock prices of technology firms in the days after the opinion was issued, particularly those with headquarters located in the Ninth Circuit.[80] On the other hand, it is now clear that this higher Ninth Circuit standard did not completely preclude a finding of scienter in cases mainly based on an inconsistency between internal and external forecasts. About five years after the *Silicon Graphics* decision was issued, the Ninth Circuit reversed the dismissal of a class action alleging securities fraud by Oracle Corporation. In that case, optimistic forecasts that the company's business would not be affected by a recession were contradicted by a contemporaneous internal sales report indicating a "major slowdown in sales."[81]

The critics of the PSLRA feared that the heightened burden on plaintiffs to describe fraudulent intent would mean that many securities frauds would go unaddressed. Corporate decision-making often lacks transparency. The origins of a mistake will often be lost in the bureaucratic maze of mid-level managers who implement vague instructions from high-level managers. Courts have thus dismissed cases against public companies on the ground that plaintiffs did not describe sufficient evidence that high-level managers knew of wrongdoing within a vast organization.[82] Without an opportunity to examine the company's internal documents through litigation, it can be impossible to develop sufficient allegations of fraud to satisfy a court. Opponents of the law feared that plaintiffs would only be able to bring a claim in cases where a company basically confessed to a fraud. There were questions as to whether the PSLRA meant that most securities frauds by public companies would escape scrutiny.

Did the PSLRA Succeed?

In addition to its safe harbor and fraudulent intent provisions, the PSLRA included a variety of mechanisms to reduce the incidence of frivolous securities class actions. One section creates a presumption that the court should choose the investor that suffered the largest loss as the lead plaintiff with the power to direct the litigation. This standard made it more likely that sophisticated institutional investors would control the major decisions in a case. Another section stayed discovery until a motion to dismiss was decided, reducing the pressure on defendants to settle a case to avoid litigation costs.

There was a real question about the collective impact of the PSLRA's provisions. For defenders of securities class actions, the PSLRA was a devastating blow to private securities enforcement. For supporters of the PSLRA, the statute held the promise of substantially reducing frivolous shareholder litigation. Ultimately, it turned out that while it influenced the types of securities class actions that were filed, the PSLRA did not systematically prevent shareholders from recovering damages for securities fraud.

Perhaps the clearest impact of the PSLRA was that it shifted the focus of securities class actions to "obvious" frauds. A case would be more likely to survive dismissal if the plaintiff described concrete evidence of wrongdoing supporting a "strong inference of fraudulent intent." A study found that plaintiffs were less likely to file suits without hard evidence of fraud after the PSLRA.[83] Such evidence might be an accounting restatement by the company, an SEC investigation, or evidence of abnormal insider trading. There is evidence that courts became more skeptical of cases without such evidence. Stephen Choi found that cases without hard evidence of fraud were more likely to be dismissed or result in a nominal settlement than they were before the PSLRA, even if they would have been viewed as meritorious before the PSLRA.[84]

There is thus evidence that the PSLRA succeeded in reducing litigation based solely on the failure to meet a forecast. John Coffee correctly predicted that the PSLRA's higher standard for describing fraudulent intent would result in a shift where plaintiffs would target financial statement fraud rather than missed projections.[85] Investors could avoid the safe harbor by challenging factual misstatements rather than forward-looking statements. An empirical study confirmed that cases filed against technology companies after the PSLRA were more likely to allege an accounting restatement or insider trading by management, and less likely to allege the failure to meet a forecast.[86] Institutional investors with the ability to distinguish between good and bad cases tended to become involved in such cases with hard evidence of fraud,[87] giving these cases more legitimacy.[88]

For some of the critics of securities class actions, the PSLRA was a disappointment. The number of securities class action filings fell in the first year or so after the law was passed. However, subsequent years saw an increase in the number of actions.[89] While many cases ended in dismissal, most cases still ended in a settlement. Moreover, the size of securities class action settlements increased substantially. As Joseph Grundfest, a former SEC commissioner and law professor, observed almost two decades after the passage of the PSLRA, "[m]ore than 3,200 private class action securities fraud lawsuits were filed between 1997 and 2013. Settlements in these actions generated more than $73 billion and comprise six of the ten largest settlements in class action history."[90]

The explosion of securities litigation after the passage of the PSLRA does not establish that the law failed to reduce frivolous securities litigation. The increase in filings and substantial settlements likely reflected an increase in the number of events giving rise to meritorious allegations. As noted earlier, the years after the PSLRA coincided with an unprecedented period of securities fraud enforcement by the SEC. SEC investigations often uncovered evidence that could later be used to support a private suit. More complaints may have cited restatements not only to meet the heightened requirements of the PSLRA but because the number of public companies restating their financial statements increased substantially starting in the late 1990s. Many securities fraud cases filed in the period after the PSLRA was enacted involved public companies that filed for bankruptcy,[91] where the potential investor losses were more substantial than in cases involving solvent companies. Courts were aware of the securities frauds of the late 1990s and early 2000s and may have read the PSLRA narrowly in cases they believed were meritorious. As the Ninth Circuit explained, "[i]n this era of corporate scandal, when insiders manipulate the market with the complicity of lawyers and accountants, we are cautious not to raise the bar of the PSLRA any higher than that which is required under its mandates."[92]

APPLE'S SUCCESS

Apple's future looked grim after the failure of the Lisa. After several attempts to increase sales of the business computer by cutting its price, Apple discontinued it in 1985. In 1989 it buried 2,700 unsold Lisa computers in a landfill for a tax break.[93] Apple's Macintosh computer, which was based on the Lisa's technology, was more successful but did not completely meet the company's high expectations. Just as Apple copied features from Xerox's prototype, IBM and Microsoft copied the mouse and graphical interface used by the Lisa and Macintosh. IBM came to dominate the market for office computers, and Apple became a niche company with products mostly limited to use in the home and in schools. Steve Jobs, Apple's cofounder and creative force, was pushed out of Apple soon after these failures.

Apple had another chance to succeed after Steve Jobs returned to the company in the late 1990s. This time, Apple was able to develop a set of transformative products that would make it the most valuable company in the world. In doing so, Apple at times tested the boundaries of the securities laws. In 2000, it introduced a compact desktop computer with the sleek design of a cube. The company touted the prospects of the new product despite manufacturing problems that resulted in cosmetic imperfections in many of the cubes it shipped to customers. Reviewers praised the innovative design of the desktop, but it was a commercial failure. A securities class action alleged that the company's statements describing the cube as "the coolest computer ever" and "perfect" were misleading and violated Rule 10b-5.[94] It thus raised similar allegations as the case filed more than a decade before against Apple for its optimistic claims about the Twiggy. But the more stringent standard for scienter adopted by the Ninth Circuit in *Silicon Graphics* made it more difficult for the cube computer case to proceed. A district court dismissed the case on the ground that the complaint did not describe enough facts establishing that Steve Jobs and other Apple officers knew the extent of the product's problems.

Apple used similarly aggressive tactics in promoting its greatest success, the iPhone. Like the Lisa, the iPhone was critical to building on the success of an earlier product, the iPod. Six months before the iPhone's launch in 2007, Steve Jobs demonstrated a prototype of the phone that was rigged to appear to have functionality that it did not have.[95] For example, the phone was configured to always show five bars of signal strength, even when its signal was much weaker. If the problems had not been resolved before the launch, investors surely would have had a claim for securities fraud. It is worth noting that the numerous Rule 10b-5 cases directed against technology companies over the years have not changed the reality that technology companies often scramble to put together a working product at the last minute.

In addition to touting products before they worked, Apple exhibited poor corporate governance in permitting questionable practices relating to the awarding of stock options to its executives, including Steve Jobs. Apple agreed to award Jobs options on 7.5 million Apple shares in December 2001 but fabricated documents to create the impression that the grant was approved in October 2001, when Apple's stock price was significantly lower.[96] Because the option could be exercised to purchase stock at a lower price, the backdating made it much more likely that Jobs could profit by exercising the option. Apple failed to properly account for the guaranteed profitability of the option, which would have reduced the company's earnings. The company conceded that Jobs was aware that the grant was manipulated but contended that he did not understand the accounting implications of the manipulation.[97] The SEC brought charges against two Apple executives but not Jobs, enabling him to remain with the company. While the amount of additional compensation paid to the executives through the backdated options was small relative to Apple's financial results, the practice might still have been significant to investors who would be concerned about how these actions reflected on the integrity of the company's management.[98]

Finally, Apple was questioned regarding its secrecy about the health of Steve Jobs, who tragically died of cancer in 2011. Apple delayed publicly disclosing the seriousness of Jobs' disease until it was fairly advanced. The SEC investigated the company and considered whether Jobs was so critical to Apple's success that it was misleading for the company not to disclose his illness sooner to the market. The SEC ultimately did not bring a case against Apple. In retrospect, Apple was able to thrive after Jobs' passing.

Despite its habit of running afoul of the securities laws, Apple became the world's most valuable company. Perhaps Apple's experience demonstrates that the law should give innovative companies leeway to tout their prospects to investors who should understand the risk that new technologies will not succeed. At the same time, it is difficult to deny that entrepreneurial companies manipulate investor perceptions of their future and only a few achieve spectacular success. Securities class actions can help provide a remedy when public corporations deceive investors by withholding information about significant setbacks.

THERANOS AND PROJECTIONS FRAUD IN PRIVATE MARKETS

Over time, markets evolved so that new technology companies now commonly receive more funding from private investors than public markets. Over the last decade, valuations of promising private companies soared as investors became more willing to pay for the prospect of their future earnings. The example of Theranos shows how the problem of projections fraud can be an issue in private markets.

The founder of Theranos, Elizabeth Holmes, was inspired by the example of Apple and Steve Jobs to transform the blood testing industry by creating "the iPod of health care."[99] The company's goal was to develop a machine that could perform hundreds of tests on a single drop of blood. The company began entering into contracts with national grocery and pharmacy chains to provide such testing when its prototype could only conduct tests with questionable accuracy.[100] It did not inform its partners of these challenges but orchestrated fake demonstrations of its product while actually using third party technology to conduct the blood tests.[101] It achieved a $9 billion valuation by presenting baseless projections to investors predicting it would soon generate more than $1 billion in profits.[102]

In its complaint against Holmes and Theranos, the SEC notably argued that these projections were fraudulent. The agency that had once supported a strong safe harbor for projections observed that "financial projections were important to investors because they gave the impression that Theranos had already secured contracts to deliver these revenues and that the company's business was growing rapidly."[103] The SEC's conclusion was especially notable given the tolerance in private markets for bold predictions of success. The *Wall Street Journal* reporter who uncovered the Theranos fraud drew parallels to the "vaporware" in the 1980s.[104] He observed that "[h]yping your product to get funding while concealing your true progress and hoping that reality will eventually catch up to the hype continues to be tolerated in the tech industry."[105] It is unclear whether the SEC's legal theory against Theranos will be applied more broadly to police the integrity of projections in private markets.

Allegations similar to those raised in the Apple and Theranos cases are often asserted in cases against pharmaceutical companies.[106] Because of the long and uncertain approval process of drugs by the Food and Drug Administration, the prospects of what seems like a promising medicine can quickly dim. When side effects or other problems emerge and become known, investors often fault drug companies for not disclosing such problems sooner. The defendant corporation will typically respond that it continued to hope that the drug would work, but it failed despite the company's best efforts. Just as the Apple case turned on whether the company had specific knowledge that its disk drive was a failure, the success of a securities class action against a pharmaceuticals company will depend on whether it knew of significant problems with a product but withheld such information from public investors.

***

The issues raised in the securities class action against Apple continue to be relevant in modern securities litigation. Because entrepreneurial companies are valued based on the prospects of the new products they are developing, they are often accused of fraud when a project does not come to fruition. Courts continue to grapple with the question of when the failure to disclose a significant setback to investors is fraudulent.

5

Enron and Sarbanes–Oxley

It is not true, as Skilling claims, that the Government's theory at trial was that Skilling made bad business decisions; its argument was that Skilling hid those bad business decisions from investors.

US Court of Appeals for the Fifth Circuit, 2011

[P]laintiffs have alleged a fraud of a magnitude only rarely seen – at least until recent years.

US District Court for the Southern District of New York, 2004

Like Penn Central more than thirty years before, the energy conglomerate Enron was the largest US company to ever fall into bankruptcy when it filed in December 2001. Enron's crisis was most directly caused by two accounting restatements that prompted a downgrade of its credit rating. For a company that claimed to have generated $100 billion in revenue the prior year, the accounting errors were arguably small – each restatement involved around $600 million in revenue.

But Enron's stock price assumed that its revenue would grow at double digit rates, and after it admitted to misstatements, the market no longer trusted its reporting. Enron had actively created the impression that it could generate exceptional growth by developing transformative new projects (like Xerox in the 1960s, Apple in the 1970s, and the internet companies that were booming at the time). It signaled its strength with high projections for growth that it consistently met (like Xerox in the 1990s). When Enron could no longer meet its projections, it utilized questionable methods such as creating the appearance that it was generating revenue by selling assets when in fact it did not transfer the risk of owning those assets (like Penn Central).

Without Enron and the collapse of WorldCom about half a year later, the SEC's enforcement effort against earnings fraud at the turn of the century likely would have run its course without substantial federal reform. Just six months before Enron's bankruptcy filing, an article in the *Harvard Business Review* noted that the SEC's chief accountant "isn't convinced that earnings management is rampant, and he's in a position to know."[1] Enron and WorldCom made securities fraud a national issue and spurred the passage of the Sarbanes–Oxley Act of 2002 (Sarbanes–Oxley),[2] which for better or worse made the prevention of securities fraud a requirement for public company status. The best argument for the law is that it addressed the structural pressure to commit fraud to meet the expectations of markets that constantly assess the future performance of public companies.

ENRON'S SECURITIES FRAUD

A common perception is that Enron committed securities fraud because of its accounting violations. While Enron's financial statements were riddled with massive errors, its accounting misrepresentations are only part of the story. Just as important was the false story of its ability to generate extraordinary growth that it supported by consistently meeting its ambitious quarterly projections. If it had not insisted on this unrealistic narrative, it would not have needed to violate generally accepted accounting principles (GAAP). Even if its executives were not aware of every technical mistake in its accounting, they knew that Enron's businesses had significant problems that were not apparent to investors.

Enron's CEO, Jeffrey Skilling, who resigned a few months before the restatements, argued vigorously that Enron did not commit securities fraud. First, like Xerox's executives, he cited the fact that Enron's auditors had approved its various tactics. Because of the complexity of its accounting, Enron's managers claimed they relied in good faith on the judgment of experts and thus did not act with fraudulent intent. Second, many of the major aspects of the company's accounting transactions had been disclosed in its SEC filings. Enron's investors should have known that its financial reporting was complex, aggressive, and not completely transparent.

There is some tension between these two arguments. On the one hand, Enron claimed that it could not have been expected to understand the technical details of its accounting. On the other hand, Enron argued that investors should have been on notice about the nature of its accounting practices.

Even if Enron's executives did not know that its financial reporting violated the details of complex accounting rules, they must have known at some point that the company's performance could not support the aggressive projections that it had issued. Enron knew that many of its major projects were failing and could not meet earlier forecasts without misstatements. Like Xerox, there was evidence that it pushed its auditor to approve questionable transactions and withheld information from its auditor. Far from turning solely on the propriety of the energy conglomerate's accounting, the securities fraud theory against Enron raised a similar allegation as was made against Apple, that it conveyed optimism about its situation while hiding knowledge of serious problems.

Enron had a clear motive to deceive investors about its prospects. It feared that if it told the truth, it would fall off the valuation treadmill on which it had willingly run. There was evidence of specific instances where high-level Enron managers used improper transactions to generate enough revenue to meet projections. While the revenue produced in these transactions was relatively small, it permitted Enron to maintain its false narrative of smooth earnings growth. Enron's securities fraud thus can only be understood within a modern valuation system that prizes meeting quarterly projections. The SEC's earlier scrutiny of earnings misstatements established the framework within which the actions of companies like Enron were decisively condemned as securities fraud.

An Entrepreneurial Conglomerate

Enron is best understood as a company that combined the elements of a conglomerate (like Penn Central) and an entrepreneurial technology company (like Apple). It attempted to create the impression that it could develop innovative new businesses while using its presence in a diverse range of industries and its risk management skills to deliver smooth earnings. Its talented management distinguished it from other companies that could either innovate or manage risk but not do both.

At least initially, Enron was a company that operated solely within the domestic energy industry, owning and managing natural gas pipelines. As energy markets were deregulated, Enron shifted its strategy to create trading markets for natural gas.[3] Enron's management thought it could use its experience in gas markets to trade other commodities such as electricity and water, and that it could even create new markets in weather and broadband access. Enron expanded internationally and invested in assets like Nigerian barges and a power plant in India. Enron not only sought to innovate with respect to commodities but attempted to develop new businesses such as an online video streaming service. In a book published the year the company filed for bankruptcy, an accounting professor included Enron in a group of "companies that leverage major innovations to gain leading positions in their industries and sometimes even creat[e] new fields (energy and bandwidth trading, in Enron's case)."[4]

Because it seemed to innovate like a technology company and manage risk like a sophisticated conglomerate, Enron was able to convince markets that it would consistently generate significant growth in its revenue. Rather than package itself as an old-line energy company, Enron claimed it was comparable to the pioneering internet companies that were valued highly by markets at the time.[5] Its market value was tied to the expectation that Enron's projects would succeed and generate revenues and profits. It sought to provide its employees with the freedom and incentive to take initiative in developing their own ideas. The credibility of Enron's managers was especially important because its ventures would only pay off if they continued their superior execution. While its high market value permitted Enron to expand its business and reward its talented managers, it also left the company vulnerable if the market lost faith in its story.

Enron's Story of Extraordinary Growth

Enron created a false narrative that its combination of businesses and talent would result in extraordinary growth. It did so primarily through two methods. First, it reported strong revenue growth using questionable assumptions. Second, it issued optimistic projections for further growth in revenue and earnings that had little basis. Its past performance convinced markets that its forecasts for growth were a reliable basis for valuing the company.

Enron's reported revenue exploded from about $13 billion in 1996 to more than $100 billion in its final set of annual income statements as a public company in 2000. Its revenue numbers earned it the seventh highest spot on the Fortune 500. Enron reached a market valuation of around $70 billion that year, an ambitious amount considering that its earnings were slightly under $1 billion. The market was buying Enron stock based not on its actual earnings, but the hope that its rapid revenue growth would produce higher and higher profits in the years to come. The revenue Enron reported was not a historical fact, but rather based on assumptions about its future performance.

One way of looking at accounting fraud is that it reports facts about a company's past performance. For example, a company records revenue based on the sales it made over a period. But financial statements not only report past facts – they include predictions about future events. For example, a seller of goods will have to estimate the percentage of goods that will be returned by customers and recognize the cost of those returns in reporting its profits. Similarly, a company might create a reserve of funds to cover the estimated costs associated with a merger. Managers are typically given significant discretion with respect to developing financial estimates, but they can also go too far and abuse that discretion.

One way that Enron inflated its revenue was through aggressive assumptions about what it would earn from long-term energy contracts. For a time, the energy assets owned by Enron were conservatively reported at book value, the price at which they had been purchased. As energy markets became deregulated, prices fluctuated more, supporting the argument that contracts to provide energy should be valued based on market prices. Enron got approval from the SEC to use mark-to-market accounting to report the value of its natural gas contracts. It aggressively projected strong performance for these contracts over long periods and booked the present value of those revenues immediately.[6] As it later became apparent that Enron's assumptions were unrealistically high, Enron had to reverse the revenue that had been recorded earlier. Enron responded by using more questionable transactions to create the appearance that its revenue was growing. While Enron did not always violate accounting rules through its aggressive estimates, its decision to make unrealistic predictions about its revenue contributed to high expectations that could only be maintained by questionable accounting.

Enron's reporting of revenue highlights how estimation is pervasive in financial reporting. Estimates are used not only to predict what a company will earn in a future period but are also used to generate the company's reported revenue for a current period. Markets find such forecasts useful because they reflect the superior knowledge and expertise of corporate managers. But such trust can be exploited by a company that abuses its discretion to make estimates that are without basis. And it can be very difficult for outsiders to assess when such predictions are made in bad faith.

Enron's mark-to-market revenue tactics became more problematic as they were extended outside of its core competency of energy. Enron attempted to develop a video-on-demand service in partnership with Blockbuster Video. Despite the uncertainties about whether such a service was viable at the time, Enron booked all the revenue it estimated it could earn for the life of the project immediately.[7] The SEC later observed that this revenue accounted for $53 million of the $63 million earnings in its broadband subsidiary (which Enron hyped to investors as a promising source of growth) for the fourth quarter of 2000.[8]

By demonstrating revenue growth through its questionable estimates, Enron justified aggressive projections of growth. In its last annual report, Enron boldly claimed: "we see our market opportunities company-wide tripling over the next five years."[9] It could only credibly make such statements because it had produced extraordinary growth in the past. But such numbers were illusionary because they were founded on revenue representing estimates that were not made in good faith.

Rather than offer reasonable forecasts grounded on sound assumptions, Enron disseminated projections to the market that had little basis in reality. Journalists Bethany McLean and Peter Elkind alleged that Skilling would base Enron's projections not on "a rigorous budget process" but rather "solely on what Wall Street wanted."[10] The class action brought against Enron by investors claimed that Skilling set "budget targets . . . based on the numbers necessary to meet or exceed analysts' expectations, not on what could be realistically achieved by legitimate business operations."[11]

The PSLRA safe harbor protected Enron's forward-looking statements that were accompanied by meaningful cautionary statements (a federal district court dismissed some criminal charges against Enron's executives for issuing misleading projections because they were covered by the safe harbor).[12] But Enron's knowledge that its projections were unrealistic supports the argument that it was engaged in a fraudulent course of conduct. The unfounded projections meant that the company had to push and overstep the boundaries of acceptable accounting to meet its projections. Put another way, they created an incentive for the company to misstate its financial statements.

Enron's Fraudulent Transactions

Enron's misrepresentations concerning its present performance were necessary because the company's estimates of future revenues were unrealistic. As its investments did not perform as planned, the company had to write-down the value of assets and recognize losses. For example, Enron's stock price had surged after it predicted that its broadband business would add $40 billion of market value to the company's stock, but it soon became clear that the venture was failing. If Enron did not deliver continued revenue growth, the market would reverse those gains.

Enron committed securities fraud by using a variety of tactics so that investors would not know that its earlier portrayal of the company's prospects was inaccurate. Like Penn Central, Enron attempted to generate revenue by selling assets. Enron transacted with special purpose entities (SPEs) that appeared to be independent entities but were in fact completely controlled by individuals affiliated with Enron.[13] Enron often purported to "sell" assets to its SPEs and booked the money it received as revenue.

Enron represented that the SPEs were essentially independent actors that purchased the asset and took on the risk that its value might decline. But in many cases, Enron failed to comply with even the nominal requirement that a small percentage of the SPE be owned by an independent investor. Because Enron's SPEs were not independent, Enron was able to use them to execute transactions that a rational investor would not have agreed to. As the district court that heard the Enron securities class actions noted, the arrangement "provided Enron with the opportunity in the future to do non-arm's-length-transactions with an Enron-controlled entity that no independent entity would have done nor agreed to do and which provided a stream of sham profits onto Enron's books."[14] Enron's board claimed that it understood that the SPEs were not functionally independent and that it had set up procedures to ensure that the transactions were fair to Enron. However, the board did not ensure that the procedures were followed and thus failed to prevent Enron from using the SPEs to distort its financial reporting.

Enron often used its SPEs to create the impression that it was continuing to meet its projections. For example, at times, Enron would purport to sell an asset to an SPE to recognize revenue prior to the end of a quarter and then buy back the asset soon after.[15] Many of these SPE transactions involved modest amounts relative to Enron's total business. Two of the SPE transactions highlighted by the SEC in its complaint against Enron executives each involved $65 million in revenue, and a third transaction generated just $28 million in cash flow. The SPE transactions were significant not because of their size, but because they were "needed to meet budget targets and earnings-per-share goals."[16] Enron's tactics again reflected the influence of valuation methods that emphasized the company's ability to consistently deliver smooth earnings growth. Consider that Enron's Value Line Investment Survey Earnings Predictability score in June 2001, just a few months before it restated its earnings, was 90 (Xerox's score was 75 before its problems).[17] Enron continued to rely on these tactics to the point where 96 percent of its earnings in 2000 was attributed to questionable transactions with its SPEs.[18]

Several years after it was widely condemned as a securities fraud, the public intellectual Malcolm Gladwell provocatively asked whether Enron truly withheld information from investors.[19] He pointed out that the basic elements of Enron's aggressive accounting, such as its use of SPEs to move assets off its balance sheet, were disclosed in SEC filings. Just as the Xerox fraud was initially uncovered by the *Wall Street Journal* rather than regulators, reporters using public sources and a few tips from short-selling hedge funds were the first to raise questions about Enron's accounting. Gladwell argued that Enron is best categorized as a mystery – where sufficient information to ascertain the truth was available but not easily understood – rather than as a puzzle – where there was a basic lack of information that prevents understanding. If Enron's complexity was basically disclosed to markets in compliance under its obligations under the securities laws, it is more difficult to argue that it defrauded investors who did not make sufficient effort to understand its complexity.

Gladwell's argument drew heavily on points made in a law review article by Jonathan Macey. For Macey, the problem was not that Enron hid information from investors, but that investors were unable to process the available public information correctly. He asserted that "Enron did make disclosures that should have led reasonable market participants to uncover grave problems within the company."[20] Donald Langevoort made a similar point, noting that "most all the general features of what are now assumed to be [Enron's] manipulations were left in plain view – only the details and precise strategies were obscured."[21] Indeed, after the company's collapse, a number of institutional investors noted that they had questioned Enron about some of its more aggressive accounting but remained invested in the company.[22]

The claim that investors simply did not understand Enron highlights the difficulties of modern valuation. If one were to accept the efficient markets hypothesis in its strongest form, there would be no need for securities fraud regulation because investors would always know when a company's disclosures are misleading. But experience has shown that the complexity of businesses makes it difficult to truly understand their ability to generate profits over time. Investors thus rely heavily on the integrity of management in reporting financial results that permit them to assess the performance of a business. There is an argument that corporate managers should have greater obligations in such conditions to provide meaningful and accurate disclosures to investors. It is even more important for them to exercise their discretion in good faith, because it is difficult for markets to second-guess their judgment.

The depth of the problems with Enron's SPE transactions was not apparent until they were fully investigated. There were not just issues with the independence of the SPEs, there were also basic violations of accounting rules that an outsider could not have detected. For example, Enron claimed to be generating revenue by selling its assets to the SPEs, but in fact, it never actually transferred the risk of owning the assets to those entities. Enron guaranteed payments on the debt issued by the SPE to purchase Enron assets. Enron was thus ultimately responsible for the debt, and in effect had borrowed money backed by the asset it claimed to have sold. The lawyers who were required to sign off on the legitimacy of the SPE sales could not conclude that they were "true sales," yet Enron proceeded to improperly recognize the SPE transactions as sales. As the examiner appointed by the bankruptcy court concluded after extensive inquiry, these transactions were "from both an economic and risk allocation perspective, a loan rather than a sale of asset."[23]

Moreover, Enron's disclosures did not warn investors of many important details concerning the transactions. While Enron had disclosed that it had "entered into transactions with limited partnerships … whose general partner's managing member is a senior officer of Enron,"[24] Enron's disclosures "did not reveal that Enron was obligated to repay the amounts borrowed to fund" the SPE transactions.[25] A special investigative committee observed that "[a]ny readers of [Enron's] disclosures should have recognized that these arrangements were complex, the dollar amounts involved were substantial, and the transactions were significant for evaluating the Company's financial performance," but its "disclosures were obtuse, did not communicate the essence of the transactions completely or clearly, and failed to convey the substance of what was going on between Enron and the partnerships."[26] While investors were aware that the company used SPEs, the number of such transactions was not transparent. As one research analyst testified before Congress, analysts "never saw or were even aware of these deals," and he thought that Enron had just a handful of SPEs rather than hundreds of them.[27]

Once the SPE transactions were unraveled, it was clear that Enron had not been consistently meeting its projections, undermining the narrative that its revenue was growing exponentially. Moreover, the revenues generated from the SPE transactions were effectively loans, meaning that Enron had more than twice the amount of debt that it had disclosed to investors. This revelation affected the company's credit rating, reducing its ability to act as a market maker in its various trading businesses. Enron's stock collapsed both because investors realized its narrative of exceptional growth was untrue and because the company debt burden was greater than they realized.

Enron's Defense

In testifying before Congress, Enron's former CEO described the company's failure as a "classic run on the bank." He maintained that Enron's accounting restatements did not involve "big numbers in the grand scheme of Enron Corporation" and that they could have turned the company around if they "had time."[28]

But even if Enron's misreported revenue was small relative to its total revenue, its misstatements had a significant impact on the market's evaluation of its prospects. Enron's stock traded at a high multiple to its earnings, and its managers encouraged such a valuation. Thus, the impact of relatively small misstatements could result in significant adjustments to its market value. Consider a company with a stock price trading at a multiple of ten times its earnings per share. The reversal of a misstatement that overstated its earnings by $10 million would reduce its market value by $100 million. Now consider a company with a stock price trading at a multiple of a hundred times its earnings per share. The reversal of a misstatement that overstated its earnings by $10 million would reduce its market value by $1 billion.

The willingness of investors to value Enron at a high multiple reflected their faith in the exceptional talent of Enron's managers. When this faith was lost, the company's market value disintegrated. Enron was similar to Penn Central in that both companies were unable to access the capital markets once their true financial condition was known. Each company believed that it could have survived if investors had not panicked and withheld the funds that it needed to continue operating. However, the decision to withhold funds was not an arbitrary and irrational decision. Investors realized that Enron's managers had acted recklessly and that Enron's market value was a sham that could not support additional investment.

Perhaps it would be unfair to hold Enron accountable for the willingness of investors to assign it a high valuation. Its stock rose during an unprecedented time of speculation. As the economic historian Charles Kindleberger has documented, in times of economic expansion, investors become less risk averse and "more eager to pursue profit opportunities that pay off in the distant future."[29] When stock prices become irrationally high, as Michael Jensen has argued, managers are trapped by the pressure to meet unrealistic market expectations. [30]

According to its defenders, Enron did its best to navigate difficult economic conditions using innovative techniques that were blessed by its auditors. As reported by Enron's bankruptcy examiner, "[w]hen many of the officers were asked whether Enron's disclosure of the results of the [SPE] transactions was misleading, reliance on Andersen's approval of Enron's accounting for those transactions was a common response."[31] In a remarkable interview with Harvard Business School professor Eugene Soltes, Enron's chief financial officer (CFO), who engineered many of Enron's questionable transactions while enriching himself, echoed this view. He argued that if Enron wanted to cheat, it could have done so in much simpler ways. Instead, he asserted that it "cheated fair and square."[32]

The main flaw with Enron's defense is that the company was not a passive victim of market expectations. It full-heartedly embraced a flawed system and for a time thrived within it. Enron and its managers did not attempt to lower market expectations when warranted but consistently drove them higher. Indeed, it actively encouraged the narrative that it should be valued as an exceptional company.[33] At some point, Enron and its managers knew that it could not deliver the growth that it had promised. Rather than inform the market of the truth, they pushed through questionable transactions to misrepresent Enron's true condition. When the market understood that Enron's accounting was false, it could no longer trust the company's integrity.

ENRON'S EXECUTIVE COMPENSATION

As noted earlier, the conventional story is that public company securities fraud in the 1990s was driven by the interests of individual executives who wanted to boost the company stock price so they could sell their stock at an inflated price. Viewed in this way, fraud is a subset of the problem of agency costs, where the interests of managers diverge from the interests of the corporation and its shareholders. As the amount of executive compensation increased significantly over the 1990s, company executives were more susceptible to the allegation that they had a personal incentive to commit securities fraud.

The argument that Enron's top executives committed securities fraud for personal reasons was bolstered by the fact that they sold significant amounts of Enron stock in the year before the company collapsed. Kenneth Lay, the chairman of Enron's board, sold $65 million in Enron stock in 2001.[34] Skilling sold $62 million in Enron stock from 2000 to 2001.[35] The sales supported the narrative that these two individuals knew the company's market value was distorted. Moreover, the sales were the basis for independent charges of criminal insider trading against the two defendants.

For much of the twentieth century, the CEO of a large public corporation was a salary man tasked with maintaining rather than growing a business. A study published in 1945 observed that CEOs of large corporations were not expected to be risk-takers. Large corporations had advanced past the entrepreneurial stage, and CEOs were "men whose job is to carry on rather than to build up a new organization."[36] Thus, "the chief executive in our largest corporations is not ordinarily the type of creative and aggressive business leader who is both famous and infamous in the annals of American industry."[37] Because the goal was stability rather than growth, "the executive's compensation is relatively stable, and he is likely to have a high degree of security of tenure."[38] It was possible to describe "[t]he goal of business leadership [as] not profit-*making* but profit-*receiving*."[39]

Corporate managers were motivated mainly by the prestige and security of their jobs rather than the hope of accumulating tens of millions of dollars in compensation. They generally received a fixed salary and did not own substantial amounts of stock in their firm. Financial economists Michael Jensen and Kevin Murphy found that executives typically held a small percentage of their company's stock through the 1970s and 1980s. During the period from 1969 to 1973, CEOs on average held 0.21 percent of their company's stock. In contrast, during the period from 1979 to 1983, CEOs on average held only 0.11 percent of their company stock.[40] They thus concluded that "the relation between CEO wealth and shareholder wealth is small and has fallen by an order of magnitude in the last 50 years."[41] As a result, the incentive of executives was not to increase a company's stock price by maximizing profits but to increase the size of their companies through acquisitions to reduce the risk of failure. Such a strategy would result in a safe but moderately performing investment for shareholders and job security for the company's executives.[42]

Over the 1980s and 1990s, public companies awarded executives larger amounts of equity through stock grants and options.[43] Two economists documented an "explosion of stock option issuance that occurred during the 1980s and 1990s."[44] By the mid-1990s, the mean stock option grant to a CEO increased almost seven-fold, making executive compensation more sensitive to stock price movements. Just a 1 percent increase in price on average translated into an increase of $124,000 in CEO wealth. A significant decline in a company's stock price could make the options worthless. Other forms of executive compensation also increased with the average salary and bonus of public company CEOs doubling. By 2001, stock and option compensation accounted for about two-thirds of total CEO pay for the median company, while in 1984 it accounted for less than 1 percent.[45] On the other hand, it is worth noting that Jensen and Murphy still maintained well into the 2000s that "[o]n average, corporate America pays its most important leaders like bureaucrats."[46]

The personal enrichment of executives was not always understood as a significant driver of securities fraud. A study published in 1996 examined accounting enforcement cases brought by the SEC from 1982 through 1992.[47] It concluded that the primary motivation for the frauds uncovered in such cases was to obtain external financing at a lower cost. It found that the SEC did not often allege that a fraud was part of a scheme by managers to receive a higher bonus or to sell their stock at an inflated price. The relative absence of allegations directed at individual managers prior to the 1990s illustrates how significantly the system changed by the end of the decade.

Many commentators now believe that public company securities fraud is primarily driven by the desire to inflate executive compensation. Just four years after noting the absence of a link between executive compensation and securities fraud during the 1980s, one of the authors of that study wrote: "as stock market valuations . . . increased during the 1990s, especially in conjunction with the increased importance of stock-based compensation, managers have become increasingly sensitive to the level of their firms' stock prices and their relation to key accounting numbers such as earnings. Consequently, their incentives to manage earnings to maintain and improve those valuations have also increased, which arguably explains why earnings management has received so much recent attention."[48] Finance professors Bengt Holmstron and Steven Kaplan observed after the Enron and WorldCom scandals: "as executive stock and option ownership has increased, so has the incentive to manage and manipulate accounting numbers in order to inflate stock market values and sell shares at those inflated values."[49] A number of studies published in the mid-2000s found positive correlations between the number of options awarded to executives and the likelihood of a company restatement or accounting error.[50] On the other hand, one study found no link between equity incentives and an SEC accusation of accounting fraud.[51] John Coffee argued that equity compensation was a more likely explanation for Enron's fraud than the pressure of meeting projections.

He noted that Enron's management could have issued less ambitious projections and that it did not do so because "[a]ggressive forecasts drove the firm's stock price up and enabled management to sell at an inflated price."[52] As public companies increased compensation through stock options, and such options created incentives to manage earnings, the regulation of executive compensation became an important part of securities and corporate law.

An important implication of linking executive compensation to securities fraud is that such frauds can be understood as mainly driven by individual managers who seek to maximize their own pay packages. If that is the case, then there is an argument that securities fraud enforcement should be mostly directed at individuals rather than corporations. Executive compensation reform rather than enhancing accuracy of public company disclosure might be more effective in reducing securities fraud.

On the other hand, it is difficult to argue that securities fraud in public companies is solely the result of bad individual incentives. While there may be some cases where executives issue misstatements because of personal greed, there are others where they act to further corporate goals. As accounting professor Baruch Lev observed, "[w]hile the image of managers who feather their own nests attracts an understandably large share of attention ... my sense is that the more common reason for earnings manipulation is that managers, forever the optimists, are trying to 'weather out the storm' – that is, to continue operations with adequate funding and customer/supplier support until better times come."[53] There is a general corporate incentive to maintain a high valuation. Shareholders may prefer that corporate managers pursue a strategy that inflates the company's stock price. An economic model by James Spindler envisions such a situation where managers commit fraud simply to increase shareholder payoffs and concludes that corporate liability for such fraud is an appropriate deterrent.[54]

If valuation methods had not changed as corporate managers were increasingly paid in stock, would they have still had an incentive to commit securities fraud? If investors valued companies based on their long-term strategies and did not emphasize short-term financial results, executives would have been less able to boost the value of their personal stock holdings by issuing misleading periodic disclosures. While executive compensation plays a role in creating personal incentives to issue misrepresentations, valuation pressure also is a factor and is arguably a more important driver of securities fraud.

WERE ENRON'S MANAGERS CRIMINALS?

Unlike the Penn Central, Apple, and Xerox cases, several of Enron's top executives were criminally charged and convicted of securities fraud.[55] Even though it was clear that Enron and its managers deceived investors to an extent that supported a finding of civil liability, it was harder to establish that Enron's managers acted with criminal intent. A criminal violation of the securities laws requires a determination that an individual "willfully and knowingly" violated those laws. It was one thing to conclude that Enron's former CEO was reckless in his belief that Enron's use of SPEs to meet earnings targets was consistent with GAAP. It was another to conclude that he actually knew that the SPEs violated GAAP. While there was sufficient evidence to support a criminal conviction of Skilling,[56] the conviction was based on just a handful of the company's questionable transactions where there was specific proof of his personal involvement. Notably, the prosecutors argued that many of these transactions permitted Enron to meet projections. Because in other cases such evidence is often not available, it is difficult to use the criminal law to single out and punish individuals for public company securities fraud.

Not all of the securities frauds that emerged around the time of Enron triggered substantial government sanctions. Consider the example of Global Crossing. Like Enron, Global Crossing was a large public company (its market capitalization approached $50 billion at its peak) that unexpectedly filed for bankruptcy. Prior to its filing in January 2002, the market took comfort in the fact that it was meeting its revenue projections. Investors did not know that much of Global Crossing's revenue came from questionable "reciprocal transactions" where it would sell telecommunications services to other carriers, which only purchased them because Global Crossing agreed it would buy an equivalent amount of services from the same carriers. The transactions were a wash, but Global Crossing could report revenue that would meet market expectations, hiding its inability to generate revenue through legitimate transactions. As an SEC investigation later reported, "[w]ithout these reciprocal transactions, [Global Crossing] would not have met securities analysts' estimates for its first and second quarter 2001 pro forma results."[57]

Not only did Global Crossing and its executives escape criminal sanction, the SEC never imposed a penalty on the company. It fined three of the company's officers $100,000 each. The press speculated that Global Crossing avoided more severe condemnation because regulators were focusing their efforts on Enron.[58]

There is a more substantive reason why Global Crossing was treated differently. It was not completely clear that these reciprocal transactions violated GAAP. Global Crossing was not the only telecommunications company to use this accounting maneuver. A leading auditor wrote a memo that pitched the idea to the industry. On the other hand, the transactions were clearly deceptive.[59] As the district court that heard a securities class action against the company noted, "these exchanges were essentially unnecessary mirror-image transactions created with the specific intention of inflating the [company's] revenues and deceiving investors into thinking the company was financially sound when it was, in fact, in increasingly perilous straits."[60] Indeed, the court held that the misleading nature of the transactions was sufficient to permit a civil securities fraud claim to go forward.

In contrast, the CEO of another telecommunications company, Qwest, used similar tactics as Global Crossing and was criminally convicted and sentenced to six years in prison. Qwest also used reciprocal transactions to meet unrealistically high revenue projections.[61] Rather than claim that the transactions were material misstatements that misled investors, federal prosecutors argued that Qwest's CEO avoided losses by selling substantial amounts of stock before the company's inflation of its revenue numbers was revealed.[62] Instead of using the CEO's insider trading to show that a misstatement was motivated by fraudulent intent, the prosecutors successfully brought a stand-alone claim of insider trading against him. The government achieved a harsh sanction by advancing a theory that did not rely on establishing an accounting violation of which the CEO had knowledge.

Enron's former CEO, Skilling, was also convicted on one count of insider trading,[63] but in his case, the government also alleged criminal securities fraud. This was a more challenging charge to establish because it required prosecutors to prove that Skilling was involved with Enron's misrepresentations and knew that they were materially misleading. As noted earlier, Skilling argued that he genuinely believed in the promise of Enron's business and that he did not know that Enron's financial statements were misstated.

In the end, Skilling's securities fraud conviction hinged on specific evidence of his knowledge that certain transactions were improper. For example, the company's former CFO, who ran the SPEs that purchased assets from Enron so it could meet its earnings, testified that Skilling personally guaranteed that the SPEs would not lose money on these transactions.[64] Such a guarantee would mean that the assets had not truly been sold to the SPE. If the CFO's testimony was credible to the jury, this claim directly implicated Skilling in willful fraudulent conduct. While it is certainly possible that the CFO lied to reduce his own sentence, there was testimony that corroborated his account, and criminal sentences are commonly based on the testimony of cooperating witnesses.

It is worth noting that Skilling's criminal conviction for securities fraud was based on a fraction of the improper conduct that occurred at Enron. The SPE transactions at issue in the criminal trial were modest in size and were mainly important because they permitted Enron to meet quarterly projections. These transactions were not the sole or even primary cause of Enron's failure. However, they did deceive investors and likely supported Enron's inflated market valuation. The idea that a relatively small misstatement permitting a company to meet investor expectations could support a Rule 10b-5 violation was first seen in the Penn Central case, where the company improperly recognized revenue so it could report a quarterly profit. By the 2000s, such a misstatement could support a criminal conviction.

In contrast, the criminal conviction of the CEO of WorldCom, Bernard Ebbers, was based on much larger transactions. Like Enron, WorldCom's fraud was primarily motivated by the pressure to meet its quarterly earnings projections. The company had grown exponentially from its humble beginnings as an upstart reseller of long-distance telephone services, and its stock price soared as the market expected the company's growth to continue. In an April 1999 press release, WorldCom commented on its "impressive" quarterly results and predicted that "incremental capital spending combined with more aggressive selling and marketing efforts will continue to propel strong top-line sales growth in our core communications services for the foreseeable future."[65] The year before its collapse, it continued reiterating aggressive projections for a 12–15 percent increase in revenue.[66] A report by the special investigative committee of WorldCom's board later concluded that the company had an institutional process where accounting was manipulated to make up the difference between its actual results and projections.[67] The controller of the company explained that he "was instructed on a quarterly basis by senior management to ensure that entries were made to falsify WorldCom's books to reduce WorldCom's reported actual costs and therefore to increase WorldCom's reported earnings."[68]

As with the Enron defendants, the criminal conviction of Ebbers hinged on specific testimony provided by the company's CFO. The criminal trial revealed multiple occasions where WorldCom's CFO warned Ebbers that WorldCom could not meet its projections and that the company should lower market expectations. Ebbers refused to do so and instead instructed the CFO to hit the numbers. To accomplish Ebbers' orders, the CFO improperly failed to properly report billions of dollars in expenses. Ebbers ignored the company's internal reports that it could only achieve growth of 5.5 percent and instead claimed that the company had met its target of a 12 percent growth rate. Even if Ebbers did not know the precise way in which the company's financial statements were misleading, the CFO's testimony established that the CEO knew that its results were fabricated to hit financial targets. As Judge Ralph Winter, who was a leading corporate law scholar before becoming a federal appellate judge, wrote in affirming Ebbers' criminal conviction, the company's accounting decisions were based "on the financial targets needed to keep share price high" and "were used for the express purpose of intentionally misstating WorldCom's financial condition and artificially inflating its stock price."[69]

Major criminal convictions of executives for public company securities fraud are not the norm. In many cases, high-level executives can credibly argue that they did not have actual knowledge of false financial statements. The criminal convictions at Enron and WorldCom depended on specific information that top executives knew that corporate statements were misleading. While the criminal law can at times play a role in sanctioning individuals responsible for a fraud, in many cases the evidence will not be available to support a criminal verdict.

SECURITIES FRAUD AND CORPORATE GOVERNANCE REDUX

Much like Penn Central almost thirty years before, the Enron and WorldCom frauds were viewed as partly the fault of passive boards that did not do enough to prevent the companies from hiding their declining performance from investors.

These two cases, along with the many other examples of securities fraud that were being uncovered, thus raised broad questions about public company governance.

As noted earlier, the adequacy of corporate governance in public companies was criticized starting in the 1970s. Corporate scandals like Penn Central shook the managerialist assumption that large corporations would never fail and helped lead to proposals to increase the independence of company boards.[70] Academic commentators observed that the interests of managers diverged from the interests of shareholders and thus the board should be composed of independent directors who monitored management. The SEC made efforts to regulate corporate governance through its enforcement efforts. It required some companies that violated the securities laws to agree to governance changes. But efforts by federal regulators to reform governance became dormant by the early 1980s. The SEC during the Reagan administration made it a point to de-emphasize public company governance and focused instead on narrower issues of individual wrongdoing like insider trading.

During the 1980s, the problem of securities fraud was mainly viewed as affecting emerging companies. Newly public companies are more susceptible to fraud because they tend to be small, do not have the resources to develop reliable internal reporting, and because they may not have experienced management. An influential study of securities fraud that covered the period from 1987 to 1997 noted that most of the fraudulent financial reporting cases resolved during this period involved companies that were not traded on a stock exchange and had assets or revenues well under $100 million. The authors of the report concluded that "[t]he relatively small size of fraud companies suggests that the inability or even unwillingness to implement cost-effective internal controls may be a factor affecting the likelihood of financial statement fraud."[71] Toward the end of the 1980s, the collapse of the Savings and Loan (S&L) industry revealed substantial fraud, but these S&Ls generally did not have widely traded stocks. As will be discussed in Chapter 6, the looting of S&Ls was mainly viewed as an issue of corporate waste and self-dealing rather than securities fraud directed at public markets.[72]

The initial wave of securities frauds uncovered during the 1990s at companies like Cendant, Sunbeam, and Waste Management prompted corporate governance reform by the industry groups that make rules for the stock markets. The New York Stock Exchange (NYSE) and National Association of Securities Dealers formed a Blue Ribbon Committee on Improving the Effectiveness of Corporate Audit Committees in September 1998. The committee issued a report in early 1999 proposing that companies listed on a stock market with a market capitalization over $200 million have an audit committee composed solely of independent directors. It argued for a tighter definition of independence for such directors. Finally, it proposed that at least one member of the audit committee meet a standard of financial literacy.[73] Soon after the report was released, the major stock markets proposed rules that adopted many of these recommendations.

The SEC also responded by passing rules relating to public company audit committees in early 2000. In doing so, it referred to the "increasing pressure to meet earnings expectations" as necessitating "strong audit committees" to "oversee[] and monitor[] management's and the independent auditors' participation in the financial reporting process."[74] The SEC's approach did not directly regulate the composition of the audit committee but required disclosure if a company chose to include a nonindependent member on that committee. This disclosure approach was consistent with the philosophy of the securities laws, which have traditionally been reluctant to directly regulate corporate governance.

After these initial efforts, SEC Chairman Levitt expressed optimism that the new rules were working. He reported in 2000 that "I can't have a conversation with a corporate board member without hearing how active and revitalized audit committees have become."[75] A few months later, the SEC's chief accountant reported he had "heard about audit committees that have undertaken with renewed enthusiasm their role in corporate governance."[76]

The collapse of Enron and WorldCom about a year after these statements created pressure to implement stronger reforms. After filing its complaint against WorldCom, the SEC issued a remarkable order asking for "written statements, under oath, from senior officers of certain publicly traded companies ... with revenues during their last period of greater than $1.2 billion" confirming the accuracy of company financial statements.[77] The high profile of these failures and the size of the financial misstatements at issue resulted in extensive investigations. As with Penn Central, these inquiries naturally asked why the boards of Enron and WorldCom failed to prevent the fraud.

The report of the special investigative committee of Enron's board pointed to board failure as enabling the fraud.[78] The report observed that some of the SPE transactions had been reviewed by Enron's board. The board raised questions about the transactions and attempted to put in place procedures to manage the conflict of interest created by the fact that these SPEs were controlled by Enron's CFO. However, those procedures were not effectively implemented. For example, the company's audit committee was supposed to review the transactions between Enron and the SPEs but only examined the transactions "in a cursory way." The report also noted problems with the board's access to information. It reported that while "Enron's outside auditors supposedly examined Enron's internal controls," it "did not identify or bring to the Audit Committee's attention the inadequacies in their implementation."

A special investigation by a committee of two WorldCom directors appointed after the company filed for bankruptcy concluded that, "WorldCom's collapse reflected not only a financial fraud but also a major failure of corporate governance."[79] A report by WorldCom's bankruptcy examiner, former US Attorney General Richard Thornburg, described a company that grew too quickly and was completely controlled by its management. The company's decision-making was criticized as ad hoc and lacking in coherence. As WorldCom made acquisition after acquisition, its "management systems, internal controls and other personnel did not keep pace with that growth." Because of the company's early success, the CEO of the company, Ebbers, "appears to have dominated the course of the Company's growth, as well as the agenda, discussions and decisions of the Board of Directors."[80] The examiner's report faulted WorldCom's board for its lack of oversight. Its board failed to act even though it was uncomfortable with the significant loans extended to Ebbers by the compensation committee.[81] The company's audit committee "rarely scratched below the surface of the issues that arose" and instead took "at face value" the representations of WorldCom's CFO.[82] WorldCom's earnings fraud "went undetected for so long" because of "substantial problems with the Company's internal controls."[83]

Many commentators criticized these boards. Jeffrey Gordon suggested that Enron's board should have been particularly alert given what it knew about the company. He argued that "the interaction of Enron's high-powered stock-based compensation structure, the corresponding managerial temptation to manipulate financial results that would affect the stock price, and a financial disclosure approach that made the firm's financial performance substantially opaque to public capital markets, created an unusual risk that should have called forth unusual, intense Board monitoring of business results and financial controls."[84] A congressional report documented the board's knowledge of the company's aggressive accounting and emphasis on smoothing income.[85]

The portrayal of Enron and WorldCom as governance failures was not surprising given the extent of the frauds at these companies. Because they were significant public companies that quickly shed billions of dollars in market value, there was concern about why their corporate directors did not do more. On the other hand, a skeptic might contend that these reports simply reiterated common criticisms of company boards. Earlier corporate governance proposals provided ready-made solutions that could be applied by the investigators who were tasked with quickly explaining the complex causes of two high-profile frauds.

The collapse of Enron and WorldCom most directly spurred passage of federal corporate governance reform, but the new governance requirements were also the culmination of several years of grappling with a problem that affected many public corporations. These efforts expressed the view that securities fraud in public companies had systemic causes that could not be addressed solely through enforcement.

SARBANES–OXLEY

The severity of securities frauds at companies like Enron and WorldCom shook faith in the efficiency of stock markets. If billions of dollars could simply evaporate, how could investors trust the valuations of other public companies? As Urska Velikonja has noted, the securities frauds at these two companies not only affected stock markets but a variety of corporate stakeholders.[86] Workers lost their jobs and saw their 401(k) accounts dissipate. WorldCom's fraud also affected competitors who could not keep up with its fictitious performance. The CEO of Sprint complained: "[w]e kept asking ourselves what we were doing wrong because we couldn't generate the numbers WorldCom reported . . . As we discovered, the margins were a hoax but the devastating effect on our industry was very, very real."[87] AT&T reported that it laid off "tens of thousands [of its employees] in the late 1990s as it tried frantically to match WorldCom's infuriatingly low costs."[88]

Building on the earlier reforms adopted by the SEC and stock markets, Congress responded by passing Sarbanes–Oxley, which mandated a variety of corporate governance and company reporting measures to prevent securities fraud in public corporations. The statute was a remarkable intervention considering that less than a decade before, the Private Securities Litigation Reform Act reflected doubt that private securities litigation typically asserted strong claims of securities fraud against public companies. Sarbanes–Oxley has been a controversial law and soon sparked a significant backlash that will be described more extensively in a later chapter of this book.

Sarbanes–Oxley contains a wide variety of provisions aimed at public companies. Parts of the statute addressed the accuracy of financial reporting. It strengthened the regulation of auditors by requiring them to increase their independence from public company clients and establishing a new entity to govern them.[89] It required heightened disclosure relating to SPEs.[90] Other parts of the law more broadly regulated corporate governance. It prohibited personal loans by a public company to its directors and executive officers and also required that the CEO and CFO return bonuses and securities sale profits based on financial statements that were restated as "a result of misconduct."[91] It required disclosure about whether a company has adopted a code of ethics.[92]

Two of the most important Sarbanes–Oxley provisions relating to public company obligations to prevent securities fraud sought to increase the accuracy of financial statements by regulating public company audit committees and requiring public companies to invest significant amounts of time and resources in assessing their internal controls to prevent material misstatements.

Sarbanes–Oxley and Audit Committees

The legislative history supporting the passage of Sarbanes–Oxley was explicit that the new law sought to address the wave of securities fraud in public companies. The House report for an early version of the law noted that "the bankruptcies of Enron Corporation and Global Crossing LLC, and restatements of earnings by several prominent market participants" had raised questions about the adequacy of the securities laws.[93] A later Senate report stated that the law was prompted by "recent corporate failures" and was meant to "improve investor protection in connection with the operation of public companies."[94]

Building on the scrutiny of audit committees after the initial wave of earnings frauds, Congress increased regulation of public company audit committees. It departed from the SEC's initial inclination to pass a disclosure rule that allowed a company some leeway in the composition of its audit committee. Instead, it imposed a mandatory requirement that all public companies trading on a national stock market have independent audit committees. The Senate report cited and Congress essentially adopted the recommendation of the Blue Ribbon Commission in requiring all audit committee members to be independent.[95] An independent director may not "accept any consulting, advisory, or other compensatory fee" from the company or be affiliated with the company.[96]

The hope of this provision was to make it more difficult for management to influence the company's audit. The SEC later explained in passing the rules implementing the independence requirement that "[a]n audit committee comprised of independent directors is better situated to assess objectively the quality of the issuer's financial disclosure and the adequacy of internal controls than a committee that is affiliated with management." The SEC referenced the "pressures to satisfy market expectations" as a factor that might warp management's judgment.[97] Jonathan Macey later observed that "[b]y empowering the board to obtain information necessary to monitor management without management's participation in the information production process, [the audit committee] rules represent the most ambitious attempt to date to deal with the problem of board capture."[98]

In addition to mandating independence, the Act centered responsibility for supervising the audit of the company's financial statements in the audit committee. The audit committee is required to set forth procedures to receive and respond to complaints relating to the company's accounting practices. The audit committee is also empowered to hire outside advisors to assist it in its duties. The company must disclose whether at least one member of the audit committee is a "financial expert," encouraging companies to choose a director qualified to supervise the audit.[99] These provisions sought to transfer control over the audit process from management to the company's board. James Cox noted that these provisions "impose a dialogue between the audit committee and the outside accountants for the purpose of eliciting any warning signs in the reporting system or management's disclosure policies and practices."[100] As accounting professor William Beaver noted, these reforms "substantially increase the reliance on the audit committee and financial reporting as a mechanism for effective corporate governance."[101] Stephen Bainbridge and Todd Henderson observed that after Sarbanes–Oxley, "[t]he board is in a sense the agent of not just the shareholders but also society writ large."[102]

Sarbanes–Oxley's provisions were supplemented by additional independence requirements passed by the exchanges. At the prompting of the SEC, the NYSE commissioned an extensive study of possible corporate governance reforms that was published in June of 2002.[103] The major stock markets soon after adopted rules: (1) requiring that a majority of directors on the board for a listed company be independent; (2) tightening the definition of independence; (3) requiring separate meetings for independent directors; (4) requiring independence for the committees that nominate directors and set executive compensation; and (5) mandating that all of the directors serving on the company's audit committee be financially literate, with one member having "increased financial sophistication."

Sarbanes–Oxley and Internal Controls

In addition to reforms directed at the board, Sarbanes–Oxley sought to regulate the process of verifying the accuracy of financial reports. The law requires public companies to invest significant resources to prevent securities fraud.

Perhaps the most controversial aspect of Sarbanes–Oxley is its mandate that public companies assess on a yearly basis the internal controls that help ensure that the company's financial reports are reliable. While public companies had been required to keep accurate books and records and maintain adequate internal controls since the passage of the Foreign Corrupt Practices Act, which was passed in the 1970s partly because of frauds at companies like Penn Central, there was no federal requirement that the company check the effectiveness of the controls on a yearly basis. As noted earlier, the SEC signaled that it would not bring enforcement cases to ensure that such controls were adequate. Sarbanes–Oxley increased the importance of internal controls by requiring that public companies stand by the reliability of their financial statements in two ways.

First, the highest executives of the company, the CEO and CFO, must personally certify the integrity of the company's annual and quarterly SEC filings. They must represent that they reviewed the company's disclosure, that "the report does not contain any untrue statement of a material fact," and that the "financial statements ... fairly present in all material respects the financial condition and results of operations of the issuer." The requirement that a company fairly present its condition to investors was drawn from a famous decision written by Judge Henry Friendly in *US* v. *Simon*,[104] which held that financial statements can be misleading even if they technically comply with accounting rules. Moreover, the signature of these officers represents that they "designed such internal controls" to alert them to "material information" about the company, and that they "have evaluated the effectiveness" of these controls. The officers must also certify that they have disclosed to its auditors and audit committee "all significant deficiencies in the design or operation of internal controls" and "any fraud, whether or not material, that involves management or other employees who have a significant role in the issuer's internal controls."[105] The certification provision is meant to increase the expectation that management will take personal responsibility for preventing substantial fraud. Robert Thompson and Hillary Sale have argued that the certification requirement essentially imposes a duty of care on a company's highest officers.[106] In contrast, Lisa Fairfax was skeptical that the certification would impose any substantive requirement.[107]

Second, the company must annually file with the SEC a report on its internal controls. That report must notably "contain an assessment ... of the effectiveness of the internal control structure and procedures" relating to the company's financial reports. Section 404(b) of Sarbanes–Oxley requires the company's auditor to "attest, to, and report on, the assessment made by the management" of the company. Such an assessment requires the auditor to essentially verify the representations of management.

This provision is significant in that it essentially overturned the SEC's decision at the start of the Reagan administration to view the extent of a company's internal controls as a matter of managerial business judgment. The assessment of the controls must now be conducted in accordance with SEC rules and standards set forth by a Public Company Accounting Oversight Board (PCAOB). The SEC in its rulemaking later stated that management must identify the framework it used to assess the controls. It pointed specifically to an internal controls framework promulgated by the Committee of Sponsoring Organizations (COSO) of the Treadway Commission that had earlier highlighted the problem of accounting fraud in the late 1980s.[108] The PCAOB also published auditing standards relating to its expectations for assessing internal controls. These standards notably provide guidance to auditors on how controls can address the risk of securities fraud. Such controls may scrutinize: (1) "significant, unusual transactions, particularly those that result in late or unusual journal entries"; (2) "journal entries and adjustments made in the period-end financial reporting process"; (3) "related party transactions"; (4) "significant management estimates"; and (5) "incentives for, and pressures on, management to falsify or inappropriately manage financial results."[109] Internal controls are thus directed in part at the valuation pressure of meeting projections that contributed to Xerox, Enron, and other securities frauds.

Sarbanes–Oxley's increased regulation of public company internal controls demonstrates how perceptions of securities fraud have evolved over the decades. As noted earlier, securities fraud was mainly viewed as a problem for small companies that could not afford to invest in internal controls. As investors increasingly valued public companies based on their future performance, the incentive to commit securities fraud increased. It was not enough for public companies to have internal controls; such controls needed to be assessed for their effectiveness on a periodic basis. Public companies became largely distinguished from private companies based on their ability and willingness to invest in measures to prevent securities fraud. As Donald Langevoort and Robert Thompson explained, "[t]he new requirement for internal controls produced the sharpest cleavage in terms of differentiating public companies."[110]

The importance of monitoring for wrongdoing did not end with federal law. Delaware, the state where most large public companies are incorporated, quickly responded to show that it understood that monitoring the corporation for misconduct is an important function of the board. The Delaware Court of Chancery had recognized such a basic duty in its 1996 decision in *Caremark*,[111] where it held that directors have a fiduciary duty to monitor the corporation for wrongdoing. That case had been influential, but it was not until 2006 that the Delaware Supreme Court officially recognized this corporate law duty to monitor.[112] Delaware was careful not to make the monitoring duty too burdensome. It can be fulfilled by setting up a minimal system of controls. But it is telling that Delaware formally adopted an internal controls requirement several years after the passage of Sarbanes–Oxley. As the years have passed, *Caremark* has provided Delaware courts with a vehicle to assess whether a board should bear some responsibility for failing to prevent a corporate crisis.

* * *

When the SEC backed the ability of public companies to issue projections without fear of liability in the mid-1990s, it could not have anticipated that less than a decade later, it would be routinely imposing significant sanctions on large companies for misstating earnings to meet such projections. Enron was the most visible of a string of securities frauds that were viewed by securities regulators as meritorious. While its collapse can be tied to corporate mismanagement, the company's deceptive portrayal of its prospects could only be supported by questionable accounting. Even if Enron's high-level executives were not aware of every detail of the deception, they knew that the company's financial statements did not reflect reality. Sarbanes–Oxley, which was passed to prevent securities frauds like Enron, casts a shadow over all public companies. Unlike the initial set of reforms prompted by Penn Central, Sarbanes–Oxley has mostly persisted for the last two decades. As will be discussed later in this book, part of the reason for the stickiness of the statute is that the valuation pressure that contributed to Enron's fall continues. Whether the statute will be effective in preventing the next Enron remains to be seen.

6

Citigroup and the Financial Crisis of 2008

What does solvent mean?

JP Morgan CEO Jamie Dimon, 2010

A little more than five years after the passage of the Sarbanes–Oxley Act of 2002 (Sarbanes–Oxley),[1] many of the nation's largest financial institutions failed or were pushed to the brink of failure. An unprecedented decline in housing prices reduced the value of securities backed by housing loans owned by many banks. The resulting insolvency of some of the most significant Wall Street giants prompted the worst financial turmoil since the Great Depression. The crisis raised serious questions about the efficiency of markets as hundreds of billions of dollars in market capitalization suddenly disappeared. The losses suffered by investors were more severe and long lasting than those that came out of the market crisis that helped give rise to Sarbanes–Oxley.

Some of the banks affected by the crisis misrepresented their exposure to the housing market. The financial conglomerate Citigroup misstated the amount of the subprime mortgage assets it owned by around $40 billion. Investors filed a Rule 10b-5 class action claiming securities fraud against the company. But for the most part, Wall Street's brush with death was not viewed through the lens of securities fraud. The SEC's complaint against Citigroup alleged that its statements were inaccurate but was careful not to claim that the company acted with fraudulent intent. Despite extensive efforts to investigate the financial sector, criminal prosecutions were not brought against the top executives of the major banks for securities law violations.

Courts and regulators generally rejected broad claims arguing that the failure of financial institutions to warn the market about the massive losses they incurred in their housing-related assets was fraudulent. Like in the Apple case, some investors argued that banks like Citigroup hid a serious problem from the market. The banks did not disclose that the excessive amount of risk on their balance sheets would put them in danger of insolvency. Just as Apple's optimistic statements about the Twiggy disk drive were misleading given its problems, financial institutions were arguably too optimistic about the value of their housing securities.

The narrowness of the viable claims against Citigroup highlights the boundaries of securities fraud liability. To commit securities fraud, corporate managers must have superior knowledge relative to investors with respect to information that will affect the company's financial performance. In earlier cases, there was a stronger argument that defendants knew that their financial statements or representations about their products created a misleading appearance of growth. The need to meet the expectations of the valuation treadmill provided a compelling narrative that misstatements of revenue and earnings were part of a fraudulent scheme.

In contrast, after the financial crisis of 2008, there was a reasonable case that bank officials were just as surprised by the extent of the crisis as investors.[2] It was challenging to construct a compelling argument that the failure of managers to anticipate that the value of what were viewed as safe securities would evaporate was securities fraud. As the crisis unfolded over more than a year, it was unclear whether the turmoil would be temporary or would persist and grow worse. Under one view, many financial institutions were essentially insolvent because their housing assets had declined significantly in value. Under another view, these large banks were solvent because the value of their assets could be expected to rebound after a return to normalcy. It was difficult to link investor losses to a clear misrepresentation at one point in time because the situation was continually evolving.

Rather than address the underlying causes of the failure of financial institutions through securities fraud enforcement and holding specific firms and executives accountable for investor losses, the main response to the financial crisis was extensive regulation directed at preventing the next crisis. While most of the statute that implemented these measures, the Dodd–Frank Wall Street Reform and Consumer Protection Act (Dodd–Frank),[3] was meant to ensure the stability of the financial system, it also continued the work of Sarbanes–Oxley. Dodd–Frank increased regulation of executive compensation, which has been viewed as a significant driver of securities fraud, and provided incentives for public company whistleblowers to come forward. The combination of Sarbanes–Oxley and Dodd–Frank increased the distinction between public companies, which must devote significant resources to prevent securities fraud, and private companies, which are not so obligated.

A FINANCIAL CONGLOMERATE

By the 1980s, investors generally viewed the strategy of conglomeration as a failure.[4] Managers found it difficult to apply their general expertise to master the nuances of multiple industries. Large corporations became bureaucratic and inefficient and were averse to innovation. Foreign competitors exposed these problems as they produced superior products and captured market share. Management theory shifted and concluded that companies were more likely to create value if they developed expertise in a specific industry. Investors could easily achieve the diversification benefits offered by a conglomerate by investing in a mutual fund. There is evidence that a conglomerate discount emerged where the market value of a conglomerate was less than the market value of its individual businesses.

The financial services industry was a notable exception to the new bias against conglomerates. As markets became more international, there was an argument that US banks needed to grow larger to compete globally. German, Swiss, and Japanese banks were expanding in size. American financial institutions needed to keep pace to work with large corporate clients that themselves were becoming larger and more international. Small banks simply could not offer the range of specialized services that were demanded by multinational corporations.

Citigroup emerged to become the largest US banking conglomerate by the end of the 1990s. It was formed through the merger of two other large financial conglomerates – Citicorp and Travelers Group. Citicorp was already the largest commercial bank in the United States and was known as the "megaconglomerate of American banking."[5] It could trace its origins to a bank formed two centuries ago by shareholders of the First Bank of the United States after Congress permitted its charter to expire.[6] As Michael Perino has recounted, in the 1930s, it operated as National City Bank and was scrutinized for its sales practices and trading in its own stock during the Pecora hearings that laid the foundation for the passage of the federal securities laws.[7] It was Penn Central's largest lender, and its CEO reportedly made a call urging the federal government to bail out the railroad but was rebuffed.[8] It was notable for making an ambitious promise in the early 1970s to increase its earnings by 15 percent a year to keep pace with growth companies like Xerox.[9] This was an early sign of the shift to valuing public companies based on their future earnings. Travelers Group was not only an insurance company but had acquired two investment banks – Smith Barney and Salomon Brothers. It was led by a management team that ruthlessly cut costs to boost earnings. Because a Depression-era law, the Glass-Steagall Act, separated commercial and investment banking, Citicorp and Travelers Group had to lobby Congress to repeal the law for the merger to close.

The merger was justified on the promise of: (1) synergies that would be created by melding different businesses and (2) the safety of a diversified financial conglomerate. The CEO of Travelers, Sandy Weill, had long had the ambition of creating a financial supermarket.[10] He believed that cross-selling diverse financial products would create opportunities to increase revenue. For example, Citigroup might provide a client with advice on a merger while also providing financing for the transaction through bank loans and securities sales. Its banking branches could offer customers both a mortgage and investment advice. Moreover, diversification and size could reduce the risk of failure during a downturn.[11] Bank failures have always been a reality of the industry and Citicorp had struggled in the early 1990s from significant loan losses in its Latin America business.[12] Weill argued that "[o]ur company will be so diversified and in so many different areas that we will be able to withstand these storms."[13]

As with Penn Central, opponents of the merger argued that the company would become too big to fail.[14] Because of Citigroup's size and complexity, it would be impossible to adequately manage the many risks on its balance sheet. Because of its status as a public company, Citigroup was subject to pressure to produce earnings and could not be expected to act conservatively and avoid risk. Indeed, many of the same management techniques used by Weill to increase shareholder value at Travelers were applied to the financial giant created by the merger. As one account described the way Citigroup was managed, "[e]ach division is required to deliver a certain amount of profits to the corporate coffers, ensuring that the company meets earnings targets."[15] Over time, Citigroup continued to grow and prosper. Its balance sheet grew from $1.1 trillion in 2002 to $2.2 trillion in 2007, the eve of the crisis that almost destroyed it.[16]

CITIGROUP'S SUBPRIME MORTGAGES

Financial institutions such as Citigroup were exposed to the collapse in housing prices largely through their ownership of securities backed by real estate loans. Prior to the crisis, banks created hundreds of billions of dollars in collateralized debt obligations (CDOs), which pooled diverse securities backed by mortgages and other assets and sold bonds backed by those securities to investors. CDO bonds were issued in tranches, where safer senior bond tranches suffered losses only after riskier lower bond tranches effectively become worthless. Most of the CDOs were sold to investors, but banks kept some on their balance sheet for investment purposes or because they were unable to sell them. As housing prices declined and mortgage defaults increased, the CDOs fell in value. Banks with significant assets related to the housing market faced billions of dollars in losses.

On July 20, 2007, about a year before the most significant economic turmoil, Citigroup discussed with investors its exposure to CDOs with securities backed by subprime mortgages, which were typically made to borrowers with low credit scores and a greater risk of default. At least initially, the decline in housing prices was thought to be a problem mainly for such riskier loans. Citigroup represented in a conference call discussing its prior quarterly earnings that it had reduced its exposure to subprime mortgages from $24 billion at the end of 2006 to $13 billion.[17] It thus created the impression that its exposure to turmoil in the housing market was low and unlikely to substantially affect its financial results.[18] It reiterated this statement a week later to investors on another call.[19]

Citigroup failed to disclose that it had an additional $39 billion of exposure to subprime CDOs. Most of this exposure was from liquidity puts on subprime CDOs sold by Citigroup giving the purchaser the right to sell the CDO back to Citigroup at the price it had paid for the security. Such liquidity puts were meant to address the possibility that a market for CDO securities might not exist during a financial crisis. If investors exercised the puts as CDO prices collapsed, Citigroup would have to buy back an asset at full price when it was likely to be worth much less. It would have to acknowledge such losses, which would reduce the value of the assets on its balance sheet and reduce its earnings. Citigroup did not mention the liquidity puts in discussing its subprime exposure because at the time, it believed that the risk that the puts would be exercised was low. Citigroup also did not include the value of super senior tranches of subprime CDOs it owned that it viewed as unlikely to suffer losses. In July 2007, it excluded the senior tranches and liquidity puts from its own internal analysis of its subprime exposure.[20]

Prior to its next earnings conference call, Citigroup's management discussed whether it should provide additional disclosure about its subprime risk. It concluded that "because the super senior tranches of CDOs previously had not been discussed and because of a request by the investment bank that the IR [investor relations] member understood to be a request not to discuss those tranches, there was no choice other than to let listeners conclude that the investment bank's total subprime exposure was $13 billion."[21] Despite knowing of these subprime assets, because it had not mentioned them earlier, Citigroup did not amend its earlier statement during an October 1, 2007 call.[22] It was only a month later, on November 4, 2007, that it issued a press release disclosing its full exposure after credit rating agencies lowered the ratings on subprime CDOs, forcing Citigroup to recognize $8–11 billion in losses.[23] The *Wall Street Journal* reported that the revelation "came as a surprise even to some analysts who cover the company closely."[24] Citigroup's stock price fell by more than 10 percent in the week after its disclosure.

Over the next year, Citigroup's market capitalization declined by more than 90 percent as the housing market deteriorated and it suffered more losses on housing-related securities.[25] Citigroup was only saved from failure by federal intervention that included billions of dollars of government loans and a guarantee of hundreds of billions of dollars in loans on its balance sheet.

Citigroup investors filed a securities class action in federal district court that eventually advanced two major theories. First, they offered the narrow theory that Citigroup's statements in July and October 2017 and several other instances misrepresented its exposure to subprime mortgages. Second, they offered the broader theory that Citigroup knew that it held low-quality assets on its balance sheet and that it failed to acknowledge the risks in its business that resulted in its collapse.[26]

Citigroup's defense was much weaker with respect to the first claim. It argued that the market knew that it had some exposure to subprime CDOs.[27] It claimed that it had no duty to disclose in detail every one of its potential liabilities.[28] The district court rejected this argument in refusing to dismiss the claim. It noted that the extent of Citigroup's exposure was important to investors and its disclosure had not been complete about that exposure.[29] Because Citigroup had specifically disclosed facts about its subprime exposure, the bank had a duty to ensure that those facts were not misleading, especially as it became clear that there was a real risk that the puts would be exercised. The court explained that "disclosure of Citigroup's CDO holdings was necessary to prevent other statements – such as the boilerplate statement that the company *may* have such exposure – from being false or misleading."[30] Citigroup's claim that it had only $13 billion in subprime exposure was at best a half-truth, and there was evidence that its managers did not correct the figure earlier because it was wary of investor reaction to an acknowledgment that the disclosure was incomplete.

Citigroup also argued that the failure to disclose was not material or fraudulent because it genuinely believed that it would never suffer losses on the super senior CDO tranches.[31] The plaintiffs responded that these specific securities were not so safe because of the way they were structured by Citigroup to make lower tranches of the CDO more appealing to investors.[32] They also argued that Citigroup overstated the value of its subprime CDOs in light of the turmoil in the market for such securities. The district court agreed that the complaint sufficiently described action-able allegations on these points.[33]

Citigroup had a stronger argument with respect to the second claim. The allega-tions that it generally held low-quality assets and knew of problems in its mortgage lending business were too vague to support a claim of securities fraud. The district court found that Citigroup's disclosures were adequate with respect to its non-CDO assets and that the complaint did not describe enough specific evidence that high-level officials knew of the extent of the problems in the company's lending prac-tices.[34] It also rejected claims that Citigroup generally knew that the assets on its balance sheet were overvalued to the extent that it would face insolvency as the market crisis grew.[35]

A well-established line of cases had cautioned against finding securities fraud liability against a financial institution merely because it became distressed after losses in its loan portfolio. In a Rule 10b-5 case filed against Chase Manhattan Bank in the late 1970s after defaults on many of its loans to developing countries, US Court of Appeals for the Second Circuit Judge Henry Friendly explained that the complaint could not go forward because it merely "alleged fraud by hindsight." Put another way, courts should be wary of assuming that bank managers had knowledge of the likelihood of a significant investment loss based solely on the fact that the loss occurred. Judge Friendly noted that a viable claim requires more than "vague allegations" that "the corporation's true financial picture was not so bright ... and that the defendants knew, or were reckless in failing to know, this."[36] About a decade later, Judge Frank Easterbrook cited Judge Friendly's earlier decision in affirming the dismissal of securities litigation against the auditors of Continental Illinois Bank (where Enron's CFO started his career),[37] which needed a government bailout after depositors withdrew their funds after the bank suffered losses on bad energy loans (securities class actions against Continental and its officers recovered about $45,000,000).[38] The fraud by hindsight doctrine recognizes that corporate managers are not omniscient. They cannot predict the future perfectly and can be surprised by unexpected events.

On the other hand, it is understandable that investors in a failed bank can be suspicious that it intentionally kept information that its situation was deteriorating from markets. A bank may have understood that its investments were distressed but avoided disclosure in the hope of a miraculous turnaround (as Arlen and Carney's last period agency costs theory would predict). Courts have thus found securities fraud liability when specific public statements by bank managers were clearly contradicted by internal reports. The key question in such cases is whether statements about the valuation of an asset were untrue when they were made, rather than proven untrue by subsequent events.[39]

Citigroup argued that it did not have contemporaneous knowledge that its asset valuations were false. It claimed that it could not have foreseen the extent of the market upheaval that resulted in a catastrophic decline in its market value.[40] Corporate executives at the bank contended that they had little if any informational advantage over markets with respect to how macroeconomic conditions would evolve. Indeed, even after its November 2007 announcement of CDO losses, Citigroup raised billions of dollars through public offerings and private placements to sophisticated investors, such as sovereign wealth funds, who may have believed that the bank's stock was undervalued because the crisis would subside.

Whether or not one finds Citigroup's argument persuasive, the district court's decision to dismiss the plaintiffs' broader theories was consistent with the heightened pleading standard instituted by the PSLRA. Congress decided that it is not enough for a complaint to make general allegations that defendants had knowledge of adverse developments. It is possible that Citigroup officials knew more than they admitted, but without evidence that they knew the company was in danger of insolvency that would require a government bailout, there was arguably not enough to permit a securities fraud claim with respect to those allegations to proceed.

Citigroup settled the securities class action for an amount that was significant but only covered a fraction of investor losses. It paid $590 million to settle claims by shareholders and $730 million to settle claims by bondholders.[41] The significant recovery by bondholders reflected the extent of the bank's financial troubles as bondholders generally do not suffer large losses unless the value of a company's equity is essentially wiped out. Indeed, as I have documented in an earlier study, bondholders became more involved in securities litigation as the losses associated with securities fraud increased during the early 2000s.[42] The Citigroup bondholders had an advantage over shareholders in that they purchased their securities directly from Citigroup in various bond offerings and could thus invoke Section 11 of the Securities Act of 1933, which does not require the showing of fraudulent intent necessary to prevail under Rule 10b-5.

In addition to the private litigation, the SEC filed an enforcement action against Citigroup alleging a narrow theory that the company had misled investors about its subprime exposure. This case was settled for $75 million (far more than what Xerox paid but not at the top of the range of SEC settlements by that time). Notably, the SEC did not take the position that the bank had acted with fraudulent intent. Instead, it charged the company under securities law provisions that did not require establishing such intent.[43] Citigroup's settlement was thus seen by some knowledgeable observers as less serious than earlier settlements that involved statutory charges requiring a showing of scienter.[44] The SEC also did not bring cases against senior executives of Citigroup other than the company's CFO (who paid a penalty of $100,000). It took the position that the other executives had not been involved in making the inaccurate statements to investors.[45]

In addition to the Citigroup case, the SEC brought a few similar cases involving other major financial institutions. Two government-sponsored mortgage lenders issued statements downplaying their exposure to subprime mortgages. The Federal National Mortgage Association (known as Fannie Mae) maintained that its subprime exposure was about $4.8 billion when it had more than $40 billion in such loans.[46] The Federal Home Loan Mortgage Corporation (known as Freddie Mac) claimed that it had an exposure to subprime loans of $2 billion to $6 billion when in fact it was $141 billion and grew to $244 billion.[47]

In contrast, the SEC did not pursue a case against Lehman Brothers (which filed for bankruptcy in the fall of 2008 as the value of its housing-related assets declined) or its managers, despite evidence that they had gone to elaborate lengths to hide risk relating to the company's balance sheet.[48] A report by the bankruptcy examiner concluded that the most viable theory of deception against the company involved questionable transactions that created the impression that it had fewer risky assets on its balance sheet. Lehman raised funds to finance its operations through the repo market, where it would temporarily sell assets at a small discount while promising to repurchase those assets at full value the next day. The assets essentially serve as collateral for a short-term loan. Because Lehman knew that it would be buying back the assets, they should have remained on its balance sheet. Instead, Lehman used an accounting tactic that it called Repo 105 to structure the transactions so they would temporarily remove the assets from its financial statements.[49] It argued that if it sold the assets at a larger discount than normal, receiving $100 for every $105 in assets it sold (a discount of approximately 5 percent, which was higher than the typical 2 percent discount), it would effectively have given up control of the asset and could book the transaction as a sale.[50] Lehman would execute Repo 105 transactions at the end of the quarter so that it could report that its balance sheet held lower amounts of risky assets. It removed about $50 billion in assets from its SEC filings through this tactic. The Lehman Brothers Bankruptcy Examiner concluded that there was "no articulated business purpose" for the transactions other than to make Lehman's books look better. The report noted that "Lehman did not disclose its use – or the significant magnitude of its use – of Repo 105 to the Government, to the rating agencies, to its investors, or to its own Board of Directors."[51]

Lehman Brothers, like Citigroup, downplayed the riskiness of its assets, but its disclosure was arguably accurate under accounting rules. The company was able to obtain a "true sale" letter opining that the transactions were sales under English law (but was not able to get such a letter under US law) and routed the transactions through London. While there was an argument that it should have disclosed its use of this tactic, it was not clear that it was required to make such a disclosure. Other banks such as Bear Stearns used similar methods to obscure balance sheet risk, but the SEC did not bring cases to penalize such tactics.[52] Rightly or wrongly, there was an argument that there was not a clear enough accounting violation to justify a finding of securities fraud against the investment bank and its managers.

The issue of whether the banks misled the public about the extent of their losses was more extensively litigated through securities class actions. The officers and directors of Lehman Brothers paid $90 million to settle a securities class action after a federal district court held that the complaint alleged sufficient facts that the Repo 105 tactics created a "misleading picture of the company's financial position at the end of each quarter."[53] The SEC did not bring a case against Bear Stearns, but a securities class action won a $275 million settlement against the company. A judge found that the plaintiffs in that case sufficiently alleged that the company misled investors by recording its mortgage-backed assets "at full value even while privately acknowledging the declining value to its counterparties."[54] The insurance company AIG paid nearly $1 billion in settlements to investors after a ruling denying a motion to dismiss a claim alleging that it had misrepresented the risks of credit default swaps it had sold insuring the value of mortgage bonds.[55]

LOSS CAUSATION AND THE COLLAPSE OF THE HOUSING MARKET

The Citigroup case also involved a dispute about an important element of a Rule 10b-5 securities fraud claim – loss causation.[56] That doctrine only permits investors to recover for losses that are sufficiently linked to the fraudulent statements at issue in a case. The law governing causation in securities fraud cases is vague and difficult to apply. Jill Fisch has described the case law on this element as "inconsistent, unfaithful to the common law, and largely incoherent."[57] Citigroup and other banks claimed that a good portion of the losses suffered by bank investors during the financial crisis of 2008 was caused by something other than the misstatements by the banks that the courts found actionable under Rule 10b-5.

As in the Penn Central scandal, the misleading disclosures by Citigroup related to issues that were not the sole cause of its failure. The bank would likely have been pushed to the brink of collapse in 2008 whether or not it had an additional $39 billion in subprime exposure a year earlier. Citigroup argued that the plaintiffs' losses were caused by an unprecedented decline in the value of housing-backed securities, rather than its disclosure decisions.[58] Nine other banks had significant write-downs of their assets, and Citigroup was only in the middle of the pack of this group.[59] Citigroup's subprime exposure was overshadowed by the fact that its other vast holdings were threatened by the financial crisis as the value of even nonhousing investments declined because of a loss of market confidence. More than a year after it disclosed its subprime exposure, the US government provided Citigroup with a guarantee covering $300 billion in its assets.

Perhaps an argument could be made that Citigroup's misstatement set the initial tone for the way that investors viewed its stability. The fact that it initially claimed it had little exposure to subprime risk and later had to retract that statement affected the credibility of the bank. As conditions worsened, markets were not willing to give the company another chance. If it had not bungled its disclosure, perhaps its later troubles would have been viewed in a different light. Such an argument is plausible but difficult to prove in the context of a litigation.

SECURITIES FRAUD AND CORPORATE MISMANAGEMENT

While it is true that Citigroup did not predict the extent of its losses, its troubles were unusual. Not all of the major banks required a government guarantee to survive.[60] Some regulators noted that Citigroup was the financial institution that was in the worst shape during the crisis and the primary reason for the controversial bailout of Wall Street.[61] They admitted that they trusted too much in the competence of Citigroup's management, which failed to prevent the crisis.[62] The company's history of high profitability helped insulate it from serious regulatory scrutiny.[63] In retrospect, the company was so large that it was too difficult to manage. As the Financial Crisis Inquiry Commission reported, Citigroup was "an organization in which one unit would decide to reduce mortgage risk while another unit increased it. And it was an organization in which senior management would not be notified of $43 billion in concentrated exposure – 2% of the company's balance sheet and more than a third of its capital – because it was perceived to be 'zero-risk paper.'"[64] Notably, just a few years before the financial crisis, Citigroup had responded to a prohibition against major acquisitions after a prior scandal by initiating a program that emphasized internal controls and risk management.[65] Either these efforts were not fully implemented, or the internal controls (which were one of the main reforms required by Sarbanes–Oxley) had little impact on the company.

While an argument could be made that the company failed to disclose that its internal management of risk was insufficient,[66] such a claim is difficult to distinguish from a basic claim of corporate mismanagement. The Supreme Court has clearly stated that Rule 10b-5 does not generally regulate all types of corporate misconduct and only governs securities fraud.[67] Citigroup's complexity likely shielded many of the company's top executives from securities fraud liability because they were not aware of the misrepresentation concerning its subprime exposure. It is notable that a corporate law derivative claim brought against

Citigroup's board of directors and officers – alleging that the company's internal controls inadequately protected shareholders – was dismissed by the Delaware Court of Chancery for failing to adequately allege a strong enough claim so that plaintiffs could proceed with the case without making a demand on the board.[68]

On the other hand, several cases directed at mortgage lenders found them liable for failing to disclose bad underwriting practices that resulted in loan defaults in their portfolio. Countrywide was one of the largest mortgage lenders in the years leading up to the crisis and claimed in its SEC filings that it used strict underwriting standards to only make high-quality loans. Over time, it loosened these standards to issue riskier loans that began to default at higher rates. The SEC brought a case alleging that the company's executives misrepresented the quality of its lending practices, which resulted in investor losses as the value of Countrywide's loan holdings declined.[69] The SEC brought similar cases against managers of the housing lender New Century.[70]

The SEC appeared to draw a distinction between lenders that directly made loans to risky borrowers and the financial institutions that held securities backed by those questionable mortgages. The lenders had an obligation to disclose to the market that their underwriting standards were deficient and could result in significant losses. The financial institutions, in contrast, were not generally liable for failing to disclose their ability to manage risk in their portfolios. A legitimate question could be asked as to why the SEC expected lenders to predict and disclose their losses but not the financial institutions. Perhaps the lenders were in a better position to understand that their practices on the ground were questionable and that borrowers would default. On the other hand, given their supposed expertise in risk management, it is understandable why some commentators believed that financial institutions should have disclosed more about the risks posed by their housing assets.

A FAILURE TO PROSECUTE?

Some significant enforcement proceedings were brought against financial institutions after the 2008 crisis, but critics have argued that banks and their executives were not sufficiently held accountable for hiding the extent to which they had mismanaged their exposure to a decline in housing prices. The SEC did not bring cases against managers of companies such as Bear Stearns or Lehman Brothers that filed for bankruptcy. None of the top executives of the major financial institutions that collapsed were criminally charged. Enforcement was left primarily to private plaintiffs who had modest success in winning recoveries. Despite predictions by some commentators that Sarbanes–Oxley's provisions were a "litigation 'time bomb'" that would "explode with the next major stock market adjustment,"[71] the number of securities class action filings declined in the years after the 2008 collapse (Figure 6.1).

The question is whether the conduct of bank executives was comparable to that of the executives of companies like Enron and WorldCom who were criminally

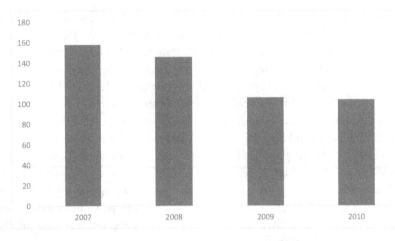

FIGURE 6.1 Securities Class Action Filings (2007–2010).

prosecuted for securities fraud. If it was, then the failure to prosecute might be explained by the risk aversion of prosecutors who feared losing a case against a well-financed opponent.[72]

While as noted earlier, there is a case that bank managers did not have superior information about the extent of the coming financial turmoil, there is also a possibility that bank managers had better access to information indicating that their institutions had taken on too much risk and were vulnerable. Rather than inform the public that they were in danger of insolvency, they took the position that their banks were well-positioned to survive the market turmoil. For example, the securities class action complaint filed against Citigroup alleged that it "repeatedly assured the market that [it] was adequately capitalized."[73] It argued that Citigroup's managers abused their discretion by not writing down the value of assets that had clearly declined, and that investors were blindsided when it was only saved by government intervention.

One argument against imposing liability, especially criminal liability, in this scenario, is that if corporate executives prematurely raise the danger of insolvency, it becomes a self-fulfilling prophecy. If there is a substantial risk of failure, there will be a run on the bank where creditors withdraw their funds. Without short-term funding, the bank will be pushed into bankruptcy. Given the difficulty of determining when a bank is insolvent,[74] banks were arguably not out of bounds in insisting that they would avoid insolvency. On the other hand, one could make a similar argument with respect to a situation where a company fails to reveal steep declines in revenue that mean it cannot meet its projections. Disclosing the truth would mean a collapse of the company's stock price that could endanger its ability to function.

Perhaps the difference is that companies have more discretion to value assets than they have in reporting earnings. As noted earlier, accounting rules acknowledge the difficulty of valuing securities that do not trade in markets and permit banks to value them using their own models. But accounting rules also give significant discretion to companies in using estimates that affect earnings. Such discretion has not kept the SEC from alleging securities fraud against companies that knowingly issued misleading estimates. As noted earlier, Xerox's securities fraud settlement was based largely on accounting decisions that arbitrarily changed estimates relating to revenue. Waste Management's executives were penalized by the SEC in part for inflating estimates of depreciation. Cendant executives were found liable for securities fraud in part for overstating reserves the company took to cover merger costs. In all of these cases, the claim was that a public company made estimates with insufficient basis. On the other hand, there are cases where the SEC has determined that the issuance of a questionable estimate does not deserve a significant sanction. For example, in 2002, the SEC brought a case against Microsoft, which used cookie-jar reserves of hundreds of millions of dollars to smooth its earnings. While it found an accounting violation, it only charged the company for violating its obligation to keep accurate books and records, which does not require a showing of fraudulent intent and does not typically trigger a penalty.[75]

Another reason why it was easier to criminally prosecute high-level managers for earnings fraud is that they were more closely involved in monitoring whether their companies could meet earnings projections. Because of the importance of meeting such projections for many companies, corporate managers are expected to keep a close eye on whether financial results will meet market expectations. When companies communicate projections to the market, upper-level management will often play a role in preparing the projections. It was thus easier to link individual officers to decisions to misstate earnings to meet a revenue or earnings projection. The Enron and WorldCom criminal convictions were possible because prosecutors were able to obtain specific testimony that linked the CEOs of those companies to incorrect accounting decisions. In contrast, it does not appear that there was sufficient evidence establishing that high-level bank executives had specific knowledge that asset valuations were objectively misstated.

Unlike the Enron and Xerox cases, the financial institutions did not inflate their earnings to create the appearance of growth. Instead, they might have obscured their increasing vulnerability to failure as the crisis progressed. While the result of these efforts was that their stock prices were higher than they should have been, there is a case that regulators should give more leeway to managers trying to navigate an unprecedented storm. The fact that the banks created the conditions for such a storm by taking on too much risk to increase their earnings was arguably corporate mismanagement rather than fraud.

It is worth noting that the earlier criminal prosecutions of executives for accounting fraud were built on the foundation of several years of civil enforcement in dozens of cases. The SEC and class action attorneys had built a coherent theory of securities fraud where accounting misstatements were motivated by the desire to meet earnings projections. In some cases, the insider trading of executives was used to justify prosecuting individual defendants. In contrast, there was no clear template of fraud that could be applied to the asset misstatements of the banks. Unlike Enron, there were not reports of high-level executives unloading unusual amounts of stock right before their institutions collapsed. Prosecutors did not have as many precedents that could be readily applied to develop criminal theories of securities fraud for the financial crisis of 2008.

Finally, aggressive enforcement would have been at odds with other governmental policies. One of the SEC's main regulatory responses to the financial crisis was to support the solvency of banks by temporarily banning short selling of the stock of certain financial institutions. Banks like Citigroup were saved from certain failure through the extraordinary intervention of the US Treasury Department. For the SEC to then sanction these institutions significantly for securities fraud would have run counter to the policy of promoting financial stability. Moreover, the SEC recognized that such penalties would essentially be covered by taxpayer funds.[76]

There were similarities between the financial crisis of 2008 and the collapse of the Savings and Loan (S&L) industry about twenty years before. S&Ls are banks that traditionally were limited by regulation to issuing housing loans. During the 1980s, the industry was deregulated to permit S&Ls to invest in riskier assets. Over time, the S&Ls took on too much risk and many of them failed as the bad loans they made defaulted. Government bailouts of the S&Ls cost $150–175 billion.[77] There were some notable instances where S&L insiders violated securities law. Charles Keating was prosecuted and convicted of securities fraud in both state and federal court for the misleading sale of risky Lincoln Savings & Loan debt (the convictions were later overturned and Keating entered into a plea agreement with respect to the federal charges). The debt was sold to ordinary bank customers who were led to believe that it was federally insured and were not told of the S&L's deteriorating financial condition.[78] Notably, Lincoln's stock was not widely traded, and so the case did not involve misleading statements to public shareholders. The bulk of the S&L losses were due to bad lending decisions.[79] While regulators brought criminal cases, the main focus of the government response was to reestablish stability. As one set of commentators noted, "the law enforcement effort was directed less at penalizing S&L offenders for their crimes than at rescuing the industry, shoring up investor confidence, and containing the loss of government-insured capital."[80] Like the S&L scandal, the main regulatory concern in responding to the failure of banks in 2008 was stopping the collapse of the financial system. While there is an argument that regulators could have brought more cases, given the lack of a clear theory of fraud, modest enforcement efforts were appropriate.

The fact that criminal securities fraud cases were not brought against the executives of public financial institutions does not mean that there was not criminality involved in the misconduct that created the conditions for the financial crisis of 2008. The transformation of questionable mortgages into low-risk securities could only have happened if some of the participants in the process committed fraud or were aware of such fraud. As the statutes of limitations to bring criminal fraud cases directed at such misconduct expired, Judge Jed Rakoff asked: "[h]ow could this transformation of a sow's ear into a silk purse be accomplished unless someone dissembled along the way?"[81] If it was possible to criminally indict an entire system, then surely such a case would have been filed.

DODD–FRANK AND SECURITIES FRAUD

Because the financial crisis was not viewed primarily as a problem of securities fraud, the legislative response mainly consisted of measures to reduce the risk that banks will fail and endanger the financial system. Dodd–Frank thus required significant financial institutions to set up a plan to liquidate their assets in an orderly matter if necessary and subjected them to periodic stress tests. Several of the law's provisions increased corporate governance regulation in ways that might indirectly address the risk of securities fraud. For example, it built on the precedent of Sarbanes–Oxley by regulating public company executive compensation to reduce the incentive of managers to take on excessive risk that could result in setbacks that are hidden to deceive investors.[82] Dodd–Frank thus requires public companies to have independent executive compensation committees; conduct periodic advisory shareholder votes on the compensation of their executive officers; and disclose the ratio of their CEO's compensation to the compensation of their median employee.

The Dodd–Frank provision with the most direct effect on securities fraud enforcement provides financial incentives for whistleblowers to report securities law violations and prohibits employers from retaliating against them.[83] Sarbanes–Oxley provided protection for whistleblowers of public companies but did not provide an incentive to report violations.[84] Under Dodd–Frank, individuals who provide information resulting in SEC sanctions over $1,000,000 can receive a payment equal to between 10 and 30 percent of the sanction collected by the SEC. The whistleblower provision recognizes that employees within the company are in a better position to discover fraud than regulators and investors. Recall that the Xerox investigation was prompted by an employee who alerted the SEC of questionable practices that originated from the company's headquarters. As Amanda Rose explains, increasing the prospect that internal whistleblowers will come forward will increase the likelihood that a fraud will be reported to the SEC and thus increase the expected cost of such fraud for the company. However, offering a monetary award could also reduce the incentive for whistleblowers to immediately report such fraud internally.[85] While the Dodd–Frank whistleblower law applies to both public and private companies, because large sanctions relating to securities fraud are more likely in cases involving public companies, its most significant impact is likely with respect to public company securities fraud. As of 2020, the SEC had paid over $500 million to whistleblowers who reported information, resulting in $2.7 billion in monetary sanctions, with $850 million of such sanctions going back to investors.[86]

THE NEW PUBLIC CORPORATION

The combined impact of Sarbanes–Oxley and Dodd–Frank established a starker distinction between public and private companies.[87] Public companies are expected to invest significant resources in internal controls that reduce the risk of securities fraud. They are required to comply with uniform corporate governance standards. These measures are best justified on the ground that public corporations are subject to the continuous pressure of market expectations while private companies are not. The increasing potency of the valuation treadmill prompted ex ante measures to prevent fraud to meet market expectations.

The net effect of these reforms is that public corporation status has become a mark of merit rather than just a commitment to take on disclosure obligations. As public companies have become more complex and difficult to understand, investors must depend on the experience and competence of corporate managers. Because valuation increasingly relies on accurately projecting future performance, public company managers must not only manage internal capital markets but also navigate external capital markets. Only companies with the resources and infrastructure to operate in public markets can access funds from public investors. As the SEC's Advisory Committee on Smaller Public Companies reported, "public companies today must be more mature and sophisticated, have a more substantial administrative infrastructure and expend substantially more resources simply to comply with the increased securities regulatory burden."[88]

The heightened federal regulation of large public companies reflects their social importance. Donald Langevoort and Robert Thompson note that one purpose of the securities laws is to "create more accountability of large, economically powerful business institutions."[89] As noted earlier, the rapid value destruction caused by the revelation of a fraud not only affects investors, it can destroy jobs and affect local communities.[90] While it may be rare that a fraud by itself is entirely responsible for a corporate bankruptcy, a fraud can make the failure of a business more destructive and affect those who relied on the assumption that the business would continue to prosper.

To some extent, greater obligations for public companies are made possible by the alternative of a private market. Private companies can still raise funds by selling securities so long as they limit the sale to sophisticated investors. An extended period of low interest rates after the financial crisis of 2008 helped increase the availability of money for promising start-ups. If a company has access to substantial amounts of private capital, it need not take on the burden of periodically updating investors with truthful disclosure that validates its market valuation. Companies can weigh the costs and benefits of going public, and if the costs are too high, they can choose to avoid regulation by remaining private.[91] On the other hand, there are undeniably benefits to selling securities to the public. Arbitrarily denying smaller companies access to capital will mean that deserving businesses will find it more difficult to succeed.

Statutes like Sarbanes–Oxley not only deter private companies from going public, they reduce the incentive of public companies to remain public. A public company can end its obligations to file periodic reports, check internal controls, and comply with federal corporate governance requirements if it has fewer than 300 record owners of its stock. Studies have shown that the number of public companies going private increased substantially in the years immediately after the passage of Sarbanes–Oxley.[92] In addition to going private, companies have the option to "go dark" in that they deregister their securities from SEC obligations, but their stock trades to some extent in over-the-counter markets. One study found that Sarbanes–Oxley was likely a substantial factor in an increase in companies going dark, but they found that the increase mainly involved companies that "are smaller and have poorer stock market performance, higher leverage, and fewer growth opportunities than the population of firms that could but choose not to [deregister]."[93]

Another concern has been that regulatory obligations to prevent securities fraud could deter foreign companies from seeking public company status in the United States. But it appears that these fears have not come to fruition. A study looked systematically at listing decisions by foreign companies from 1995 through 2006.[94] It found that large foreign companies did not change their preferences after Sarbanes–Oxley between listing in the United States relative to London. However, smaller firms were more likely to choose London over the United States after the Act's passage. A 2017 survey by Ernst & Young found that the number of foreign companies listed on US exchanges has remained fairly constant since the passage of the Act, and that the United States is still the leader in attracting companies that list outside of their home country.[95]

Even if the trend to go private or dark primarily affects smaller companies, there is a question of whether the burdens of public regulation have resulted in a suboptimal number of public companies. The companies trading on a stock exchange in the United States fell from a high of about 8,000 in the mid-1990s to around 4,000 by the end of the 2010s.[96] Between 1980 and 2000, an average of 300 companies conducted an initial public offering each year. Since 2000, this average has declined to 100 companies a year.[97] While a substantial part of this trend predated the passage of Sarbanes–Oxley,[98] or might be attributed in part to increasing acquisitions,[99] it is possible that the combination of Sarbanes–Oxley and Dodd-Frank have contributed to the smaller number of public companies today.

While regulation may have played a part in these trends, it is important to recognize that it is not just federal regulation that is being rejected when a company chooses to remain private. The valuation treadmill itself is a strong deterrent. A 2012 *Economist* article claimed that the public company is "endangered" and that "[c]-orporate chiefs complain that the combination of fussy regulators and demanding money managers makes it impossible to focus on long-term growth."[100] Founders may prefer to keep control of the governance of their companies rather than be required to constantly meet the expectations of public shareholders.

Responding to concerns about the number of new public companies, Congress passed the Jumpstart Our Business Start-Ups Act (the JOBS Act) in 2012. The law's provisions attempt to reduce the gap in the ability of public and private companies to sell securities. The statute was based in part on proposals issued in a report by an IPO Task Force of venture capitalists and entrepreneurs.[101] The group cited the need to support "innovative, high-growth companies" given the increased cost of going public for such companies. While noting that the problem could be traced to a number of sources, it observed that "well-intentioned but 'one-size-fits all'" laws were passed "to address market issues created exclusively by the behavior of, and risks presented by, the largest companies." These regulations had "unintended adverse effects on emerging growth companies looking to access public capital."[102] It cited regulatory costs of about $2.5 million for a company to go public and ongoing costs of about $1.5 million a year to remain a public company, which could lower a company's market capitalization by tens of millions of dollars.[103]

The JOBS Act thus created an "on-ramp" for start-up companies wishing to go public. It amended the securities laws to create a new regulatory category of emerging growth companies with annual revenue of less than $1 billion. Such companies would receive special treatment to ease their transition to full public company status. An emerging growth company is not required to provide the three years of financial statements required for other companies. They are exempt for five years from internal control requirements as well as corporate governance require-ments. They thus have a grace period before they are required to invest heavily in measures to ensure the accuracy of their financial reports.

The JOBS Act is likely only the first of what will be continuing efforts to bridge the gap between public and private companies. There is an argument that Sarbanes–Oxley and Dodd–Frank, which were passed in response to unprecedented company failures, need some additional fine-tuning. On the other hand, the burdens of these regulations have not prevented many of the most promising entrepreneurial companies from selling shares to the public. The benefits of redu-cing securities fraud will continue to be weighed against the costs of such efforts.

CITIGROUP AFTER THE FINANCIAL CRISIS

More than a decade after the financial crisis of 2008, Citigroup's market capitaliza-tion is a fraction of what it was before the crisis. While it is still a significant financial institution, it has yet to persuade investors that it has moved beyond its past problems. Citigroup eventually repaid the government loans that saved it, and the US Treasury profited from its investment. The company escaped serious criminal and civil sanctions in its securities fraud cases. But Citigroup has paid a high price for its failure to prevent losses that destroyed hundreds of billions of dollars in shareholder value.

Citigroup's stagnation is typical of other large financial institutions that were valued conservatively by stock markets after Dodd–Frank (though in the last year, the market values of some of the surviving firms seem to be recovering their luster). The statute's regulation has reduced the ability of financial institutions to take on risk that will generate exceptional growth in profits. Moreover, investors understand that it may be impossible to adequately comprehend the financial statements of the largest banks. As Frank Partnoy and Jesse Eisinger argue, even after the passage of Dodd–Frank, major banks do not provide much detail about billions of dollars of risk on their balance sheets.[104] In 2020, the Federal Reserve fined Citigroup $400 million for persistent problems with its internal controls and risk management. The fine highlights the continued difficulty of running large financial conglomerates. Despite all of the company's efforts, it has not been able to assure regulators that it is adequately managed. Far from being safer because of their size and diversity, banks like Citigroup pose substantial risks to shareholders that have not been easily forgotten.

7

General Electric and the Problem
of Earnings Management

78% of the surveyed executives would give up economic value in exchange for smooth earnings.

Graham, Harvey & Rajgopal, 2005

Over the last twenty years, as memories of the crisis that spurred the passage of the Sarbanes–Oxley Act of 2002 (Sarbanes–Oxley) faded, public company securities fraud receded as a matter of national concern. The stock market losses arising out of the financial crisis of 2008 were only partly linked to securities fraud, and the slow economic recovery afterward did not generate many spectacular investor losses that could be firmly tied to a corporate misrepresentation. There is some evidence that companies responded to Sarbanes–Oxley by adopting more conservative financial reporting policies. Stronger internal controls may have been successful at checking obvious accounting rule violations.

Even if there are now fewer companies transgressing generally accepted accounting principles (GAAP) to meet projections,[1] the continuing potency of the valuation treadmill is evidenced by the many public corporations that manage their earnings in facially legal ways to manage market expectations. The possibility that public companies might sacrifice long-term prosperity to meet short-term metrics was noted as early as the Penn Central case, where the SEC observed: "Penn Central was focused, by the immediate pressures for income, to take actions because of the short term advantages, although from a longer term viewpoint the action was detrimental to the company."[2] In modern times, studies have documented that companies work to meet quarterly projections by cutting research and development; offering discounts to move products right before the end of a quarter; selling assets; and making other operational decisions that they would not engage in if they were not trying to meet a projection. These tactics are often referred to as *real earnings management* because while they generate real revenue and cash flow, they are motivated mainly to meet an earnings target.[3]

There is a long-standing question about whether real earnings management can support a claim for securities fraud. On the one hand, by definition, such management involves real transactions that are properly recorded under accounting rules. It is thus difficult to find a clear misrepresentation that would support a Rule 10b-5 claim. On the other hand, real earnings management can obscure problems in a company's business and create the false impression that the company is generating smooth earnings. To the extent that such management sacrifices significant long-term value, investors may later be surprised by losses. The question of whether and when real earnings management is fraudulent provides another opportunity to examine the boundaries of the concept of securities fraud.

The case of the prominent public conglomerate General Electric (GE) illustrates how real earnings management operates and how it arguably deceives stock markets. For years, investors rewarded GE for its ability to deliver smooth earnings. Because it always met its quarterly projections of increasing earnings, the company was an exception to the rule that the stock of a conglomerate should trade at a discount. Remarkably, it was an open secret that the company managed its earnings to meet forecasts. Over the 1990s, it increasingly relied on its financial services subsidiary, GE Capital, to allocate resources among its various businesses to consistently meet market expectations. Investors viewed GE's prowess at meeting financial projections as evidence that the company had superior management that would reliably grow the company's profits over time. When GE's businesses performed well, this strategy was sustainable, but by the end of the 2010s, GE found itself in a position where its earnings management delayed the reporting of significant losses to investors.

In 2017, GE revealed billions of dollars of losses in its power and insurance businesses that made it impossible to continue the perception that its long-standing success would continue. Its stock price plummeted around 75 percent in the wake of the disclosure, erasing more market value than Enron and WorldCom combined. The extent of the company's fall was captured by two *Wall Street Journal* reporters, who wrote: "[a] share of GE stock was once an essential component of the beginner investor's portfolio, but is now perceived as a speculative bet."[4] Toward the end of 2020, the SEC alleged that GE had misrepresented its financial performance. Notably, none of the reporting decisions highlighted by the SEC's complaint involved violations of GAAP. While the SEC did not conclude that GE had acted with fraudulent intent, it signaled the seriousness with which it viewed the company's transgressions by requiring the company to pay a $200 million penalty to resolve the matter.

The example of GE illustrates the dangers of real earnings management. By delaying the recognition of losses, a company risks the possibility that it cannot engineer a turnaround, and its losses accumulate until they are large enough so that they must be disclosed to the shock of investors. Even though real earnings management does not involve clear misstatements, it can be as deceptive to investors as accounting fraud. As the valuation treadmill continues to affect the incentives of public companies, regulators will need to develop strategies to address a wider range of questionable practices.

THE PREVALENCE OF REAL EARNINGS MANAGEMENT

Many of the securities frauds discussed in this book involved a public company violating accounting rules to report higher earnings. There are other methods that can achieve the same goal. Corporate managers can in some circumstances generate earnings to meet projections by exercising their wide discretion to make business decisions. For example, a corporation could increase income in a quarter by selling an asset that has appreciated in value. It could widely distribute coupons on products to boost sales. It might reduce costs by trimming R&D or marketing expenses.[5] Such real earnings management can be inefficient if it sacrifices the future to create a rosier portrayal of the company's business.[6]

Evidence that public companies engage in real earnings management is long-standing. Several studies looking at research and development expenditures over the 1980s found that companies adjusted such expenditures to meet market expectations and report positive earnings.[7] Another study examined a sample of companies from the late 1980s and found that they sold assets to offset decreasing earnings.[8] A 1990 survey of 649 company managers concluded that a "large majority of managers use at least some methods to manage short-term earnings." [9] The survey found that while only 5 percent believed it was ethical to increase short-term earnings through accounting misstatements, 57 percent believed it was ethical to increase short-term earnings through changes in operations. It also found that 80 percent believed it was ethical to sell an asset to meet an earnings target. One study looked at firms from 1987 to 2001 for evidence of real earnings management such as price discounts to increase sales; overproduction of inventory to report lower costs; and cutting discretionary expenses.[10] It found that such tactics were less likely in companies with a high percentage of institutional shareholders.

The risk of earnings management may have become more significant as public companies increasingly invested in intangible assets that are difficult to value. Several commentators have noted that during the mid-1980s, overseas competition and advances in information technology spurred a shift from manufacturing to businesses that develop intangible assets.[11] Such assets might include patents, trademarks, and goodwill from acquiring another company. For example, Apple is now one of the world's most valuable companies because of its intellectual property in transformative products for which consumers will pay a premium to own. Enron's market value was based on the expectation that its entrepreneurial culture would create opportunities in different markets. Intangible assets can have less certain value than physical assets, which trade in markets and can be easily compared with similar assets. As a result, managers of companies with substantial intangible assets have a significant informational advantage over investors.[12] They can exploit that advantage and the subjectivity of valuing intangible assets to manage corporate earnings.

As Sarbanes–Oxley increased the scrutiny of internal controls directed at accounting fraud, companies may have generally reduced both accounting misstatements and real earnings management. At least initially after the law was enacted, companies that consistently met their projections were viewed with suspicion by investors.[13] One study found a decrease in real earnings management in the year immediately after the passage of Sarbanes–Oxley.[14] Another study examined companies from 2002 through 2006 and found that fewer companies reported earnings per share within 1 cent or less of their forecasted earnings per share than they did prior to 2001.[15] Put another way, fewer of these companies just barely met their projections with the aid of earnings management. A 2019 study from the American Accounting Association concluded that audits of internal controls are "a highly effective warning system for corporate fraud."[16]

On the other hand, the pressure to meet projections did not abate after Sarbanes–Oxley. A policy report on corporate earnings guidance observed in 2015, "[t]here is often a stock market reward for meeting or beating expectations and a penalty for failing to do so."[17] With greater confidence in the reliability of financial reports, markets could place even more weight on quarterly results. As one accounting professor noted in a *Wall Street Journal* interview, "[i]f you believe Sarbanes–Oxley has teeth, you can put more faith in the numbers now."[18] A 2018 SEC enforcement action opined that accounting misstatements by the car rental company Hertz "occurred within a pressured corporate environment where, in certain instances, there was an inappropriate emphasis on meeting internal budgets, business plans, and earnings estimates."[19]

There is evidence that after Sarbanes–Oxley, companies continued to engage in real earnings management. One study found that while some types of earnings management declined from 2002 to 2005, activities associated with real earnings management increased during that period.[20] A 2005 survey of chief financial officers found widespread evidence of real earnings management. It reported that "[p]redictability of earnings is an over-arching concern among CFOs" and that "78% of the surveyed executives would give up economic value in exchange for smooth earnings."[21] The study found that "80% of survey participants report that they would decrease discretionary spending on R&D, advertising, and maintenance to meet an earnings target."[22] Moreover, "[m]ore than half (55.3%) state that they would delay starting a new project to meet an earnings target, even if such a delay entailed a small sacrifice in value."[23] A 2016 article argued that companies were not as likely to commit accounting fraud, but were "Cooking the Decisions, Not the Books."[24]

GE AND THE DANGERS OF EARNINGS MANAGEMENT

Throughout the 1990s, GE was praised for its strong management and ability to generate consistent earnings growth. Its stock price rose, creating billions of dollars of shareholder value. Investors believed that GE's ability to consistently meet market expectations justified a high valuation that assumed its steady growth in profits would continue. And for a time, perhaps that narrative was true. But at some point, it became clear that the company's consistency was achieved through tactics that masked significant risks that could not be managed away. Even a company with GE's storied past could not escape the pressure of the valuation treadmill.

A Modern Conglomerate

The struggles of GE are significant because the company exemplifies the evolution of the modern public corporation over more than a century. One can trace the increasing influence of the valuation treadmill by looking at the history of GE. Like Xerox and Apple, it initially leveraged a new technology to dominate a market and rapidly create significant shareholder wealth. Like Citigroup and Penn Central, it pursued a strategy of diversification that it believed would shield it from market turmoil that could disrupt its consistent earnings. Like Enron, GE fostered an expectation that its exceptionalism would produce earnings growth.

GE's corporate lineage can be traced back to 1878, when Thomas Edison raised $50,000 from investors to conduct experiments that resulted in the incandescent lamp.[25] The light bulb was patented in 1880, and by 1889 Edison brought litigation against imitators to enforce his patent on "a high-resistance carbon filament in a sealed glass container which formed a nearly perfect vacuum."[26] GE was formed a few years later in 1892, when Edison's companies merged with a competitor, the Thomas-Houston Electric Company, which had rapidly grown from 40 to 4,000 employees and was viewed as having superior organization and management.[27] GE was from its inception a conglomerate that did business in "nearly everything electric, a manufacturer of fans, dynamos, light-bulbs, trolley cars and locomotives, motors, and heaters."[28] Edison opposed the merger and largely moved on to other ventures after the companies were combined.[29]

Electricity was the first technology that required capital investment on par with the railroad industry.[30] It had a social impact "analogous to that of the microprocessor and information and communication technology, which revolutionized enterprise management and much of daily life during the twentieth century."[31] GE initially focused on providing equipment to utilities and companies (notably it electrified the Pennsylvania Railroad), but by the 1920s diversified into making household electrical appliances.[32] By 1929, GE had a market capitalization of $2.8 billion (around $45 billion in 2021 dollars).[33]

Over time, GE began moving away from its origins as an electricity company. In 1968, about 80 percent of its revenue came from electrical equipment. By 1979, that percentage had fallen to 47 percent.[34] Like Penn Central and other companies during this timeframe, GE sought to diversify into other businesses. GE became involved in industries such as nuclear energy, computers, commercial jet engines, chemicals, entertainment, housing, and financial services.[35] Its CEO at the time described its business as "generating new businesses."[36]

Rather than rely on its dominance in one industry, GE's comparative advantage became its superior management. The company had long recognized the importance of training and management skills for the success of its business. A 1929 book by a former employee noted GE's system of ranking employees based on criteria such as Imagination, Judgment, Personality, Knowledge, Experience, and Physical Energy. The company noted an additional factor, Intellectual Honesty, which was "Indispensable, therefore not weighted."[37] As the company grew larger and extended into other businesses, strong management became even more essential. As its organizational structure became more decentralized, the company increasingly delegated power to department managers.[38] In 1956, it started a Management Development Institute that would provide managers with training that would provide some uniformity within this decentralized structure.[39]

Budgeting and forecasting became an important element of managing GE as it grew. A 1958 book, *Business Forecasting*, explained GE's process for developing projections in some detail. Every one of the "100 departments prepares a budget in the fall, showing estimated operations by month for the following year and annually for the succeeding four years, together with a forecast of the tenth and twentieth year ahead." [40] These budgets included sales forecasts that are then used to "estimate costs and operating expenses, plant and equipment expenditures, and other investment requirements."[41] Each of the individual budgets is consolidated at the central headquarters. Throughout the year, "monthly actual operations are compared with each department's budget at the headquarters' level, and the amount and percentage of deviation are presented to higher levels of management as a basis for reviewing each department's operations."[42]

The importance of forecasting was also emphasized in a 1978 article on GE published in *Management Today*. The article reported that "the technique uppermost in the minds of GE top management is *planning*, a preoccupation in which GE is again an acknowledged master and innovator among corporate giants."[43] Public companies were attempting to move beyond the earlier perception that forecasting was a "dubious exercise" because of the general unpredictability of change.[44] The article noted that the "strategic planning function" was an area where "the leading corporations have made the most impressive intellectual contributions in recent years."[45]

GE's Shift to Stock Markets

During the 1950s, GE was one of the first companies to create an investor relations department. This early step foreshadowed a world where external capital markets would significantly influence the management of public companies. As one former employee described the department, "[t]his organization's job was to help create realistic expectations among the investment analysts and then communicate the expectations internally so that the operating and executive officers understood the right level of profitability to achieve."[46] GE thus made an effort to communicate with investors during the managerialist era, when many corporate managers did not consider attending to the needs of their investors as an essential part of their job.

Even before projections became an important way of judging company performance, companies like GE were concerned with profits. In the early 1960s, the company was widely condemned for its participation in a conspiracy to fix prices on electrical equipment. One former employee testified that these antitrust violations were driven by corporate pressure "to get more business, make better profits."[47] Decades earlier in 1911, the federal government had accused GE of fixing the prices it charged for its incandescent lamps. The Supreme Court eventually dismissed the government's complaint, but the case showed that the company was willing to engage in questionable practices to increase its earnings.[48]

But at least in the first half of the twentieth century, GE was known for balancing profitability with concern for its stakeholders. It created innovative programs for workers such as a pension, health and life insurance, and profit-sharing.[49] The company's leaders in the 1920s and 1930s were "among the first to recognize a new conception of management's responsibilities – a conception of management, not as an agent of the owners, but as a trustee of all groups vitally interested in industry – owners, employees, and the general public, including customers. It was their determination to guard the interests of all three groups."[50]

Even as GE increased its communications with investors, it was not rewarded with an increasing stock price. While the company grew over the 1960s, such growth did not generate significant increases in profits.[51] Like other conglomerates, GE's push for diversification resulted in questionable investments in businesses that were not successful. Over the 1970s, in a languid stock market, the company's stock price was stagnant for years.[52] By the early 1980s, the scientific management methods that had been its strength in earlier years were viewed as creating an inefficient bureaucracy that was too slow in making important decisions.[53]

Starting in the 1980s, under the leadership of its new CEO Jack Welch, GE focused increasingly on improving its efficiency and profitability.[54] It attempted to shake up its complacent culture and expand internationally. Welch famously declared a policy of only keeping businesses that were either first or second in their industry. GE divested businesses that sold products that had been a long part of its history and laid off thousands of workers. It adopted management techniques such as Six Sigma that emphasized efficiency. It instituted metrics for evaluating its employees and periodically pushed out underperformers.

Investors actively sought to obtain the information that companies like GE generated to manage its sprawling business. Research analysts who wanted to predict GE's earnings would find GE's internal forecasts useful in developing their own. By the 1990s, GE regularly communicated its own guidance on forecasts to analysts to help ensure that expectations would not be unrealistic.[55] As noted in earlier chapters, by that time, markets looked closely at whether companies were meeting quarterly financial projections. Public companies thus faced significant short-term pressure to meet those projections.

GE's Earnings Management

As meeting quarterly earnings projections became more important for public companies, GE developed a reputation for always delivering results consistent with market expectations. Its early efforts in investor relations came to dominate the firm's purpose. From 1995 through 2004, the company met or exceeded consensus analyst earnings predictions every quarter.[56] As an article in *Money* magazine reported, "GE enters every quarter with a specific profit goal in mind and then does everything in its power to hit that number – even if the company's actual performance turns out to be significantly better or worse." It had a policy of "no surprises for investors."[57] GE's leadership reportedly viewed meeting projections as a way of signaling that it was no ordinary conglomerate. Investors could have confidence in the company's commitment and ability to increase shareholder wealth.

GE was able to leverage its wide range of businesses to produce smoothness in its earnings. It would harvest gains in strong businesses that could be used to cover shortfalls in future years. It would sell assets and purchase new revenue-generating businesses when it needed to produce additional income for a period. As stated in the title of a *Wall Street Journal* article in 1994, the company would "Offset[] One-Time Gains with Write-Offs" and "Time[] Asset Purchases and Sales" to "Damp[en] Fluctuations in Its Earnings."[58]

Because of the company's size and complexity, investors relied heavily on the expertise of its managers. The accounting professor Baruch Lev used the example of GE's accounting to illustrate how financial reporting inherently requires significant judgment calls by corporate executives.[59] When GE puts aside $2.5 billion to cover expected losses on its receivables, investors have little basis to challenge that figure and must trust that the company is acting in good faith. Management can set such estimates hundreds of millions of dollars too high or too low and investors would not know the difference.

As the company transitioned from its manufacturing roots, it expanded into businesses with less tangible assets such as financial services that are difficult for investors to value.[60] Its GE Capital subsidiary went from contributing 8 percent of its earnings in 1980 to 40 percent in 1997.[61] GE's financing business created a vast internal capital market that could be used to reallocate resources among its various businesses to generate gains and losses as needed.[62] But GE's expansion into banking also created significant risks. The potential for losses in this business was foreshadowed in the 1990s when Kidder Peabody, an investment bank that had been acquired by GE, revealed that $350 million of the profits it had reported were fictitious. A rogue trader had entered the trades into the computer system to boost his bonus. GE escaped liability for securities fraud essentially on the ground that it could not be expected to have knowledge of every scheme hatched within its subsidiaries.[63]

Rather than raising serious concerns, many investors viewed GE's ability to meet its numbers as reflecting its exceptional management. Even if some of its methods were questionable, the company ultimately delivered real performance. GE managers were expected to produce short-term numbers but were also accountable for long-term growth. As a former CEO of the company recounted, "[i]n one meeting, the renewable energy team would cut spending to achieve a quarterly goal; in the next meeting, we would yell at them for falling behind in the area where they'd made cuts."[64] Earnings management as GE conducted it could be viewed as part of a constant struggle to balance perceptions of performance with *actual* performance.

Investors understood this tension and rewarded GE for its ability to navigate it. But an important assumption behind the acceptance of the company's real earnings management was that while GE's culture was aggressive, the company expected its employees to exercise good judgment and follow the rules. From its early years as a public company, GE had a strong reputation for integrity in its financial reporting and was known for its conservative accounting policies.[65] Like Xerox, GE's reputation for strong management training meant that investors trusted its numbers.

GE's Fall

At some point, GE's ability to grow rapidly and consistently reached its limit. Without such growth, it was more vulnerable to losses caused by the 2008 financial crisis and setbacks in its power and insurance businesses that were revealed in 2017. GE attempted to hide these adverse developments but only deferred a reckoning. When it was forced to reveal billions of dollars in losses, the faith investors had in GE's predictable growth was shaken, and the company's market capitalization disintegrated.

By the mid-2000s, GE's rate of growth had slowed. In response, its CEO set the ambitious goal of achieving 8 percent revenue growth and noted that meeting that goal was necessary for GE to remain an exceptional company.[66] As Brian Cheffins noted in a book tracing the evolution of the modern public corporation, GE did not mention the phrase "shareholder value" in its annual report until 2004.[67] Perhaps its new emphasis on achieving such value was a sign that it was no longer confident that it could continue its past success. Rather than an opportunity to convey the superiority of GE's management, the ritual of making and meeting projections came to be a burden that may have distorted the company's culture. Moreover, after Sarbanes–Oxley, GE was more limited in the range of tactics it could use to meet its projections.[68]

GE's reliance on financial services to generate earnings left it vulnerable to the financial crisis of 2008. Initially, the company's AAA credit rating protected it from the initial destruction of value that affected banks like Citigroup and Lehman Brothers during the fall of 2008. While it missed a quarterly projection in the spring of 2008 and had to raise additional capital in the fall of 2008, the company seemed to be on solid footing.[69] As late as January 2009, the company represented that it had sufficient cash to continue paying its dividend.[70] Just one month later, it surprised markets by cutting its dividend. By March 2009, it lost its AAA credit rating.[71]

In a securities class action filed after these events, investors asserted similar arguments as those asserted against Citigroup after the financial crisis. They claimed that the company issued misleading statements about its exposure to subprime assets. They argued that GE misled the public about its ability to access commercial paper markets. A district court denied a motion to dismiss the complaint,[72] finding sufficient allegations of misstatements and fraudulent intent by GE, and the case settled for $40 million (far less than the $590 million payment Citigroup made to stock investors).

At first glance, the 2008 crisis did not raise fundamental questions about GE's market value. Other large institutions were also affected, and many recovered. The 2008 crisis was not the first that threatened GE's stability. Just one year after it was formed in 1892, a sharp recession reduced its sales by 75 percent and resulted in layoffs of 5,000 of its 8,000 employees.[73] The company was only able to survive by selling securities it owned in various utility companies at a discount. While investors could expect GE to avoid losses in normal times, the 2008 financial crisis could be characterized as an exception to that rule. The company made an error in judgment by overinvesting in GE Capital but could be expected to continue to create value in other areas.

However, as it became clear that GE could not keep GE Capital, its business model had to change. The company could no longer rely on the growth generated by its financial subsidiary to smooth the results of its other businesses. It would be more difficult to manage earnings without an internal bank.

Less than a decade later, during a period when economic conditions had become more favorable, GE disclosed billions of dollars of losses in its power and reinsurance businesses. It frankly acknowledged in its 2017 annual report that "[o]ur metrics were too focused on EPS and operating profit and not enough on cash."[74] The company cut its dividend, and its stock price fell by about 75 percent between the start of 2017 and the start of 2019. The perception of GE's consistent performance was shattered.

The Deception of Real Earnings Management

GE is a company that managed its earnings for years but as far as we know did so without company-threatening violations of accounting rules. The example of GE raises the question of whether real earnings management can rise to the level of fraud. Can a public company deceive investors while complying with GAAP?

Even if GE's earnings management was consistent with accounting rules, there is an argument that it misled investors. In always meeting external analyst projections, the company created the impression that its superior management permitted it to grow while avoiding substantial losses. As an article in *Money Magazine* noted in 2000, "GE's knack for smoothing earnings has lulled investors into thinking the company is immune to the twists of fate that hurt even the best-run operations."[75] An investor in GE was not just investing in a variety of businesses but also in its human capital. While making a business decision that has the effect of permitting a company to meet a projection is not by itself deceptive, consistently using such practices over multiple years could create a misleading impression with respect to the company's business and the competency of its management.

GE's earnings management was especially problematic given its status as a blue-chip stock that could be owned by a wide range of investors. While it had been clear to sophisticated investors that the company generated its smooth results through earnings management, many retail investors did not understand that the company's consistent performance was partly manufactured. They were attracted to the company's consistent dividend and believed that its stock was safe enough to consistently generate returns without fear of significant loss.

As securities fraud enforcement has increasingly targeted misstatements that do not involve the intentional fabrication of information, the distinction between GAAP violations and real earnings management is more difficult to defend. If the SEC is willing to pursue cases involving contested determinations of whether managers acted in good faith in applying GAAP, it is not a far jump to also pursue cases against managers who act in bad faith but do not violate GAAP. Even though a GAAP violation clearly satisfies the requirement that a securities fraud involves a misstatement, courts should recognize that non-GAAP manipulations of financial reporting can also be misleading.

There is an argument that in a world where companies are valued based on their future performance, real earnings management can be deceptive. As Judge Richard Posner explained in deciding a securities class action appeal, a public company can deceive investors by masking short-term fluctuations in its performance.[76] An investor in valuing a stock will take into consideration not only the expected value of the returns from owning the stock but also the volatility of those returns. Investors will pay more for a stock that increases in value steadily than for a stock that fluctuates between losses and gains.[77] A company that hides setbacks will create the impression that the stock is less volatile, and thus inflate the price of the stock.

On the other hand, there is an argument that earnings management is only deceptive in certain circumstances. The question of whether GE's earnings management was misleading depends in part on whether it genuinely believed that it would generate consistent growth over time. If GE was truly confident in its ability to increase its earnings, then its efforts to smooth earnings could be viewed as increasing the accuracy of the company's reporting by ironing out irrelevant aberrations. However, if at some point, GE's management knew it was unable or very unlikely to deliver such growth, its tactics would be deceptive. Rather than reflecting a genuine belief in the strength of the company, managing earnings would reflect a desperate attempt to hide a weakening business. A more complicated question is whether earnings management in periods of uncertainty is deceptive. If there is a real danger that losses persist or grow larger over time, one could view smoothing over such losses as hiding significant risks that investors should know about.

The challenge of finding that real earnings management violates rules prohibiting securities fraud is that it does not typically involve a clear misrepresentation. Courts have generally focused on specific false statements by companies to satisfy the element of a misrepresentation under Rule 10b-5. An earnings figure that is incorrect because it is not compliant with GAAP when the company has committed to following GAAP, can serve as a starting point for a securities fraud claim. In contrast, real earnings management is more difficult to characterize as producing false statements. For example, plaintiffs have long challenged the practice of channel stuffing where companies heavily discount products to increase sales before the end of a quarter. A quarterly revenue figure that reflects the increase in sales is correct because the sales actually occurred, but the figure may not reflect the true health of the company's business. Courts have found that such channel stuffing by itself is not fraudulent.[78] Because the sales actually occurred, the earnings figure is accurate and thus there is no basis for concluding that investors were deceived. On the other hand, courts have not completely closed the door on the possibility that such real earnings management could be fraudulent in certain circumstances. They have acknowledged that "channel stuffing may amount to fraudulent conduct when it is done to mislead investors."[79] Moreover, the SEC has brought cases arguing that channel stuffing violates Rule 10b-5.[80] If a company acts solely to create the false impression that sales are strong, there should be a case that it has committed securities fraud.

Recall that the SEC in its report on Penn Central's securities fraud advanced a broad shareholder wealth maximization theory of securities fraud. It did not limit its inquiry to clear accounting violations and found that the company's extraordinary efforts to maximize earnings were deceptive. While such an approach has not been adopted by current case law and perhaps should not be, the basic idea that corporate cultures and policies can create a deceptive portrayal of future earnings is worth remembering.

Addressing GE's Earnings Management

It is difficult to challenge the practices of a widely admired company with a strong stock price. The SEC was surely aware of GE's aggressive practices but acted cautiously in confronting the company. It initially focused on traditional violations of accounting rules but only found a limited number of GAAP violations. As GE fell on hard times, the SEC brought a more aggressive enforcement action challenging a broader range of the company's practices that could serve as a model for addressing real earnings management.

The SEC began investigating GE's accounting around the time of the Enron bankruptcy. Like Enron, GE used special purpose entities in questionable ways. Unlike Enron, the company was able to reabsorb these entities onto its balance sheet without threatening its survival.[81] In 2009, the SEC's investigation was finally resolved with GE's agreement to pay a $50 million penalty for four accounting misstatements in 2002 and 2003. While the SEC's order noted GE's suspicious ability to meet its projections for a decade, only one of the four GAAP violations identified by the SEC permitted GE to meet a projection.[82] Because GE's accounting transgressions were not viewed as part of a concerted scheme to meet projections, it was not viewed as part of an egregious securities fraud.

After its stock price collapsed in 2017 as its insurance and power-related losses mounted, the SEC opened a new investigation into GE. In addition, private plaintiffs filed multiple securities class actions alleging that the company committed fraud by downplaying the potential for losses. An extensive report commissioned by short sellers of the stock claimed that the company was a "Bigger Fraud Than Enron."[83]

In December 2020, the SEC announced a settlement with GE where the company would pay $200 million to resolve allegations that it violated securities regulations. The SEC order describing the settlement noted two areas where GE's disclosure was inadequate for the period from 2015 to 2017.[84] The first was with respect to its power business. To meet "the forecast it provided to investors" relating to its "operating profit metric,"[85] the company substantially reduced its estimates of costs associated with various power service agreements. Moreover, in order to meet its forecasts for cash flow, the company implemented what it called a "deferred monetization" strategy where it sold receivables representing future payment obligations in order to generate cash immediately.[86] Prior to adopting this strategy, the company sold receivables due in one year or less. Under its new approach, the company sold receivables with due dates up to five years out, increasing the impact of such sales on future revenue streams.[87]

According to plaintiffs in one of the securities class actions, GE's manipulation was a continuation of real earnings management practices that created a gap between its earnings and cash flow.[88] As demand for power declined after the 2008 financial crisis, the company renegotiated long-term contracts with customers to increase its profit margin for those contracts. This permitted GE to recognize additional earnings immediately but reduced its long-term earnings and cash flow. Because of this shortfall, GE had to raise cash by selling more and more of its receivables. At some point, it was unable to use this method and was forced to reveal its losses.

The second part of the order described questionable practices by GE with respect to its insurance business. It alleged that as the rate of claims increased on its portfolio of long-term care insurance policies, the company arbitrarily changed forecasts concerning the cost of future claims. For example, it changed assumptions about the health of those covered by the policies to predict that fewer claims would be made on the policies. By doing so, GE essentially offset losses from the increase in claims that were being made in the present. The company was reportedly concerned that recognizing the losses would "derail" the division's "income target for the year."[89]

The SEC's 2020 case was notable because it did not cite specific violations of accounting rules. Indeed, the company's questionable practices affected non-GAAP measures of performance. At least one of the practices challenged by the SEC involved real earnings management. There is no accounting rule that prohibits GE from using a deferred monetization strategy. A company has discretion about whether it sells receivables for future years to generate cash flow immediately. However, because the practice was clearly meant to meet cash flow forecasts and was not disclosed, it risked misleading investors who were led to believe that GE's ability to meet its projections reflected stability in its power business.

GE's manipulation of estimates of costs relating to its power service agreements and insurance losses were closer to an accounting transgression but could also be classified as a type of earnings management. As noted earlier, managers have a significant amount of discretion in estimating losses. On the other hand, there have been cases where the SEC has brought securities fraud cases when managers abuse their discretion and issue estimates that are completely unfounded. Moreover, making major changes to the method by which estimates are calculated can deceive investors who are not aware of the change. As was the case with Xerox, a drastic undisclosed shift in GE's policies resulted in misleading financial statements.

The SEC's 2020 order against GE was similar to its order directed at Citigroup's subprime disclosures in that it did not claim that GE acted with fraudulent intent. The agency charged GE with violations of regulations that prohibit misrepresentations regardless of intent and did not bring charges under Rule 10b-5, which requires a showing of fraud. However, the size of GE's monetary penalty was on par with some of the most serious SEC fraud penalties.

While the SEC did not take the position that GE acted with deceptive intent, the private class action against the company made that argument. Parts of the case were dismissed by the district court, but claims based on its deferred monetization practices with respect to its power business survived. Recall that in the Citigroup case, the SEC did not allege fraud by the bank, but a securities class action brought by investors made the case for fraud and was settled for a significant amount. The availability of a private remedy permits further inquiry into a set of complex facts to determine whether a public company committed securities fraud.

Almost six months after it announced its settlement with GE, the SEC announced a settlement with Under Armour, as discussed in Chapter 1. In order to meet projections of 20 percent revenue growth, the sports apparel company persuaded customers to accept millions of dollars in shipments earlier than their original order. Such a practice can be classified as real earnings management and the SEC was careful to note in a footnote in its order that it did "not make any findings that revenue from these sales was not recorded in accordance with [GAAP]."[90] The SEC took the position that the practice should have been disclosed to investors because it "raised significant uncertainty that Under Armour would meet its revenue guidance in future quarters."[91] As with GE, the SEC did not allege that Under Armour acted with fraudulent intent. The company agreed to pay a $9 million penalty that was modest by today's standards but almost as much as Xerox's trail-blazing penalty. As with GE, a securities class action is now litigating the issue of whether the company committed fraud.

Whether or not the SEC's enforcement actions against GE and Under Armour signal a new approach to addressing real earnings management, they provide a model for future cases. Rather than requiring a clear accounting misstatement, securities fraud cases can be based on a broader range of conduct. The failure to disclose significant changes that affect financial reporting can be misleading to investors. The next chapter will propose that the SEC should do more to address the deception of real earnings management.

GE'S UNCLEAR FUTURE

GE has not yet recovered from the losses that shattered its aura of predictable growth. The 2020 pandemic inflicted more pain on the company and its shareholders as the shutdown in travel affected its aviation and power businesses. In November 2021, the company announced that it would split into three companies, acknowledging that it could no longer create shareholder value as a conglomerate. The company's path to recovery will be slow at best. Just as Citigroup is a shadow of itself more than a decade after it suffered unthinkable losses, GE may never completely regain credibility with investors. The company will have to do more than meet short-term metrics and create a new story of long-term growth in order for it to recapture its past glory.

8

The Future of Securities Fraud Regulation

The thesis of this book is that securities fraud became a threat to the integrity of public companies as markets increasingly valued them based on projections of their future earnings. It became important for companies to consistently validate prior forecasts of their profitability to maintain their stock price. This created a systemic incentive for corporate managers to manipulate market perceptions of their company's earnings potential. The Sarbanes–Oxley Act of 2002 (Sarbanes–Oxley) was an attempt to address this incentive by requiring all public companies to invest in measures that prevent financial misstatements. The law governing Rule 10b-5 developed as private investors and the SEC increasingly scrutinized whether misleading corporate narratives of the future were motivated by fraudulent intent.

Even with an incentive to commit securities fraud, many corporations will act ethically and not attempt to deceive investors. Many misstatements are the product of error and carelessness within a bureaucratic organization. To the extent that securities enforcers are unable or unwilling to distinguish between innocent and fraudulent mistakes, the system will impose significant costs on public companies that may outweigh the benefits of enforcement. There remain serious questions about whether the burdens of securities fraud regulation are too high.

On the other hand, there is also a case that investors do not receive enough protection from securities fraud. Corporations and their managers often receive the benefits of high market valuations that are not justified. Retail investors are the last to know that a company is at the brink of failure. Courts often dismiss securities litigation without giving plaintiffs the opportunity to conduct discovery about questionable practices.

This chapter considers the future of securities fraud regulation. It begins by describing a period of backlash directed at public company securities fraud regulation and enforcement. Commentators have criticized Sarbanes–Oxley and Dodd–Frank as imposing burdensome regulation on all public companies in response to the alleged misconduct of a handful of corporate managers. As the size of class action settlements and SEC penalties has grown, courts and policymakers have considered proposals to limit the scope of securities fraud liability. The fraud-on-the-market presumption that permits the certification of Rule 10b-5 class actions came a vote or two away from elimination in *Halliburton* v. *Erica John Fund*.[1] Despite such efforts, securities fraud regulation has remained robust, and securities fraud enforcers have continued to push for expansive securities fraud liability.

Recognizing that there are many questions about the costs and efficiency of securities fraud regulation, the chapter concludes by discussing a few possible legal reforms in light of the book's thesis and the various criticisms of such regulation. It proposes greater regulation of corporate projections to increase their transparency. It argues that securities enforcement and prevention should be more focused on punishing and deterring attempts by companies to manipulate the valuation of their shares.

BACKLASH

The combined impact of Sarbanes–Oxley and the SEC's new willingness to impose penalties on public companies for securities fraud represented a paradigm shift. Less than a decade before Sarbanes–Oxley, the perception was that securities fraud allegations were mostly contrived by class action attorneys seeking to extract a quick settlement from a deep-pocketed defendant. Now, federal law requires public companies to invest substantially to reduce the risk that they misrepresent their financial condition. The prioritization of securities fraud as a regulatory concern has been controversial and resisted vigorously. Indeed, the costs imposed on public corporations by Sarbanes–Oxley and securities fraud enforcement are substantial, and there have been efforts to reduce such costs. However, the core of the regulatory shift prompted by the' frauds of the late 1990s and early 2000s has proven to be resilient.

Sarbanes–Oxley as Crisis Law

Sarbanes–Oxley followed the pattern of many other major securities law reforms in that it was prompted by public outcry after a stock market collapse.[2] Congress considered an initial version of the law that mainly focused on the regulation of auditors after the bankruptcy of Enron toward the end of 2001, and quickly passed a more extensive law that included internal control and audit committee reforms on July 30, 2002, a few weeks after the bankruptcy filing of WorldCom on July 19, 2002 (and companies such as Global Crossing on January 22, 2002 and Adelphia on June 25, 2002).

There are two interrelated criticisms of Sarbanes–Oxley. The first is that because questionable practices are commonly uncovered after the collapse of a speculative boom, scandals like Enron and WorldCom were the natural outcome of the economic cycle. The legislation thus was an overreaction and should not have targeted all public companies. The second is that because it was passed hastily in response to a crisis, the legislation did not adopt effective measures proven to generate benefits outweighing their costs. Of these two criticisms, the second is the more persuasive.

In his classic book on market bubbles, Charles Kindleberger claimed that there was a predictable relationship between bubbles and fraud.[3] Stock market prices rise during times of optimism and prosperity. Investors are willing to fund greater risk-taking by entrepreneurs who form new companies. Older companies also expand as they have more access to capital. After early successes, additional money flows into the market in the hope of high returns. Novice investors begin borrowing money to buy stocks. Projects with little chance of success are easily able to raise funds. Opportunists take advantage of the irrational exuberance to enrich themselves. There are few skeptics who closely scrutinize companies for fraud, and those who raise questions are ignored. When the inevitable downturn comes, weaker companies can no longer maintain the appearance of success and begin to fail. As more companies file for bankruptcy, market confidence disappears and the market plummets, taking more companies with it. Evidence of questionable practices emerges, and investor confidence disappears. The public cries for reform to prevent the next bubble.

One reading of Kindleberger's account is that fraud is an inevitable part of the normal boom and bust cycle of an economy. There will always be companies that take advantage of a rising stock market to hide deceptive schemes, and we should not be shocked every time a fraud is uncovered after a market crash. It is futile to attempt to prevent fraud through reform that addresses the problems uncovered by the last bubble because the next bubble will generate new schemes. Investors should know that speculation in stocks is risky and should bear their losses.

Kindleberger is correct in observing that over the centuries there has been a tendency for wrongdoing to emerge after the market collapses, but not all periods of market decline reveal the same types of wrongdoing. The argument of this book has been that stock markets fundamentally changed toward the latter half of the twentieth century. The increasing emphasis on modeling a company's future earnings in valuing its stock has uniquely shaped the environment within which public corporations operate. These changes have fundamentally altered the incentives of large public companies, which in prior decades were not pushed to maximize profits. The law obligating public companies to prevent securities fraud developed over time as the destructive potential of such incentives became evident.

Even if the frauds of the late 1990s were exceptional, there is a legitimate question as to whether the regulatory response to these frauds was appropriate given the available evidence. Leading corporate law scholar Roberta Romano has developed this argument extensively. She explains:

Simply put, the corporate governance provisions were not a focus of careful deliberation by Congress. [Sarbanes–Oxley] was emergency legislation, enacted under conditions of limited legislative debate, during a media frenzy involving several high-profile corporate fraud and insolvency cases. These occurred in conjunction with an economic downturn, what appeared to be a free-falling stock market, and a looming election in which corporate scandals would be an issue. The healthy ventilation of issues that occurs in the usual give-and-take negotiations over competing policy positions, which works to improve the quality of decisionmaking, did not occur in the case of [Sarbanes–Oxley].[4]

As a result, Congress passed reforms that were arguably no more than cosmetic solutions that would do little to prevent the next inevitable crisis. After that next crisis, Stephen Bainbridge raised similar concerns about Dodd–Frank's regulation of corporate governance and executive compensation.[5]

Even when there is a case for federal reform, Congress is not well suited to develop effective public company regulation. Legislators are generalists who can be swayed by uninformed public opinion and whichever interest group happens to have the most influence. Congress tends to hear testimony from an assortment of experts and quasi-experts rather than systematically gathering evidence from a wide range of sources. Harvard Business School professor Malcolm Salter observed that in passing Sarbanes–Oxley, Congress heard "virtually no testimony from business leaders with deep understanding of the origin of Enron's collapse and other contemporaneous scandals" and thus "we cannot expect these new rules to protect us from future Enrons."[6]

When Congress faces pressure to act quickly, it reaches for ready-made solutions that have long been circulated by what Professor Romano refers to as policy entrepreneurs. Many of these proposals are only supported by a general intuition that they might work. For example, consider this statement from a public company's 2000 10-K:

[The company] assessed its internal control system as of December 31, 2000, 1999 and 1998, relative to current standards of control criteria. Based upon this assessment, management believes that its system of internal controls was adequate during the periods to provide reasonable assurance as to the reliability of financial statements and the protection of assets against unauthorized acquisition, use or disposition ... [The company's auditor] was also engaged to examine and report on management's assertion about the effectiveness of [the company's] system of internal controls.[7]

The company that made this disclosure of voluntary compliance with the internal control assessments later mandated by Sarbanes–Oxley was Enron, and its auditor was Arthur Andersen, which was heavily criticized for failing to stop the company's fraud. The next paragraph in the SEC filing noted that no member of Enron's audit committee "is an officer or employee of Enron."

Enron voluntarily adopted what would later become two of Sarbanes–Oxley's signature provisions, but these measures did not prevent it from committing securities fraud. To be fair, WorldCom did not conduct an annual internal control assessment, and Andersen (which was also its auditor) was criticized by a special investigative committee of WorldCom's board for "relying on the adequacy of WorldCom's control environment" without "adequately test[ing] that control environment, overlooking serious deficiencies in documentation and controls that were in fact exploited by WorldCom's fraud."[8]

Passing a law in haste can result in unintended consequences. Estimates of the cost of complying with Sarbanes–Oxley were too low. The most significant burden imposed by the statute is the requirement that a public corporation's managers and its auditors annually assess the company's internal controls for material weaknesses. Congress did not anticipate that this regulation would be particularly burdensome. A Senate committee stated that it did "not intend that the auditor's evaluation be the subject of a separate engagement or the basis for increased charges or fees."[9] The SEC's initial estimate for the average cost of the internal control provisions was about $91,000.[10] In fact, one study found that average audit fees for public companies with over $1 billion in revenue rose from $3.4 million in 2003 to $6 million in 2006. The same study found that for public companies with under $1 billion in revenue, audit fees rose from $600,000 in 2003 to almost $1.3 million in 2006. Another study focusing on smaller public companies with an average market capitalization of about $100 million found that firms subject to Sarbanes–Oxley saw their audit fees double to $697,890.[11]

As noted earlier, the cost of Sarbanes–Oxley was soon linked to the decline in the number of companies going public. A company can avoid the compliance burden of the federal securities laws by remaining private. One commentator asserted more than a decade after the passage of Sarbanes–Oxley, "[i]n part as a result of [the Sarbanes–Oxley] reforms, the number of IPOs has never returned to the level of the 1990s."[12] The number of IPOs per year fell from about 300 a year during the 1980s and 1990s to around 100 a year after the year 2000. While as noted earlier, there are many reasons for the decline in the number of public companies, it is fair to say that the costs of Sarbanes–Oxley have contributed to this trend and that Congress did not adequately consider the possibility of such an impact.

While the transition to complying with Sarbanes–Oxley was difficult given the uncertainty of what the law would require, the expense of internal control assessments has been manageable for large corporations. As John Coates explains: "Four things are clear about the costs of Sarbanes–Oxley: 1) they are substantial; 2) they are hard to estimate; 3) they have a fixed component, and so fall more heavily on small firms; and 4) they are falling over time."[13] Once a company establishes its internal controls and a process for checking them, the exercise can be basically repeated from year to year. While there is a concern that for some companies the assessment process becomes a superficial checklist that is unlikely to uncover fraud, companies that evaluate their controls in good faith may be more likely to discover problems. As one survey of about 500 public companies found, "despite responses indicating that compliance costs and the amount of time spent on SOX compliance are significant, organizations overwhelmingly report that since they initiated compliance with the Sarbanes–Oxley Act's Section 404 requirement, internal control over financial reporting has steadily improved."[4]

Over time, the government has refined the reach of Sarbanes–Oxley's internal control requirements. The SEC reduced the costs of the mandate on smaller public companies through rulemaking. Initially, internal control assessments were delayed for companies with public ownership of under $75 million while the SEC studied the issue. After finding that the costs of internal control reviews had declined, the SEC required all public companies to comply with Sarbanes–Oxley by June of 2010. But a month after that deadline, Dodd–Frank permanently exempted small companies with a public float under $75 million from section 404(b), which requires an independent auditor to assess and attest to the adequacy of the company's internal controls. Thus, managers of smaller companies must evaluate their internal controls but need not expend costs on an auditor to review that evaluation.

The fact that Sarbanes–Oxley exempts smaller public companies from some of its burdens emphasizes how the problem of securities fraud is now mainly a concern for large public companies. This is a significant change from the earlier assumption that securities regulation should be most concerned about the risk of securities fraud in smaller companies. Sarbanes–Oxley is best understood as a statute that increases the expectation that significant public companies disclose accurate financial information to markets.

The Costs of Securities Enforcement

A substantial number of securities fraud cases by both public and private enforcers were filed and litigated for several years after the passage of Sarbanes–Oxley. As these efforts generated billions of dollars in settlements, concern about the fairness and costs of such payments increased. Starting in the mid-2000s, the US Supreme Court began to frequently grant certiorari to consider appeals arising out of securities class actions. These appeals often proposed new doctrines to limit the reach of Rule 10b-5. This string of decisions culminated with a challenge to *Basic* v. *Levinson*'s fraud-on-the-market presumption that ultimately failed.

As noted in Chapter 2, as the penalties the SEC imposed for securities fraud increased in size, the agency was criticized for the arbitrary imposition of such fines. Private securities class actions, which often follow an SEC action, also required substantial payments to settle. While some suits such as the class action filed against Xerox considered a broader range of accounting problems than the SEC's case, others mainly copied evidence uncovered by the SEC to insist upon an additional payment to investors. Law firms have an incentive to file duplicative litigation with little value. Stephen Choi, Jessica Erickson, and Adam Pritchard found that almost half of securities class actions filed from 2005 to 2008 were accompanied by a parallel state corporate law suit arising out of the same conduct.[15] Their analysis concluded that such additional suits add little economic recovery for investors but are instead used to justify the payment of legal fees to additional plaintiffs' firms. Both SEC penalties and securities class actions have been criticized for imposing costs on companies that ultimately are borne by corporate shareholders who are arguably also victims of the fraud.[16]

In order to reduce the costs of private securities litigation, courts began developing additional limits to Rule 10b-5. One controversial doctrine restricted the ability of investors to sue third parties who facilitated a securities fraud. For example, some of Enron's investment banks executed problematic transactions with the company that were clearly meant to inflate the energy conglomerate's earnings. Though they did not commit fraud themselves, their assistance was necessary for Enron's fraud on public markets to succeed. Indeed, because of Enron's bankruptcy filing, which prevented investors from recovering directly from the company, much of the private litigation arising out of Enron focused on clawing back the "billions of dollars of legal, accounting, auditing and consulting fees" paid to various gatekeeper defendants.[17] Some banks settled these claims (some of which arose out of securities offerings that are governed by Section 11 of the Securities Act, which does not require a showing of fraudulent intent). But the Fifth Circuit held that cases against other banks should be dismissed because they essentially alleged that they aided and abetted a fraud, a theory that was no longer viable under Rule 10b-5 after the Supreme Court's 1994 decision in *Central Bank v. First Interstate Bank*.[18] The court reasoned that the banks "were not fiduciaries" to Enron's shareholders and thus had no "duty to disclose" that the transactions improperly inflated Enron's financial results.[19] In 2008, the US Supreme Court essentially agreed with the Fifth Circuit's approach and dismissed a Rule 10b-5 case against a company that participated in a scheme that allowed another company to improperly meet an earnings projection.[20] Notably, the court specifically referred to the problem of excessive private litigation as a policy reason for limiting the scope of Rule 10b-5 liability. It cited the concern that the fear of such litigation "may raise the cost of being a publicly traded company under our law and shift securities offerings away from domestic capital markets."[21]

Amidst continuing criticism of private securities litigation, the Supreme Court seriously considered eliminating the fraud-on-the-market presumption. Recall that this presumption permits investors to join together in a Rule 10b-5 class action against a company whose stock trades in an efficient market. The sudden evaporation of hundreds of billions of dollars in the market value of companies like Citigroup and Lehman Brothers understandably raised questions about the efficient markets hypothesis that was the foundation of the presumption. If market prices could be so wrong, can investors credibly argue that they reasonably rely on the accuracy of such prices when purchasing a stock? In a 2013 decision, *Amgen*

v. *Connecticut Retirement Plans and Trust Funds*,[22] four Supreme Court Justices signaled skepticism about *Basic* v. *Levinson's* fraud-on-the-market presumption and questioned whether it reflected economic reality.[23] Later that year, the court granted certiorari in *Halliburton* v. *Erica John Fund* to consider that argument.

In a 6–3 decision, the Supreme Court rejected the bid to eliminate the fraud-on-the-market presumption.[24] It accepted the simple theory that in an efficient market, material misstatements will generally affect the price of a security. Even if stock prices are not entirely accurate, investors can be similarly damaged if a fraudulent misstatement impacts the company's stock price. The Court reaffirmed *Basic's* premise that investors generally "invest in reliance on the integrity of [the market] price" of a public company's stock.[25] Put another way, they assume that a market price of a public company is not substantially distorted by fraud.[26] The fraud-on-the-market presumption not only permits class actions to proceed, it reflects an expectation that public companies are responsible for conveying accurate information to public investors. *Halliburton* v. *Erica John Fund* confirmed the system's commitment to the integrity of stock markets.

Even if its decision was based mainly on an unwillingness to overturn prior precedent, the accounting frauds of the late 1990s and early 2000s must have had some impact on the Supreme Court's decision. It was no longer the case that most securities class actions were viewed as questionable projections litigation. Cases like Xerox and Enron had demonstrated the prevalence of earnings misstatements to meet projections. This problem prompted not only a response from investors but also spurred the SEC and Congress to act. A majority of the Supreme Court likely believed that securities class actions often addressed real cases of fraud and was reluctant to completely do away with an important investor remedy.

A "NEW" THEORY OF SECURITIES FRAUD

After dipping for a time after the financial crisis of 2008, the number of securities class action filings gradually increased again over the 2010s. Many of the most notable cases arose out of general corporate scandals rather than accounting fraud. They were typically filed after the revelation of a legal violation by a company resulting in a government sanction and alleged that the corporation failed to adequately disclose the risk of such misconduct to investors. Because these lawsuits are typically prompted by the disclosure of an event that throws the company into turmoil, they have been generally referred to as *event litigation*. My review of securities class action filings found that complaints asserting event-driven claims increased from an average of five a year (from 2005 to 2009) to forty a year (from 2016 to 2019).[27] While initially this type of claim was advanced almost exclusively by private litigants, the SEC has also brought cases against companies for failing to disclose the risk of an adverse event. Event litigation has been described as asserting a new theory of securities fraud, but these actions raise issues of corporate knowledge similar to the Apple case where the question was whether corporate managers knew that defects in a product were serious enough to derail predictions of success.

Some event litigation is directed at general statements of a company's commitment to high standards of quality that were proven false by a product failure or corporate scandal. Courts have often dismissed Rule 10b-5 cases directed at "corporate puffery" that is too vague to be understood as a concrete guarantee. One federal appellate court thus affirmed the dismissal of securities fraud claims against Ford Motor alleging that a tire recall made statements concerning its "commitment to quality, safety, and corporate citizenship" misleading.[28] Another appellate court dismissed a complaint asserting the falsity of various statements made by an education company concerning the "financial health or performance" of its for-profit vocational colleges before they were involved in an admissions scandal.[29]

Another category of event-driven cases attempts to recover for investor losses caused by a corporate disaster.[30] In 2012, the oil company BP agreed to pay $525 million to settle an SEC action arising out of an explosion at its Deepwater Horizon oil rig. The accident spilled 4 million barrels of oil into the Gulf of Mexico. BP's stock price fell by almost 50 percent in the wake of the disaster, reflecting tens of billions of dollars in expected cleanup costs and government sanctions, as well as harm to the company's reputation. The SEC alleged that the company violated Rule 10b-5 by publishing misleading estimates about the extent of the spill.[31] A securities class action made a broader claim that BP issued material misstatements about its progress on implementing safety measures and its ability to respond to the spill.[32] After a motion to dismiss the private lawsuit failed, BP settled the case for $175 million.

Event litigation has also been prompted by government sanctions imposed on a company for major regulatory violations. For example, the German car maker Volkswagen was sued by the SEC and private investors for its failure to disclose its scheme to evade US environmental regulations governing its diesel engines.[33] The scandal resulted in close to $30 billion in fines to settle criminal and environmental actions. At least initially, a district court dismissed much of the SEC's case on the ground that the company had not misrepresented the risk of regulatory enforcement.[34] A similar theory was asserted in cases filed against Facebook for its failure to disclose that a researcher improperly sold data relating to tens of millions of users to a political consulting firm, resulting in the imposition of a $5 billion fine by the Federal Trade Commission. The SEC did not allege fraud by Facebook but claimed its disclosures were misleading because it presented the risk of such sales as hypothetical even after it became aware of an actual sale.[35] Facebook paid a $100 million fine to settle the SEC's case.[36]

As issues of workplace misconduct gained more visibility, several class actions were filed after the revelation of sexual harassment by corporate managers. Some securities fraud cases have argued that the tolerance of such behavior by a corporation meant that disclosures claiming a commitment to a strong code of ethics were misleading. Courts dismissed claims against companies like CBS and Hewlett Packard on the ground that such statements are too vague and aspirational to support a securities fraud claim.[37] In contrast, specific statements by a company denying allegations of rampant sexual harassment at a company were viewed by a federal district court as sufficiently misleading for a Rule 10b-5 class action to proceed.[38]

Event litigation reflects the importance of a firm's future performance in assessing the value of its stock. Claims that the risk of a corporate disaster was not adequately disclosed are based on the premise that companies have an obligation to fully inform investors about developments that could affect a company's future earnings. The failure to disclose specific and known risks thus arguably distorts the valuation process.

To some extent, event litigation raises similar issues as the cases filed against Apple and Citigroup. In Apple, the question was whether the company knew the Lisa would fail or whether it had a good faith belief that it would be able to overcome challenges with the product. Similarly, corporate disaster cases will often raise the issue of whether the company knew its safety measures were so inadequate that they would not work, or whether the company believed that they would prevent a disaster. In Citigroup, as with other financial crisis cases, the court concluded that the company was surprised by the extent of an unprecedented loss. In event-driven cases, companies will also often argue that they were surprised that their problems spun out of control.

Event litigation also raises the question of whether general corporate misconduct should be remedied through the securities laws. When a company violates a law, it is unrealistic to expect that it will make a confessionary disclosure of the violation in advance.[39] Corporate wrongdoing may be better addressed through corporate law, which permits shareholders to bring suit on behalf of the corporation for managerial misconduct.[40] To the extent that official corporate misconduct is discovered and punished, it is unclear that an additional sanction for failing to reveal such misconduct to investors is warranted.

The outcome of event litigation will often depend on fact-intensive inquiry.[41] Courts must determine whether there is sufficient basis for concluding that managers at some point clearly knew of a substantial risk to the company's business that should have been disclosed to investors. Federal courts have experience making such inquiries, but should be careful to avoid making the securities laws a general source of sanction for any significant corporate misconduct.

INCREASING CORPORATE ACCOUNTABILITY FOR PROJECTIONS

This section begins to explore some of the implications of this book's thesis for securities fraud regulation. Given the importance of projections for the valuation process, there is a case that more should be done to increase the transparency of such projections.

Federal securities regulation is problematic in that it emphasizes the accuracy of financial reporting of past results while doing much less to ensure the integrity of corporate projections. This is a long-standing tendency that was noted by Homer Kripke in the 1970s. In articles and a book, Kripke criticized the SEC's narrow emphasis on protecting individual investors and failure to develop a regulatory strategy that reflected the future orientation of markets.[42] There are several ways that the SEC and courts can improve the reliability of projections. First, the SEC should increase disclosure requirements with respect to public company projections. Second, courts should enforce a more stringent duty to update projections after significant new developments. Third, the SEC should act preemptively to address abusive earnings management.

Disclosing Corporate Projections

Under current regulation, public companies are permitted to disclose projections but are not required to do so. The SEC should mandate periodic disclosure of earnings and revenue projections as well as require companies to provide information about the basis for such projections. Disclosed projections should be audited to ensure that they have a reasonable basis. This proposal would provide investors with additional information that they can use to assess whether market valuations are reasonable.

Securities fraud is more likely when a company is subject to unrealistic projections that it is struggling to meet. Why do some public companies misrepresent their condition rather than acknowledge that market expectations are unrealistic? A company could issue its own projections that correct analyst projections that are too high. It could also miss the projection and allow the market to adjust its expectations.

The answer lies in the way that the valuation treadmill works. When a company's value is tied to assumptions about its future performance, even a small misstep can result in the unraveling of a company's valuation. A company like Xerox that is locked in competition with its rivals could significantly falter if it does not make and meet high expectations. Enron's high valuation was based on the belief that it could produce exceptional growth because of its superior human capital. Changing a company's narrative about its future can prompt a major reassessment of a company's stock price.

Many public company executives feel trapped by the pressure to deliver short-term results and have sought to de-emphasize the importance of market projections. Several years ago, Jamie Dimon, the CEO of JP Morgan, and the legendary investor Warren Buffett proposed that corporations should not issue their own projections to guide analyst forecasts.[43] Without such guidance, investors might not place as much weight on analyst projections, allowing public companies to step off the valuation treadmill.

But it is unlikely that reducing a corporation's communications concerning its projections would be effective in lessening the pressure to maintain a valuation. Given the importance of future earnings to stock valuations, markets will still look for a way to assess such prospects.[44] They will rely upon analyst projections even if they are less informed by corporate information. The pressure to deliver short-term results may become even greater if companies do not provide guidance with respect to projections.

The current system permits a lack of transparency around financial projections. Because some companies disclose projections and others do not, investors cannot count on receiving the best information about a company's prospects. While the SEC requires corporate managers to include a narrative description of their view of future business developments in their periodic reports,[45] such qualitative disclosure is often vague and difficult to use to make comparisons between companies. Instead of releasing projections information publicly to all investors, many companies disclose such information through informal meetings with company officials.[46] While this process has been complicated by the passage of SEC Regulation FD,[47] which prohibits selective disclosure of material corporate information to research analysts, the rule leaves significant discretion to companies in determining whether a disclosure is material and the SEC has not vigorously enforced the rule. Because analyst projections include varying degrees of insight from corporate sources, it is difficult for investors to assess the reliability of such projections. Because companies are not required to release the assumptions behind their projections, it is difficult for public investors to assess whether such projections are reasonable.

With mandatory corporate projections, public companies would have to take a public stand on estimates of their future revenue and earnings. If they also provide information about the basis for such projections, the process by which projections are set and met by public companies would become more transparent for all investors. At a minimum, such disclosure would mean that investors would have a clearer starting point for valuing public companies. They could independently scrutinize the basis for a projection to determine whether it is realistic or not. They could also take comfort in the fact that an independent auditor has reviewed the reasonableness of the projection. While research analysts already do some of this work, most investors do not have access to information that would facilitate accurate forecasting.

If they were required to provide the basis for their projections, corporations would likely issue more conservative projections. They would know that they will lose credibility if they consistently make predictions that they cannot meet. If companies disclosed realistic forecasts, there would be less pressure for them to misstate information that creates the appearance that they are meeting unreasonable market expectations.

Decades ago, the SEC considered adopting a system where projections were not only permitted in SEC filings but required. One early 1980s report described "a movement afoot for a number of years to compel the managements of listed corporations to prepare internal estimates of future earnings, and to disclose these forecasts to the public."[48] Advocates for mandatory projections disclosure believed that projections with the "official sanction" of corporate management would be more reliable than analyst projections.[49] A 1972 article in the *Harvard Business Review* coauthored by the chief accountant of the SEC, who was a professor of accounting and finance at Columbia, argued for such regulation. Importantly, the article envisioned that companies would not only disclose a bottom-line prediction, but also "a statement of the major economic and operating assumptions underlying its preparation."[50] The chairman of the Financial Analysts Federation also came to the conclusion that "every forecast statement should include a statement of the assumptions on which the forecast is based."[51]

Companies objected to the possibility of mandatory projections. They argued that some companies were not in the position to make accurate predictions, especially in times of economic uncertainty.[52] A report noted that "[e]ven if disclosure of financial forecasts expands, considerable developmental efforts would be required before the information was comparable to other accounting information." [53] However, it concluded that "if the process of preparing forecasts is standardized to the same extent as that for other accounting information, then reviews could be made of the process."[54]

There is reason to believe that public companies are now in a better position to develop and issue projections. Technology and forecasting methods have advanced. Over the years, auditors have developed guidance on reviewing corporate projections.[55] Moreover, as noted earlier, Sarbanes–Oxley effectively requires a public company to be established enough so it has developed reliable internal controls. In modern markets, it is difficult for a company to go public without the infrastructure to develop reliable forecasts.

A major objection to this proposal is that mandating corporate projections would increase the costs of public company status. But the increased burden of such a mandate could be offset by reducing other regulatory mandates.[56] For example, rather than requiring an auditor review of management assessment of internal controls every year, Sarbanes–Oxley could be amended to require such a review less frequently, perhaps once every five years. Alternatively, rather than imposing a mandate, the law could provide stronger incentives for companies to release audited corporate projections. One possibility is to grant immunity from Rule 10b-5 securities fraud liability to companies that issue such information voluntarily, except for intentional misstatements.

One concern with mandating projections is that doing so might increase the vulnerability of public companies to private litigation if they miss a projection. But this proposal would not change the current Private Securities Litigation Reform Act

(PSLRA) safe harbor, which protects projections accompanied by cautionary statements from securities fraud liability. Such protection could be expanded if the increase in the number of corporate projections triggers excessive litigation. Moreover, if companies are more likely to issue conservative projections when they must disclose them directly rather than through intermediaries, there will be less of a risk that they will miss the projection.

Strengthening the Duty to Update Projections

In addition to increasing disclosure with respect to company projections, the courts should read Rule 10b-5 as creating a strong duty to update such projections in light of major new developments. Such a duty would reduce the risk that investors will purchase stock inflated by unrealistic expectations.

Federal appellate courts have been reluctant to require public companies to update projections even when it is apparent that they are unreasonably high given new developments.[57] The US Court of Appeals for the Third Circuit has observed that "[i]ncreasing the obligations associated with disclosing reasonably made internal forecasts is likely to deter companies from providing this information – a result contrary to the SEC's goal of encouraging the voluntary disclosure of company forecasts."[58] The Seventh Circuit has taken a somewhat different approach, noting that because investors rely on projections there may be in some circumstances an obligation to correct them if they are wrong when issued, but also has not clearly adopted a general duty to update.[59] In contrast, the Second Circuit has recognized a duty to update when "opinions or projections have become misleading as the result of intervening events."[60]

If the SEC required corporations to issue projections, such a mandate would alleviate the concern of the Third Circuit that imposing liability for not updating projections would deter companies from issuing projections. Moreover, if the premise of mandating projections is that investors should have better information about a company's forecasts, a duty to update would be consistent with that goal. If there was some potential for liability for failing to update a projection, there would be an incentive for companies to issue more conservative projections.

A strong duty to update would be somewhat in tension with the PSLRA's safe harbor for projections. Rather than challenging the projection as false when issued, an investor could simply wait and argue that the company failed to update the market about events that made the projection misleading. To be consistent with the safe harbor, a duty to update should only trigger Rule 10b-5 liability if there is actual knowledge that the projection has become false. Moreover, if the projection is accompanied by meaningful cautionary language of the risks that could make the projection false, the safe harbor would apply. To the extent that there is a concern that a broad duty to update would spur excessive private litigation, such a duty might be exclusively advanced through SEC enforcement.[61]

More ambitiously, a duty to update could extend not only to corporate projections but also to projections issued by analysts.[62] A potential problem with the proposal to mandate projections is the possibility that companies would issue conservative forecasts, but analysts might continue to issue unrealistic projections, sometimes with the private encouragement of companies. A corporate duty to correct or update analyst projections when they are materially misleading would lessen the influence of unrealistically high analyst projections.

Addressing Real Earnings Management

Finally, the SEC should do more to act preemptively to target companies that persistently manage earnings to meet projections, even when such earnings management does not clearly involve a GAAP violation.

In some limited cases, public companies should be subject to securities fraud enforcement if they have a culture driven by earnings management, even without evidence of a clear transgression of GAAP. As the SEC enforcement cases against GE and Under Armour show, real earnings management can be problematic even if it does not involve clear violations of accounting rules. Sudden changes in business practices to generate results solely to meet market expectations can make a company's financial reports misleading. Companies that chronically manage their financial results can push problems into the future until they become too large to ignore. If public company securities fraud is best understood as involving the manipulation of investor perceptions of a company's prospects, there is a case that in some instances, the SEC should conclude that egregious real earnings management is motivated by fraudulent intent and violates Rule 10b-5.

At least initially, there is an argument that enforcement relating to real earnings management should be mostly prospective. The SEC could bring cases for injunctive relief against companies that engage in questionable real earnings management. Such preemptive action could stop inefficient conduct that risks significant investor losses in the future. As the SEC increasingly challenges earnings management, the boundary between proper and improper practices will become clearer. The SEC will then have a stronger basis for arguing that companies that cross the line and engage in improper earnings management acted with fraudulent intent, justifying higher sanctions.

FOCUSING SECURITIES FRAUD DOCTRINE

While in some ways this book supports a broad conception of securities fraud, in other ways it views such fraud narrowly. Securities fraud enforcement should focus on public company misstatements that materially affect the valuation process rather than on all information that might be of interest to any investor. In determining whether a misstatement was made with scienter, courts and regulators should firmly link the misstatement to a scheme to distort the company's valuation.

Materiality

One of the most important limitations on the reach of securities law is that it mainly regulates material information.[63] For a misstatement to be material, it must be important to the decision-making of the reasonable investor. If information is not material, it is generally not subject to mandatory disclosure. Securities fraud liability is only triggered by material misstatements. Internal controls are only required to prevent material misstatements. Auditors of public companies are instructed to assess whether "financial statements are free of material misstatement, whether caused by error or fraud."[64] The materiality requirement thus limits the reach of securities regulation and keeps its burden manageable.

The effectiveness of the materiality standard in limiting the costs of securities fraud regulation has been hampered by a lack of definition. Most notably, there are differing views about what information a "reasonable" investor would view as important.[65] One position is that even statements only an uninformed investor would find significant are material. Under this view, even statements of puffery by companies could be material because many retail investors would take them at face value.[66] While most courts appear to view materiality through the lens of the informed and rational investor, it is worth examining the argument for why all courts and regulators should do so.

Securities regulation should recognize the importance of valuation models for public company stock prices. Valuation models are what separates investment from gambling. While speculation and guesswork will always play a role in the movement of market prices, what has changed is the wide adoption of standard valuation methods for public company stocks. Such methods are far from perfect, but they create a basic framework that provides an anchor for the inherently uncertain process of determining the value of a stock.

Ensuring the integrity of markets where informed investors can collectively generate fairly accurate valuations is a compelling policy goal.[67] If this book is correct in that securities fraud came to threaten the integrity of public companies as valuation methods shifted to emphasize projections of future earnings, then there is a case that securities fraud regulation should mainly be concerned with policing major threats to the integrity of that valuation system. Pursuing such a clear aim is important given the high costs of securities regulation that have spurred significant backlash.

Courts, Congress, and the SEC should reinvigorate materiality as a limit on securities fraud regulation. Courts and the SEC can explicitly recognize that the reasonable investor is rational and informed. Congress could strengthen materiality as a limit on the costs of private securities fraud litigation by requiring that plaintiffs plead specific facts detailing how a misstatement was material to the valuation process. The PSLRA's requirement that plaintiffs plead specific facts establishing a strong inference of fraud has provided courts a way of separating good cases from bad. Requiring greater scrutiny of the materiality of a misstatement would provide an additional way of identifying those cases that address the type of conduct that merit the expenditure of judicial resources. While it may be difficult for judges to assess the intricacies of valuation methods, they have proven able to evaluate the presence of fraudulent intent in the context of complex business decisions.

The downside of this proposal is that it would reduce the ability of investors to recover damages for misstatements that do not have a clear impact on a company's valuation. Such a sacrifice may be necessary to maintain the viability of securities class actions. If the costs of such litigation become too great, more draconian measures to limit private litigation could regain momentum. Moreover, the heightened legal standard would only apply to investor class actions and would not restrict the SEC and state securities regulators from targeting a wider range of securities frauds.[68]

Greater clarity in the materiality definition would also make internal controls more cost-effective. The SEC should make it clear that in assessing such controls, corporate managers and auditors should mainly look at whether such controls prevent misstatements that substantially distort a company's valuation. The person making the assessment must have a deep understanding of how the assessed company is valued by markets and how the company might be expected to distort that valuation. For example, a company facing steep competition like Xerox during the 1990s will have an incentive to meet ambitious projections to convey that it is winning the competition. Companies like Apple and Enron, with valuations based on their ability to generate successful new projects, may have an incentive to hide the failure of such projects.

Scienter

As with many areas of common law, judges have developed numerous heuristics, mental short-cuts, for determining whether a company is liable for securities fraud. As Stephen Bainbridge and Mitu Gulati explain, these doctrines reflect the limited ability of generalist judges to decide complex cases.[69] Over time, such heuristics can take on a life of their own and distort judicial decision-making.

For example, in deciding whether a misstatement was motivated by fraudulent intent, some courts emphasize the presence of insider trading by corporate officers.[70] While such unjust enrichment can be a reason why managers defraud investors, as this book has shown, it is not the exclusive motivation for such fraud.

Courts in deciding Rule 10b-5 cases generally do not inquire whether the misstatement was motivated by a desire to avoid missing a financial projection. Indeed, some courts have explicitly held that meeting a projection is not a sufficient motive to support a finding of fraudulent intent.[71] Because virtually every public corporation has an incentive to meet market forecasts, there would always be a fraudulent motive in a case where a misstatement enabled a company to meet a projection.

Such an approach ignores the reality that securities fraud is often driven by structural pressures rather than individual incentives. As documented in Chapter 2, the SEC has routinely alleged that a company's misrepresentations were motivated to meet projections. The failure of some courts to acknowledge the motive to meet a projection thus results in a strange inconsistency between the SEC's bread-and-butter theory of public company securities fraud and the judicial heuristics governing scienter in private Rule 10b-5 litigation.

Courts should thus consider the pressure to meet projections in assessing whether a complaint sufficiently describes a motive that supports a conclusion that a defendant acted with fraudulent intent. However, simply alleging that a misstatement enabled a corporation to meet a projection would not be sufficient to establish scienter. The plaintiff should be required to provide specific details linking the misstatement to an actual scheme to deceive investors. Courts could ask a variety of questions in determining whether a deception was motivated to meet projections. How important was meeting projections to this particular company at the time of the misstatement? Were projections deliberately inflated to achieve a higher valuation? How egregious were the methods to meet the projection? Such inquiries would require more of judges but would ensure that cases with merit go forward.

***

Efforts to prevent and sanction securities fraud in public companies have been criticized for decades. Securities fraud regulation is imperfect and reflects the difficulty of determining when a public company intends to deceive investors. One of the problems with statutes like Sarbanes–Oxley is that they tend to implement simplistic solutions to complex problems. Once a crisis seems to be addressed, lawmakers and regulators have less incentive to continue developing better solutions. In order to better address the problem of securities fraud, regulation must become more directed at the ways in which public companies shape perceptions of their future.

9

Conclusion

At the start of 2020, the COVID-19 pandemic posed an unprecedented threat to the economy and stock market valuations. Stock prices plummeted in March 2020 as the nation shut down, and many public companies suspended their forecasts because they no longer had confidence that they could predict their financial performance. Surprisingly, the market started to recover over the spring and summer. By the fall, the S&P 500 reached the level it was at before the start of the pandemic. By the end of 2020, the market saw a significant annual gain.

The stock market's spectacular recovery highlights how modern market valuations are determined by future profitability. Even when the economy was in lockdown, investors had confidence that companies would prosper after the pandemic was contained. Big technology companies, which already commanded high valuations before the shutdown, were viewed as safe bets to continue their dominance. As government stimulus provided support for the economy, the market's confidence in the prospects of recovery for a wider range of companies grew.

As this book is nearing completion, we are in the midst of a boom in equity prices and asset valuations that has complicated the work of securities regulators. Investors are increasingly willing to speculate on digital assets and individual stocks of companies with dubious prospects, such as GameStop. The wild speculation of retail investors again raises questions about whether investors can reasonably rely upon the integrity of stock prices. As it becomes clear that the prospects of some public companies were overstated, there will likely be cries of securities fraud. Regulators and courts will have to carefully assess whether public companies manipulated the valuation process to deceive investors or whether stock declines reflect the bursting of a bubble.

Even as markets continue to follow familiar patterns, there is the possibility of significant changes in the way that investors value stocks. Investors have become more diversified and prefer to invest through index funds that hold a market portfolio. Social and environmental considerations are becoming more important to investors, and there is an increasing interest in investing in companies based on Environmental, Social & Governance (ESG) metrics. Could these developments slow down or turn off the valuation treadmill? Market pressure is unlikely to dissipate for most firms, but it is possible that large companies will face less pressure to deliver short-term results.

Securities fraud can threaten the integrity of one of our most important societal institutions, the public corporation. Without confidence in public company valuations, stock markets simply cannot function. As valuation methods have become more systematic, public companies now face pressure to produce evidence of future profitability. As a result, there is a case for regulation that counters such pressure and helps ensure the integrity of public company valuations. Without accountability for preventing securities fraud, the modern public corporation cannot prosper.

Notes

CHAPTER 1

1 In the Matter of Under Armour, Inc., Order Instituting Cease-and-Desist Proceedings Pursuant to Section 8A of the Securities Act of 1933 and Section 21C of the Securities Exchange Act of 1934, Making Findings, and Imposing a Cease-and-Desist Order (May 3, 2021).

2 SEC Rule 10b-5 reads in full:

Employment of manipulative and deceptive devices.

It shall be unlawful for any person, directly or indirectly, by the use of any means or instrumentality of interstate commerce, or of the mails or of any facility of any national securities exchange,

(a) To employ any device, scheme, or artifice to defraud,
(b) To make any untrue statement of a material fact or to omit to state a material fact necessary in order to make the statements made, in the light of the circumstances under which they were made, not misleading, or
(c) To engage in any act, practice, or course of business which operates or would operate as a fraud or deceit upon any person, in connection with the purchase or sale of any security

(17 C.F.R. § 240.10b-5).

The SEC passed Rule 10b-5 pursuant to its authority under section 10(b) of the Securities Exchange Act of 1934, which allows it to pass rules prohibiting any "manipulative or deceptive device or contrivance." 15 U.S.C. § 78j.

3 This book mainly discusses claims brought under rules and statutes that require a showing of such fraudulent intent. Some statutes impose liability for false statements even if they were not motivated by deception. See, e.g., Securities Act of 1933 § 11, 15 U.S.C. § 77k.

4 Indeed, one commentator has asserted that "fraudulent financial statements do not appear to have been proximate determinants of the Securities Acts." GEORGE J. BENTSON, *The*

Value of the SEC's Accounting Disclosure Requirements, 44 ACCOUNT. REV. 515, 517 (1969).

5 *See, e.g.*, LUCIAN BEBCHUK & JESSE FRIED, PAY WITHOUT PERFORMANCE: THE UNFULFILLED PROMISE OF EXECUTIVE COMPENSATION 10 (2004) (observing that structure of executive compensation gives managers incentive to misreport financial results).

6 John C. Coffee, Jr., *Reforming the Securities Class Action: An Essay on Deterrence and Its Implementation*, 106 COLUM. L. REV. 1534, 1572 (2006).

7 FRANK PARTNOY, THE MATCH KING: IVAR KRUEGER, THE FINANCIAL GENIUS BEHIND A CENTURY OF WALL STREET SCANDALS (2009).

8 FRANCIS X. BUSCH, GUILTY OR NOT GUILTY? THE ACCOUNT OF THE TRIALS OF THE LEO FRANK CASE, THE D.C. STEPHENSON CASE, THE SAMUEL INSULL CASE, THE ALGER HISS CASE 186–87 (1957).

9 Private Securities Litigation Reform Act of 1995, Pub. L. 104-67, 109 Stat. 737.

10 Sarbanes-Oxley Act of 2002, Pub. L. No. 107–204, 116 Stat. 745.

11 For a fuller description of these developments, see James J. Park, *From Managers to Markets: Valuation and Shareholder Wealth Maximization*, J. CORP. L. (forthcoming 2022).

12 *See, e.g.*, ASWATH DAMODARAN, INVESTMENT VALUATION: TOOLS AND TECHNIQUES FOR DETERMINING THE VALUE OF ANY ASSET (3d ed. 2012).

13 Regulators have struggled for centuries to distinguish between investment and speculation, see STUART BANNER, SPECULATION: A HISTORY OF THE FINE LINE BETWEEN GAMBLING AND INVESTING (2017), and continue to do so today, see DONALD C. LANGEVOORT, SELLING HOPE, SELLING RISK: CORPORATIONS, WALL STREET, AND THE DILEMMAS OF INVESTOR PROTECTION (2016).

14 Kenneth S. Axelson, *An Executive's Views on the Forecasting of Earnings, in* PUBLIC REPORTING OF CORPORATE FINANCIAL FORECASTS 35, 35 (Prem Prakash & Alfred Rappaport eds., 1974); NOEL M. TICHY & STRATFORD SHERMAN, CONTROL YOUR DESTINY OR SOMEONE ELSE WILL: LESSONS IN MASTERING CHANGE – THE PRINCIPLES JACK WELCH IS USING TO REVOLUTIONIZE GENERAL ELECTRIC 38–9 (1993); THOMAS J. WATSON, JR., A BUSINESS AND ITS BELIEFS: THE IDEAS THAT HELPED BUILD IBM 50 (1963).

15 AMERICAN MANAGEMENT ASSOCIATION, INC., SALES FORECASTING: USES, TECHNIQUES, AND TRENDS (1956).

16 ALEX BERENSON, THE NUMBER: HOW THE DRIVE FOR QUARTERLY EARNINGS CORRUPTED WALL STREET AND CORPORATE AMERICA (2003).

17 ALFRED RAPPAPORT, CREATING SHAREHOLDER VALUE: THE NEW STANDARD FOR BUSINESS PERFORMANCE 1, 19 (1986).

18 *See* James J. Park, *Do the Securities Laws Promote Short-Termism?*, 10 UC IRVINE L. REV. 991 (2020).

19 On the banality of corporate fraud, see Sung Hui Kim, *The Banality of Fraud: Re-situating the Inside Counsel as Gatekeeper*, 74 FORDHAM L. REV. 983 (2005).

20 In addition to the mandatory rules directly governing public companies, it is important to recognize the essential role of objective gatekeepers enlisted by the securities laws to prevent corporate securities fraud. *See* JOHN C. COFFEE JR., GATEKEEPERS: THE PROFESSIONS AND CORPORATE GOVERNANCE (2006).

21 Homer Kripke, The SEC and Corporate Disclosure: Regulation in Search of Purpose (1979).

22 Roberta Romano, *The Sarbanes-Oxley Act and the Making of Quack Corporate Governance*, 114 Yale L.J. 1521, 1528 (2005).

23 *See, e.g.*, Edward J. Balleisen, Fraud: An American History from Barnum to Madoff (2017); William A. Birdthistle, Empire of the Fund: The Way We Save Now (2016); Merritt B. Fox, Lawrence R. Glosten & Gabriel V. Rauterberg, The New Stock Market: Law, Economics, and Policy (2019).

24 Samuel W. Buell, *What Is Securities Fraud?*, 61 Duke L.J. 511 (2011).

25 *See, e.g.*, James J. Park, *Rules, Principles, and the Competition to Enforce the Securities Laws*, 100 Calif. L. Rev. 115 (2012).

26 For an excellent history of the public corporation, see Brian R. Cheffins, The Public Company Transformed (2019).

CHAPTER 2

1 John H. Dessauer, My Years with Xerox: The Billions Nobody Wanted 23 (1971).

2 Gary Jacobson & John Hillkirk, Xerox America Samurai: The Behind-the-Scenes Story of How a Corporate Giant Beat the Japanese at Their Own Game 8 (1986).

3 The Commission on Auditors' Responsibilities, Report, Conclusions, and Recommendations 54 (1978).

4 Complaint, Sec. & Exch. Comm'n v. Xerox Corp., Civil Action No. 02-272789 (DLC) ¶ 5 (S.D.N.Y. Apr. 11, 2002).

5 SCM Corp. v. Xerox Corp., 463 F. Supp. 983, 991 (D. Conn. 1976).

6 David Owen, Copies in Seconds 237 (2004).

7 *Id.* at 239.

8 According to Xerox's 1997 10-K: "Revenue Recognition. Revenues from the sale of equipment under installment contracts and from sales-type leases are recognized at the time of sale or at the inception of the lease, respectively. Associated finance income is earned on an accrual basis under an effective annual yield method. Revenues from equipment under other leases are accounted for by the operating lease method and are recognized over the lease term. Service revenues are derived primarily from maintenance contracts on our equipment sold to customers and are recognized over the term of the contracts." Xerox 1997 Form 10-K, Notes, at 56.

9 Complaint, Sec. & Exch. Comm'n v. Xerox Corp. ¶ 35.

10 *See* Michael Hiltzik, Dealers of Lightning: Xerox PARC and the Dawn of the Computer Age 24 (1999).

11 John R. Graham, Campbell R. Harvey & Shiva Rajgopal, *The Economic Implications of Corporate Financial Reporting*, 40 J. Account. & Econ. 3, 29 (2005).

12 Complaint, Sec. & Exch. Comm'n v. Xerox Corp. ¶ 8.

13 Bernard Wysocki Jr., *Xerox Recasts Itself as Formidable Force in Digital Revolution*, Wall St. J., Feb. 2, 1999, at A1.

14 Chill v. General Electric Co., 101 F.3d 263, 270 (2d Cir. 1996).

15 *See, e.g.*, Goldman v. Belden, 754 F.2d 1059, 1070 (2d Cir. 1985).

16 Novak v. Kasaks, 216 F.3d 300, 308 (2d Cir. 2000).

17 This defense has been successful in some cases. *See, e.g.*, Podraza v. Whiting, 790 F.3d 828, 838 (8th Cir. 2015) (finding "inference of scienter is contradicted by the fact that" the company's auditor concluded its "financial documents complied with GAAP").

18 *See, e.g.*, Carlson v. Xerox Corp., 392 F. Supp.2d 267, 284 (D. Conn. 2005) (rejecting defense that auditor involvement precluded finding of scienter by company).

19 Arthur Levitt, *The "Numbers Game"* (Sept. 28, 1998), *available at* https://www.sec.gov/news/speech/speecharchive/1998/spch220.txt.

20 SEC Staff Accounting Bulletin: No. 99, 17 CFR Part 211 (Aug. 1999).

21 Consolidated Class Action Complaint, *In re* HealthSouth Corp. Sec. Litig., Master File No. CV-03-BE-1500-S ¶ 3 (Aug. 2, 2004).

22 The CEO of the company was indicted but acquitted of criminal charges. However, after a civil trial in state court, he was found liable for $2.8 billion in shareholder damages.

23 Complaint, Sec. & Exch. Comm'n v. Computer Assoc. Inter., Inc., 04 Civ. 4088 ¶ 10 (E.D.N.Y. Sept. 21, 2004).

24 *The Nifty Fifty Revisited*, FORBES, Dec. 15, 1977, at 72.

25 CHARLES D. ELLIS, JOE WILSON AND THE CREATION OF XEROX (2006).

26 Dessauer, *supra* note 1, at 139–40.

27 DOUGLAS K. SMITH & ROBERT C. ALEXANDER, HOW XEROX INVENTED, THEN IGNORED, THE FIRST PERSONAL COMPUTER 48–9 (1988).

28 John Brooks, *Xerox Xerox Xerox Xerox*, NEW YORKER, Apr. 1, 1967, at 88.

29 *Id.* at 49.

30 Dessauer, *supra* note 1, at 194–96.

31 *Id.* at xiii–xiv.

32 *See* James J. Park, *From Managers to Markets: Valuation and Shareholder Wealth Maximization*, J. CORP. L. (forthcoming 2022).

33 *See* Hiltzik, *supra* note 10, at 56, 259.

34 *See, e.g.*, ANDREA GABOR, THE MAN WHO DISCOVERED QUALITY: HOW W. EDWARDS DEMING BROUGHT THE QUALITY REVOLUTION TO AMERICA – THE STORIES OF FORD, XEROX, AND GM 193–94 (1990).

35 DAVID T. KEARNS & DAVID A. NADLER, PROPHETS IN THE DARK: HOW XEROX REINVENTED ITSELF AND BEAT BACK THE JAPANESE 221–22 (1992).

36 Francois Degeorge, Jayendu Patel & Richard Zeckhauser, *Earnings Management to Exceed Thresholds*, 72 J. BUS. 1 (1999).

37 Justin Fox & Rajiv Rao, *Learn to Play the Numbers Game (And Wall Street Will Love You)*, FORTUNE Mar. 31, 1997.

38 *See* Alexander Dyck, Adair Morse & Luigi Zingales, *Who Blows the Whistle on Corporate Fraud?*, 65 J. FIN. 2213 (2001).

39 James Bandler & John Hechinger, *Executive Challenges Xerox's Books, Was Fired*, WALL ST. J., Feb. 6, 2001, at C1.

40 *Id.*

41 Mark Maremont & James Bandler, *Xerox Restates Past Three Years' Results – Relatively Small Revisions, Boost to 2000 Figures Help Cheer Wall Street*, WALL ST. J., June 1, 2001, at A3.

42 James K. Loebbecke, Martha M. Eining & John J. Willingham, *Auditors' Experience with Material Irregularities: Frequency, Nature, and Detectability*, 9 AUDITING: A JOURNAL OF PRACTICE & THEORY 1, 7 (1989).

43 Mark L. DeFond & James Jiambalvo, *Incidence and Circumstances of Accounting Errors*, 66 ACCT. REV. 643, 647 (1991).

44 Zoe-Vonna Palmrose, Vernon J. Richardson & Susan Scholz, *Determinants of Market Reactions to Restatement Announcements*, 37 J. ACCT. & ECON. 59, 61 (2004).

45 United States General Accounting Office, *Financial Restatements: Trends, Market Impacts, Regulatory Responses, and Remaining Challenges* 4 (2002).

46 Securities and Exchange Commission, Report Pursuant to Section 704 of the Sarbanes–Oxley Act of 2002 2 (2002). To be more precise, the first year of the study covered July 1997 to July 1998 and the final year of the study covered July 2000 to July 2001.

47 Harvey L. Pitt & Karen L. Shapiro, *Securities Regulation By Enforcement: A Look Ahead at the Next Decade*, 7 YALE J. REG. 149, 262–63 (1990).

48 House Committee on Energy and Commerce, H. Rep. 98-355, at 6 (1983).

49 Report of the National Commission on Fraudulent Financial Reporting 23 (Oct. 1987).

50 Ehsan H. Feroz, Kyungjoo Park & Victor S. Pastena, *The Financial and Market Effects of the SEC's Accounting and Auditing Enforcement Releases*, 29 J. ACCT. RES. 107, 108 (1991).

51 SUSAN P. SHAPIRO, WAYWARD CAPITALISTS: TARGETS OF THE SECURITIES AND EXCHANGE COMMISSION 156 (1984) (finding the SEC sought disgorgement in only 7 percent of its proceedings from 1948 to 1972).

52 On the history of SEC restitution remedies, see Donna M. Nagy, *The Statutory Authority for Court-Ordered Disgorgement in SEC Enforcement Actions*, 71 SMU L. REV. 895 (2018).

53 Report of the National Commission on Fraudulent Financial Reporting 65 (Oct. 1987).

54 *See* Senate Committee on Banking, Housing and Urban Affairs, S. Rep. No. 101-337, 101st Cong. 4 (1990) (noting that draft statute was "developed, in part, in response to certain recommendations of the National Commission on Fraudulent Financial Reporting").

55 Arthur B. Laby & W. Hardy Callcott, *Patterns of SEC Enforcement under the 1990 Remedies Act: Civil Money Penalties*, 58 ALBANY L. REV. 5, 5 (1994).

56 Monte Wetzler, *Business Forum: Curbing Stock Market Abuses: A Remedy Worse than the Problem*, N.Y. TIMES, July 23, 1989.

57 Securities and Exchange Commission, *supra* note 46, at 2.

58 Theodore A. Levine, Wayne M. Carlin & Kevin S. Schwartz, *Revisiting the SEC Corporate Penalty Policy*, 7 SEC. LITIG. REP. 1, 1 (2010).

59 *In re* Cendant Corp. Litig., 60 F. Supp.2d 354, 359 (D. N.J. 1999).

60 Cendant Corporation, Form 8-K, at 10 (Aug. 28, 1998).

61 *In re* Cendant Corp. Litig., 264 F.3d 201, 222 (3d Cir. 2001).

62 Sec. & Exch. Comm'n v. Buntrock et al., Complaint, No. 02C 2180 ¶ 19 (March 26, 2002).

63 A variant of this argument is that shareholders bear the cost of their own compensation for securities fraud. *See* James J. Park, *Shareholder Compensation as Dividend*, 108 MICH. L. REV. 323 (2009).

64 WILLIAM Z. RIPLEY, MAIN STREET AND WALL STREET 4 (1927).

65 *Id.* at 79.

66 James Bandler & Mark Maremont, *How Ex-accountant Added Up to Trouble for Humbled Xerox,* WALL ST. J., June 28, 2001.

67 Memorandum of Law in Support of Xerox Defendants' Motion to Dismiss Plaintiffs' Third Consolidated Amended Complaint, Carlson v. Xerox Corp., No: 3:00-CV-1621, at 1 (Dec. 2, 2002).

68 *See* In the Matter of KPMG LLP, Order Instituting Public Administrative and Cease-And-Desist Proceedings, Securities Exchange Act of 1934 Release No. 51574 (April 19, 2005).

69 DAVID H. WEBBER, THE RISE OF THE WORKING-CLASS SHAREHOLDER: LABOR'S LAST BEST WEAPON (2018).

70 Consolidated Amended Complaint, Carlson v. Xerox Corp., No. 3:00-CV-1621 ¶¶ 98, 130 (Aug. 8, 2006).

71 Some commentators are skeptical that projections drive securities fraud because a projection can always be revised. *See, e.g.,* JOHN C. COFFEE JR., GATEKEEPERS: THE PROFESSIONS AND CORPORATE GOVERNANCE 84 (2006). But lowering a projection will hurt the stock price, and so there is an incentive to maintain high projections.

72 Levitt, *supra* note 19.

73 Sonia A. Steinway, *SEC Monetary Penalties Speak Very Loudly, but What Do They Say? A Critical Analysis of the SEC's New Enforcement Approach,* 124 YALE L.J. 209, 209–10 (2014).

74 Another question was whether penalties should be used to compensate investors. *See, e.g.,* Verity Winship, *Fair Funds and the SEC's Compensation of Injured Investors,* 60 FLA. L. REV. 1103 (2008); URSKA VELIKONJA, *Public Compensation for Private Harm: Evidence from the SEC's Fair Fund Distributions,* 67 STAN. L. REV. 331 (2015).

75 Securities and Exchange Commission, Statement of the Securities and Exchange Commission Concerning Financial Penalties (Jan. 4, 2006).

76 Robert Tomsho, *Moving the Market: U.S. Wraps Up Its Xerox Inquiry without Any Charges Being Filed: Move Ends Criminal Probe into Company's Practices in Accounting Disclosure,* WALL ST. J., Oct. 20, 2004.

77 *Rakoff Rakes the SEC,* WALL ST. J., Sept. 15, 2009.

78 Christopher M. Matthews, *Appeals Court Says Judge Erred in Blocking SEC-Citigroup Settlement,* WALL ST. J., June 4, 2014.

CHAPTER 3

1 *See, e.g.,* Harwell Wells, *"Corporation Law Is Dead": Heroic Managerialism, Legal Change, and the Puzzle of Corporation Law at the Height of the American Century,* 15 U. PA. J. BUS. L. 305, 326–31 (2013).

2 Report of Special Study of Securities Markets of the Securities and Exchange Commission, 88th Cong., 1st Sess., House Document No. 95, Part 3 10 (1963).

3 *See, e.g.,* William W. Bratton, *The Separation of Corporate Law and Social Welfare,* 74 WASH. & LEE L. REV. 1 (2017).

4 STEPHEN B. GODDARD, GETTING THERE: THE EPIC STRUGGLE BETWEEN ROAD AND RAIL IN THE AMERICAN CENTURY 8–9 (1994).

5 Joseph R. Daughen & Peter Binzen, The Wreck of the Penn Central 252–63 (1971).

6 *Id.* at 302–3.

7 Securities and Exchange Commission, The Financial Collapse of the Penn Central Company: Staff Report to the Special Committee on Investigations 180 (1972).

8 Robert Sobel, The Fallen Colossus: The Great Crash of the Penn Central 96 (1977).

9 Daughen & Binzen, *supra* note 5, at 13.

10 *One Big Happy Railroad*, The Nation, Feb. 14, 1966, at 184.

11 *Id.* at 185.

12 *The Pennsy-Central Case: Key to Survival for U.S. Railroads*, Newsweek, Aug. 27, 1962, at 70.

13 *The Pennsylvania Railroad*, Forbes, Mar. 1, 1965, at 28.

14 Sobel, *supra* note 8, at 215.

15 Gilbert Burck, *The World's Biggest Merger*, Fortune, June 1965, at 177.

16 *Pennsy, Central Ready to Sign*, Businessweek, Apr. 28, 1962, at 80.

17 Joseph A. Schumpeter, Capitalism, Socialism and Democracy (3d ed. 1950).

18 Peter F. Drucker, The Concept of the Corporation 186–87 (1946) (Mentor ed. 1964).

19 *The Pennsy-Central Case: Key to Survival for U.S. Railroads, supra* note 12, at 71.

20 *Last Chance for the Railroads?*, US News & World Report, Apr. 30, 1962, at 79.

21 Penn-Central Merger and N&W Inclusion Cases, 389 U.S. 486, 501 (1968).

22 Wilbert E. Moore, The Conduct of the Corporation 31 (1962).

23 Securities and Exchange Commission, *supra* note 7, at 1.

24 Daughen & Binzen, *supra* note 5, at 336.

25 William D. Cohan, Money and Power: How Goldman Sachs Came to Rule the World 175 (2011).

26 Securities and Exchange Commission, *supra* note 7, at 1.

27 Oliver E. Williamson, Markets and Hierarchies: Analysis and Antitrust Implications 142 (1975).

28 Daughen & Binzen, *supra* note 5, at 139.

29 Anthony Sampson, The Sovereign State of ITT 125 (1973).

30 *Id.* at 142.

31 *Id.* at 143–44.

32 William S. Rukeyser, *Litton Down to Earth*, Fortune, Apr. 1968, at 139.

33 Sobel, *supra* note 8, at 32.

34 *Mergers That Unions Can Live With*, Business Week, May 14, 1966, at 83.

35 John Kenneth Galbraith, The New Industrial State 115 (1967).

36 Brian Cheffins, The Public Company Transformed 41 (2019).

37 *The Pennsylvania Railroad*, Forbes, Mar. 1, 1965, at 26.

38 David L. Babson, *Performance: The Latest Name for Speculation?*, 23 Fin. Anal. J. 129, 130 (1967).

39 *The Multicompanies: Conglomerate, Aggolomerate and In-Between*, Forbes, Jan. 1, 1969, at 83.

40 Henry B. Reiling & John C. Burton, *Financial Statements: Signposts as Well as Milestones*, Harv. Bus. Rev. 47 (Nov. Dec. 1972).

41 Value Line Investment Survey 258 (Apr. 24, 1970).

42 *Penn Central Sees a Light in the Tunnel*, BUSINESSWEEK, Nov. 22, 1969, at 44.

43 Interstate Commerce Commission, Docket No. 35291, Statements Concerning Penn Central Transportation Company, Statement of George K. Deller, Verified Statement No. 36, at 31 (1971).

44 In the Matter of Peat, Marwick, Mitchell & Co., 45 S.E.C. 789, 1975 SEC LEXIS 2516, at *125–26 (July 2, 1975).

45 For example, in 1968, it tried to sell the right to build an office tower over Grand Central terminal but was thwarted by the New York City Landmarks Preservation Commission, whose decision was upheld by the US Supreme Court in a famous case. *See* Penn Central Transportation v. City of New York, 438 U.S. 103 (1978).

46 Rush Loving, Jr., *The Penn Central Bankruptcy Express*, FORTUNE, Aug. 1970, at 164.

47 Abraham J. Briloff, *Six Flags at Half-Mast? Great Southwest Corp. Hasn't Exactly Raised Accounting Standards*, BARRON'S, Jan. 11, 1971, at 5.

48 ABRAHAM J. BRILOFF, UNACCOUNTABLE ACCOUNTING: GAMES ACCOUNTANTS PLAY 195–201 (1972).

49 *Id.* at 208.

50 Briloff, *supra* note 47, at 31.

51 Briloff, *supra* note 48, at 201.

52 *Id.* at 218.

53 In the Matter of Peat, Marwick, Mitchell & Co., 45 S.E.C. 789, at *111–19 (1975).

54 Securities and Exchange Commission, *supra* note 7, at 50.

55 *Id.* at 8.

56 Homer Kripke, *The Myth of the Informed Layman*, BUS. LAW. 631, 633 (1973).

57 ABRAHAM J. BRILOFF, MORE DEBITS THAN CREDITS 6 (1976).

58 Ray Ball & Philip Brown, *An Empirical Evaluation of Accounting Numbers*, 6 J. ACCOUNT. RES. 159, 160 (1968).

59 Securities and Exchange Commission, *supra* note 7, at 180.

60 *Id.* at 4.

61 *Id.* at 30–1.

62 Loving, Jr., *supra* note 46, at 164.

63 Securities and Exchange Commission, *supra* note 7, at 35.

64 Report of the Trustee of Equity Funding Corporation of America 141 (Oct. 31, 1974).

65 RONALD L. SOBLE & ROBERT E. DALLAS, THE IMPOSSIBLE DREAM: THE EQUITY FUNDING STORY: THE FRAUD OF THE CENTURY 12 (1975).

66 *Id.* at 138–39.

67 In the Matter of McKesson & Robbins, SEC Accounting Release No. 19 (Dec. 5, 1940).

68 Report of the Trustee of Equity Funding Corporation of America, *supra* note 64, at 6.

69 Soble & Dallas, *supra* note 65, at 20.

70 Report of the Trustee of Equity Funding Corporation of America, *supra* note 64, at 12.

71 *Id.* at 105.

72 LEE J. SEIDLER, FREDERICK ANDREWS & MARC J. EPSTEIN, THE EQUITY FUNDING PAPERS: THE ANATOMY OF A FRAUD 302 (1977).

73 Soble & Dallas, *supra* note 65, at 132.

74 *In re* Equity Funding Corp. of America Sec. Litig., 438 F. Supp. 1303, 1319 (1977).

75 Kenneth H. Bacon, *Penn Central Co. and Ex-Officers Are Charged with Fraud by SEC*, WALL ST. J., May 3, 1974, at 3.

76 *See* Complaint, Sec. & Exch. Comm'n v. Penn Central Co., 1974 WL 391, at ¶ 30 (E.D. Pa. May 2, 1974).

77 *Id.* ¶ 43.

78 *Id.* ¶¶ 38–46.

79 *Former Chairman of Penn Central Co. Accepts Fraud Ban,* WALL ST. J., July 30, 1974.

80 *In re* Penn Central Sec. Litig., 347 F. Supp. 1327, 1332 (E.D. Pa. 1972).

81 *In re* Penn Central Sec. Litig., 416 F. Supp. 907, 912 (E.D. Pa. 1976).

82 Complaint, Sec. & Exch. Comm'n v. Penn Central Co., 1974 WL 391, at ¶ 31.

83 Cohan, *supra* note 25, at 175.

84 JOHN C. COFFEE JR., GATEKEEPERS: THE PROFESSIONS AND CORPORATE GOVERNANCE n.27 (2006).

85 Cohan, *supra* note 25, at 182–83.

86 *Id.* at 178–85.

87 Jennifer Arlen & William J. Carney, *Vicarious Liability for Fraud on Securities Markets: Theory and Evidence,* 1992 U. ILL. L. REV. 691.

88 *Id.* at 694.

89 *Id.* at 703.

90 Securities and Exchange Commission, *supra* note 7, at 9.

91 *Id.* at 245.

92 The Penn Central Failure and the Role of Financial Institutions, Part V, Trading in Penn Central Stock: Financial Institutions and Privileged Information, Staff Report of the Committee on Banking and Currency House of Representatives 92nd Congress, First Session 8–9 (Mar. 29, 1971).

93 *See* James J. Park, *Insider Trading and the Integrity of Mandatory Disclosure,* 2018 WIS. L. REV. 1133.

94 401 F.2d 833 (2d Cir. 1968) (en banc).

95 Just a few years after Penn Central's bankruptcy filing, a major insider trading case arose out of the Equity Funding case. A research analyst covering the insurance company, Raymond Dirks, learned of the company's fraudulent practices from an insider. Dirks informed his institutional investor clients, who exited their positions before the company collapsed. The New York Stock Exchange and the SEC both sought to discipline Dirks for disseminating inside information to his clients without disclosing the information to the public. Initially, a federal appeals court agreed that Dirks violated the prohibition of insider trading. It was not until 1983 that the US Supreme Court disagreed and held that Dirks' distribution of insider information did not violate Rule 10b-5. *See* Dirks v. Sec. & Exch. Comm'n, 463 U.S. 646 (1983). Dirks did not act deceptively because he did not have a duty to Equity Funding's shareholders that would be violated by passing on its information to others.

96 *See* Complaint, Sec. & Exch. Comm'n v. Penn Central Co., at ¶¶ 55–9.

97 *In re* Cabletron Systems, Inc., 311 F.3d 11, 24 (1st Cir. 2002).

98 The Penn Central Failure and the Role of Financial Institutions, Part III, Penphil: The Misuse of Corporate Power, Staff Report of the Committee on Banking and Currency House of Representatives 92nd Congress, First Session (Feb. 15, 1971).

99 *See* James J. Park, *Reassessing the Distinction between Corporate and Securities Law,* 64 UCLA L. REV. 116 (2017).

100 Securities and Exchange Commission, *supra* note 7, at 7.

101 Interstate Commerce Commission, Docket No. 35291, Statements Concerning Penn Central Transportation Company, Statement of George K. Deller, Verified Statement No. 36, Appendix (1971).

102 MELVIN ARON EISENBERG, THE STRUCTURE OF THE CORPORATION (1976).

103 RALPH NADER, MARK GREEN & JOEL SELIGMAN, TAMING THE GIANT CORPORATION 259 (1976).

104 Roberta S. Karmel, *Realizing the Dream of William O. Douglas – The Securities and Exchange Commission Takes Charge of Corporate Governance*, 30 DEL. J. CORP. L. 79, 86 (2005).

105 *In re* Four Seasons Sec. Litig., 58 F.R.D. 19, 25 (1972).

106 Arnold Lubasch, *Year in Jail Given for Stock Fraud*, N.Y. TIMES, Sept. 19, 1973, at 65.

107 *Settlement Following U.S. Financial Collapse Is Approved by Court*, WALL ST. J., Nov. 29, 1978, at 37.

108 *U.S. Financial Inc. Accused of Fraud to Create Profit*, WALL ST. J., Feb. 26, 1974, at 12.

109 *Walter, Ex-Chairman of U.S. Financial Inc., Gets 3-Year Sentence*, WALL ST. J., Feb. 4, 1976, at 7.

110 Tamar Lewin, *Peat, Marwick Settles in N.S.M. Holders Suit*, N.Y. TIMES, Sept. 11, 1982, at 37.

111 *Two Auditors in National Student Case, Company's Founder Receive Jail Terms*, WALL ST. J., Dec. 28, 1974, at 11.

112 Robert D. Hershey, *White & Case Agrees to Settle S.E.C. Suit in Anti-Fraud Action*, N.Y. TIMES, May 3, 1977, at 59.

113 William J. Casey, Toward Common Accounting Standards (May 19, 1972).

114 Subcommittee on Reports, Accounting and Management, The Accounting Establishment, S. Doc. No. 34, 95th Cong., 1st Sess. 2 (1976).

115 Coffee Jr., *supra* note 84, at 133.

116 Report of the Securities and Exchange Commission on Questionable and Illegal Corporate Payments and Practices, 94th Congress, 2d Session, at 3 (May 1976).

117 Securities Exchange Act of 1934 § 13(b)(2)(A).

118 *Id.* at § 13(b)(2)(B).

119 Report on Foreign Corrupt Practices, at *8.

120 ROBERT C. CLARK, CORPORATE LAW 134 (1986).

121 Foreign Corrupt Practices Act of 1977, Statement of Policy, SEC Release Notice, Release No. 17500, at *1 (1981).

122 *Id.* at *6.

123 *Id.* at *7.

124 *Id.* at *3.

125 Loving, Jr., *supra* note 46, at 165.

126 STEPHEN B. GODDARD, GETTING THERE: THE EPIC STRUGGLE BETWEEN ROAD AND RAIL IN THE AMERICAN CENTURY 228–29 (1994).

127 Sobel, *supra* note 8, at 331.

128 Securities and Exchange Commission, *supra* note 7, at 33.

129 *See, e.g.*, Cheffins, *supra* note 36, at 215 (observing that during the 1980s, "fraud and illicit self-dealing were not a major concern in the public company context").

CHAPTER 4

1 *See, e.g.*, Tom Nicholas, VC: An American History 236–38 (2019).

2 Private Securities Litigation Reform Act of 1995, Pub. L. 104-67, 109 Stat. 737.

3 Michael Hiltzik, Dealers of Lightning: Xerox, PARC and the Dawn of the Computer Age 333 (1999).

4 For an account of the passage of this rule, see Brian T. Fitzpatrick, The Conservative Case for Class Actions 8–12 (2019).

5 Report of Special Study of Securities Markets of the Securities and Exchange Commission, 88th Cong., 1st Sess., House Document No. 95, Part 3 96 (1963).

6 Arthur Fleischer, Jr., *Corporate Disclosure/Insider Trading*, Harv. Bus. Rev. 129, 134 (1967).

7 Adam C. Pritchard & Robert B. Thompson, *Texas Gulf Sulphur and the Genesis of Corporate Liability Under Rule 10b-5*, 71 SMU L. Rev. 927 (2018).

8 Sec. & Exch. Comm'n v. Texas Gulf Sulphur, 401 F.2d 833, 860 (2d Cir. 1968).

9 *See, e.g.*, Financial Industrial Fund, Inc. v. McDonnell Douglas Corp., 474 F.2d 514, 515 (10th Cir. 1973) (describing case arising out of failure to meet six-month projections in the 1960s); Herbst v. Able, 47 F.R.D. 11, 16 (S.D.N.Y. 1969); Reeder v. Mastercraft Electronics Corp., 297 F. Supp. 815 (S.D.N.Y. 1969) (alleging misleading financial statements and annual report); Spayregen v. Livingston Oil Co., 295 F. Supp. 1376 (S.D.N.Y. 1968) (alleging misleading income projection in speech). In addition, a number of early major cases relating to fraud by companies going public involved financial statement fraud. *See* Feit v. Leasco Data Processing Equip. Corp., 332 F. Supp. 544 (E.D.N.Y. 1971); Escott v. Barchris Construction Corp., 283 F. Supp. 643 (S.D.N.Y. 1968).

10 Herbst v. Able, 47 F.R.D. 11, 16 (S.D.N.Y. 1969).

11 *See, e.g.*, Blackie v. Barrack, 524 F.2d 891, 902 (2d Cir. 1975); In re LTV Securities Litig., 88 F.R.D. 134 (N.D. Tx. 1980); *see also* Daniel Fischel, *Use of Modern Finance Theory in Securities Fraud Cases Involving Actively Traded Securities*, 38 Bus. Law. 1 (1982).

12 485 U.S. 224 (1988).

13 The protection of sophisticated investors who trade in such markets is an important function of securities law. *See* Zohar Goshen & Gideon Parchomovsky, *The Essential Role of Securities Regulation*, 55 Duke L.J. 711 (2006).

14 507 F.2d 485 (1974).

15 *Id.* at 488.

16 *Id.* at 489.

17 *Id.* at 490.

18 *In re* Apple Computer Sec. Litig., 886 F.2d 1109, 1113 (9th Cir. 1989).

19 *Id.* at 1115.

20 *Id.*

21 Esther Dyson, *Beware the Hypervapor!*, Forbes, July 13, 1987, at 478.

22 Memorandum of Defendants A.C. Markulla, Jr. and John Vennard in Support of Motion for Judgment Notwithstanding the Verdict, *In re* Apple Sec. Litig., Master File No. C-84-20148, at 3 (July 19, 1991).

23 *Id.* at 4.

24 Ken Siegmann, *Apple Verdict Stuns Lawyers*, S.F. Chron., June 1, 1991, at B1.

25 Victoria Slind-Flor, *Spoils of Apple*, 14 Nat'l L.J., Apr. 14, 1992, at 2.

26 Charles McCoy & G. Pascal Zachary, *Apple Computer Settled Holder Suits For $19.8 Million*, WALL ST. J., Dec. 23, 1991, at B5.

27 *See* PATRICK DILLON & CARL M. CANNON, CIRCLE OF GREED 197 (2010).

28 John C. Coffee, Jr., *Companies' Projections Pose Problems*, 15 Nat'l L.J., Feb. 8, 1993, at 19.

29 Hanon v. Dataproducts Corp., 976 F.2d 497 (9th Cir. 1992).

30 James D. Beck & Sanjai Bhagat, *Shareholder Litigation: Share Price Movements, News Releases, and Settlement Amounts*, 18 MANAGERIAL & DEC. ECON. 563 (1997).

31 Willard T. Carleton, Michael S. Weisbach & Elliott J. Weiss, *Securities Class Action Lawsuits: A Descriptive Study*, 38 ARIZ. L. REV. 491, 501 (1996).

32 Jennifer Francis, Donna Philbrick & Katherine Schipper, *Shareholder Litigation and Corporate Disclosures*, 32 J. ACCT. RES. 137 (1994).

33 This data was compiled from the Institutional Shareholder Services Securities Class Action database.

34 *See, e.g.*, Provenz v. Miller, 102 F.3d 1478, 1488 (9th Cir. 1996) (predicting a profit despite information that there would be a loss); *In re* Ames Dept. Stores Inc. Stock Litig., 991 F.2d 953, 959 (2d Cir. 1993) (alleging prediction of increase in annual earnings was misleading because internal projections showed a loss); *In re* Compaq Sec. Litig., 848 F. Supp. 1307, 1318 (S.D. Tx. 1993) (noting prediction that "the company expected its domestic revenue to exceed general market growth" contradicted internal projection of decline in revenue); Alfus v. Pyramid Tech. Corp., 764 F. Supp. 598, 603 (N.D. Cal. 1991) (finding allegation that "financial projections were made while defendants were in possession of contradictory information" supported Rule 10b-5 claim).

35 *See In re* Warner Comm. Sec. Litig., 613 F. Supp. 735, 739 (S.D.N.Y. 1985).

36 *Id.* at 742–43.

37 *In re* Warner Comm. Sec. Litig., 798 F.2d 35, 36 (2d Cir. 1986).

38 *See, e.g.*, Grassi v. Info. Res., Inc., 63 F.3d 596, 600 (7th Cir. 1995) (describing evidence that projections were the result of "the company's annual budget planning process"); Kirby v. Cullinet Software, Inc., 721 F. Supp. 1444, 1452 (D. Mass. 1989) (finding forecast was reasonably based on "internal forecasting system").

39 *In re* Time Warner Inc. Sec. Litig., 9 F.3d 259, 267 (2d Cir. 1993).

40 Backman v. Polaroid Corp., 910 F.2d 10, 16 (1st Cir. 1990).

41 Report of the Advisory Committee on Corporate Disclosure to the Securities and Exchange Commission D-14 (Nov. 3, 1977).

42 Douglas J. Skinner, *Do the SEC's Safe Harbor Provisions Encourage Forward-Looking Disclosures?*, 51 FIN. ANAL. J. 38, 42 (1995).

43 J. Carter Beese, *Now It's SEC vs. the Lawyers*, WALL ST. J., Oct. 28, 1994, at A16.

44 17 C.F.R. § 230.175(a) (2011).

45 Safe Harbor for Forward-Looking Statements, Sec. Act Rel. No. 7101, 57 SEC Docket 1999, at 16 (Oct. 13, 1994).

46 Raab v. General Physics Corp., 4 F.3d 286, 291 (4th Cir. 1993).

47 DiLeo v. Ernst & Young, 901 F.2d 624, 627 (7th Cir. 1990).

48 *In re* Donald J. Trump Casino Sec. Litig., 7 F.3d 357 (3d Cir. 1993).

49 Rubinstein v. Collins, 20 F.3d 160, 167 (5th Cir. 1994).

50 Donald C. Langevoort, *Disclosures that "Bespeak Caution,"* 49 BUS. LAW. 481, 503 (1994).

51 S. Comm. on Banking, Hous., and Urb. Affairs, Private Securities Litigation Act of 1995, S. Rep. 104-98, at 38 (1995).

52 H. Comm. on Commerce, Common Sense Legal Reforms Act of 1995, H. Rep. 104-50, at 15 (1995).

53 H.R. Report No. 101-369, at 43 (1995).

54 Safe Harbor for Forward-Looking Statements, Sec. Act Rel. No. 7101, 57 SEC Docket 1999, at 9 (Oct. 13, 1994).

55 *Id.* at 15.

56 Testimony of Arthur Levitt, Concerning Litigation Reform Proposals Before the Subcommittee on Telecommunications and Finance Committee on Commerce, at 1 (Feb. 10, 1995).

57 H.R. Report No. 101-369, at 43 (1995).

58 Richard A. Rosen, *The Statutory Safe Harbor for Forward-Looking Statements after Two and a Half Years: Has It Changed the Law? Has It Achieved What Congress Intended?*, 76 WASH. U. L.Q. 645, 646 (1998).

59 JOEL SELIGMAN, THE TRANSFORMATION OF WALL STREET 657 (2003).

60 Private Litigation Under the Federal Securities Laws: Hearings Before the Subcomm. on Securities of the Senate Comm. on Banking, Housing & Urban Affairs, 103d Cong., 1st Sess., at 113 (1993).

61 *See* Michael Perino, *Fraud and Federalism: Preempting Private State Securities Fraud Causes of Action*, 50 STAN. L. REV. 273 (1998).

62 Securities and Exchange Commission Office of the General Counsel, Report to the President and the Congress on the First Year of Practice under the Private Securities Litigation Reform Act of 1995 3 (April 1997).

63 Statement by the President on Securities Litigation Act, 1998 WL 767340 (Nov. 4, 1998).

64 Seligman, *supra* note 59, at 671.

65 The PSLRA safe harbor also expanded the types of statements protected from Rule 10b-5 liability. The prior safe harbor only applied to projections contained in documents filed with the SEC. It did not cover the projections that companies often conveyed through press releases and informal communications. Congress evidenced a policy of encouraging all projections, regardless of whether they were part of a company's SEC filings.

66 Seligman, *supra* note 59, at 671.

67 President of the United States, Veto of H.R. 1058, 104th Cong., 1st Sess., House Doc. 104-150 (Dec. 20, 1995).

68 Slayton v. American Exp. Co., 604 F.3d 758 (2nd Cir. 2010).

69 *See, e.g.*, Lormand v. US Unwired, Inc., 565 F.3d 228 (5th Cir. 2009); *In re* See Beyond Tech. Corp. Sec. Litig., 266 F. Supp.2d 1150 (C.D. Cal 2003).

70 *See, e.g.*, Asher v. Baxter Intern. Inc., 377 F.3d 727 (7th Cir. 2004).

71 Marilyn F. Johnson, Ron Kasznik & Karen K. Nelson, *The Impact of Securities Litigation Reform on the Disclosure of Forward-Looking Information by High Technology Firms*, 39 J. ACCT. RES. 297 (2001).

72 Carol Anilowski, Mei Feng & Douglas J. Skinner, *Does Earnings Guidance Affect Market Returns? The Nature and Information Content of Aggregate Earnings Guidance*, 44 J. ACCT. & ECON. 36, 38 (2007).

73 *See Pleading Securities Fraud with Particularity under Rule 9(b)*, 97 Harv. L. Rev. 1432, 1432 (1984).

74 *See* Goldman v. Belden, 754 F.2d 1059 (2d Cir. 1985).

75 Wexner v. First Manhattan, 902 F.2d 169, 172 (2d Cir. 1990).

76 Goldman, 754 F.2d at 1070.

77 *See, e.g.*, William C. Baskin II, *Using Rule 9(b) to Reduce Nuisance Securities Litigation*, 99 YALE L.J. 1591, 1593–94 (1990).

78 *In re* Silicon Graphics Inc. Sec. Litig., 183 F.3d 970, 988 (9th Cir. 1999).

79 *Id.* at 988.

80 Adam C. Pritchard, Marilyn F. Johnson, & Karen K. Nelson, *In re Silicon Graphics Inc.: Shareholder Wealth Effects Resulting from the Interpretation of the Private Securities Litigation Reform Act's Pleading Standard*, 73 S. CAL. L. REV. 773 (2000).

81 Nursing Home Pension Fund Local 144 v. Oracle Corp., 380 F.3d 1226, 1231 (9th Cir. 2004).

82 *See, e.g.*, Mizzaro v. Home Depot, Inc., 544 F.3d 1230, 1250-51 (11th Cir. 2008).

83 Stephen J. Choi, Karen K. Nelson, & A. C. Pritchard, *The Screening Effect of the Private Securities Litigation Reform Act*, 6 J. EMP. LEGAL STUD. 35 (2009).

84 Stephen J. Choi, *Do the Merits Matter Less after the Private Litigation Reform Act?*, 23 J. L. ECON. & ORG. 598 (2006).

85 John C. Coffee Jr., *The Future of the Private Securities Litigation Reform Act: Or, Why the Fat Lady Has Not Yet Sung*, 51 BUS. LAW. 975 (1996).

86 Marilyn F. Johnson, Karen K. Nelson & A. C. Pritchard, *Do the Merits Matter More? The Impact of the Private Securities Litigation Reform Act*, 23 J. L. ECON. & ORG. 627 (2006).

87 Stephen J. Choi, Jill E. Fisch & Adam C. Pritchard, *Do Institutions Matter? The Impact of the Lead Plaintiff Provision of the Private Securities Litigation Reform Act*, 83 WASH. U. L. Q. 869 (2005); James D. Cox, Randall S. Thomas & Dana Kiku, *Does the Plaintiff Matter? An Empirical Analysis of Lead Plaintiffs in Securities Class Actions*, 106 COLUM. L. REV. 1587 (2006); Michael Perino, *Institutional Activism through Litigation: An Empirical Analysis of Public Pension Fund Participation in Securities Class Actions*, 9 J. EMP. LEG. STUD. 368–92 (2012).

88 There was some debate about whether law firms could influence state pension funds to appoint them as lead plaintiff through political contributions. Compare David H. Webber, *Is "Pay-to-Play" Driving Public Pension Fund Activism in Securities Class Actions? An Empirical Study*, 90 B.U. L. REV. 2031 (2010) and Stephen J. Choi, Drew T. Johnson-Skinner & Adam C. Pritchard, *The Price of Pay to Play in Securities Class Actions*, 8 J. EMP. LEGAL STUD. 650 (2011).

89 *See, e.g.*, Michael Perino, *Did the Private Securities Litigation Reform Act Work?*, 2003 U. ILL. L. REV. 913, 930–32.

90 Joseph A. Grundfest, *Damages and Reliance under Section 10(b) of the Exchange Act*, 69 BUS. LAW. 307, 308 (2014).

91 *See* James J. Park, *Securities Class Actions and Bankrupt Companies*, 111 MICH. L. REV. 547 (2013).

92 No. 84 Employer-Teamster Joint Council Pension Trust Fund v. America West Holding Corp., 320 F.3d 920, 946 (9th Cir. 2003).

93 Owen W. Linzmayer, Apple Confidential 2.0: The Definitive History of the World's Most Colorful Company 80 (2004).

94 *See In re* Apple Computer, Inc., Sec. Litig., 243 F. Supp.2d 1012 (N.D. Cal. 2002).

95 Freg Vogelstein, *And Then Steve Jobs Said, "Let There be an iPhone,"* N.Y. Times Mag. (Oct. 4, 2013).

96 Sec. & Exch. Comm'n v. Heinen & Anderson, Complaint, Case No. 07-2214 ¶ 33.

97 Charles Forelle, James Bandler & Nick Wingfield, *Jobs Knew Apple Manipulated Some Option Grants*, Wall St. J., Oct. 5, 2006.

98 On the process of granting stock options, see Iman Anabtawi, *Secret Compensation*, 82 N.C. L. Rev. 835 (2004).

99 John Carreyrou, Bad Blood: Secrets and Lies in a Silicon Valley Startup 30 (2019).

100 Sec. & Exch. Comm'n v. Balwani, Complaint, Case No. 5:18-cv-01603 ¶ 51 (Mar. 14, 2018).

101 Sec. & Exch. Comm'n v. Holmes and Theranos, Inc., Complaint, Case No. 5:18-cv-01602 ¶¶ 30–1 (Mar. 14, 2018).

102 *Id.* ¶¶ 83–9.

103 *Id.* ¶ 89.

104 Carreyrou, *supra* note 99, at 296.

105 *Id.* at 297.

106 *See* Dechert LLP, Dechert Survey: Developments in Securities Fraud Class Actions against U.S. Life Sciences Companies (2018).

CHAPTER 5

1 Harris Collingwood, *The Earnings Game: Everyone Plays, Nobody Wins*, Harv. Bus. Rev. (June 2001).

2 Sarbanes-Oxley Act of 2002, Pub. L. No. 107–204, 116 Stat. 745.

3 *See, e.g.*, Vince Kaminski & John Martin, *Transforming Enron: The Value of Active Management*, 13 J. App. Corp. Fin. 39, 42–4 (2001).

4 Baruch Lev, Intangibles: Management, Measurement, and Reporting 16 (2001).

5 As later described by two accounting professors, the perception at the time was that "with the exception of revenues, traditional financial statement information is not relevant for the valuation of Internet stock prices." Elizabeth Demers & Baruch Lev, *A Rude Awakening: Internet Shakeout in 2000*, 6 Rev. Account. Stud. 331, 336 (2001).

6 Second Interim Report of Neal Batson, *In re* Enron Corp., No. 01-16034, at 22–8 (Jan. 21, 2003).

7 *Id.* at 28–32.

8 Second Amended Complaint, Sec. & Exch. Comm'n v. Lay, Skilling, Causey, No. H-04-0284 ¶ 62 (S.D. Tx. July 2004).

9 Enron 2000 Annual Report 2.

10 Bethany McLean & Peter Elkind, The Smartest Guys in the Room 126–27 (2003).

11 Second Amended Complaint, Sec. & Exch. Comm'n v. Lay, Skilling, Causey ¶ 17.

12 *See* Memorandum Opinion and Order, U.S. v. Causey, Skilling & Lay, No. Crim. H-04-025-SS, 2005 WL 2647976, at *20 (Oct. 17, 2005).

13 For an extensive description of Enron's improper transactions with its SPEs, see First Interim Report of Neal Batson, Court-Appointed Examiner, *In re* Enron Corp., No. 01-16034 (Bankr. S.D.N.Y. Sept. 21, 2002).

14 *In re* Enron Corp. Sec., Deriv. & ERISA Litig., 235 F. Supp.2d 549, 616 (S.D. Tex. 2002).

15 Special Investigative Committee of the Board of Directors of Enron Corp., Report of Investigation 12 (2002) ("Enron Special Committee Report").

16 Second Amended Complaint, Sec. & Exch. Comm'n v. Lay, Skilling, Causey, at ¶¶ 30, 32.

17 Value Line Investment Survey 454 (June 22, 2001).

18 Second Interim Report of Neal Batson, *In re* Enron Corp., No. 01-16034, at 3 (Jan. 21, 2003).

19 Malcolm Gladwell, *Open Secrets*, New Yorker (Jan. 8, 2007).

20 Jonathan R. Macey, *A Pox on Both Your Houses: Enron, Sarbanes-Oxley and the Debate Concerning the Relative Efficacy of Mandatory Versus Enabling Rules*, 81 Wash. U. L. Q. 329, 331 (2003).

21 Donald C. Langevoort, *Resetting the Corporate Thermostat: Lessons from the Recent Financial Scandals about Self-Deception, Deceiving Others and the Design of Internal Controls*, 93 Geo. L.J. 285, 287 (2004).

22 Aaron Lucchetti, *When Bad Stocks Happen to Good Mutual Funds: Enron Could Spark New Attention to Accounting*, Wall St. J., Dec. 13, 2001, at C1.

23 First Interim Report of Neal Batson, at 17.

24 Enron 2000 Annual Report 48.

25 Appendix C to Final Report of Neal Batson, *In re* Enron, Case No. 01-16034, at 51 (June 30, 2003).

26 William C. Powers, Jr., Raymond S. Troubh & Herbert S. Winokur, Jr., Report of Investigation by the Special Investigative Committee of the Board of Directors of Enron Corp. 17, 187 (Enron Special Investigative Committee Report).

27 Hearing before the Subcommittee on Oversight and Investigations of the Committee on Energy and Commerce, The Financial Collapse of Enron – Part 2, Serial No. 107–88, at 25 (Feb. 7, 2002).

28 Committee on Commerce, Science, and Transportation, Collapse of the Enron Corporation, S. Hrg. 107-1141, at *35 (Feb. 26, 2002).

29 Robert Z. Aliber & Charles P. Kindleberger, Manias, Panics, and Crashes 21 (2015) (7th ed.); *see also* John C. Coffee Jr., Gatekeepers: The Professions and Corporate Governance 329 (2006) (noting that future expectations matter more in a bubble than past performance).

30 Michael C. Jensen, *Agency Costs of Overvalued Equity*, Fin. Mgmt. 10 (2005).

31 Third Interim Report of Neal Batson, Court-Appointed Examiner, *In re* Enron, Case No. 01-16034, at 31 (June 30, 2003).

32 Eugene Soltes, Why They Do It: Inside the Mind of the White-Collar Criminal 242–43 (2016).

33 *See, e.g.,* Frank Partnoy, Infectious Greed: How Deceit and Risk Corrupted the Financial Markets 306 (2003).

34 Second Amended Complaint, Sec. & Exch. Comm'n v. Lay, Skilling, Causey, at ¶ 92.

35 *Id.* ¶ 112.

36 ROBERT AARON GORDON, BUSINESS LEADERSHIP IN THE LARGE CORPORATION 72 (1945) (1961 edition).

37 *Id.* at 71.

38 *Id.* at 311.

39 *Id.* at 336.

40 Michael Jensen & Kevin J. Murphy, *Performance Pay and Top-Management Incentives*, 98 J. POL. ECON. 225, 258 (1990).

41 *Id.* at 261.

42 Yakov Amihud & Baruch Lev, *Risk Reduction as a Managerial Motive for Conglomerate Mergers*, 12 BELL J. ECON. 605, 606 (1981).

43 A number of developments relating to tax and accounting encouraged public companies to pay managers with stock and options. First, the deductibility of cash salaries was limited to $1 million in the early 1990s, making it more attractive for tax reasons to pay executives in stock and options rather than salary. Second, companies lobbied for and won a battle about whether stock options should be reported as an expense when awarded. The industry argued that options may not directly cost the company because unless the company's stock price increases, the options will have no value. Moreover, options were a common way for start-up companies without significant funds to attract talented employees. The counterargument was that options are a potential cost for shareholders if they are profitably exercised. As employees buy more shares at the lower option price, the ownership interest of the prior shareholders is diluted. Chairman Arthur Levitt, who later argued for more conservative accounting, ultimately sided with proponents of a more aggressive accounting policy that would not count options as expenses. A company could thus reduce expenses and increase earnings by paying its employees in options rather than cash.

44 Brian J. Hall & Jeffrey B. Liebman, *Are CEOs Really Paid Like Bureaucrats?*, 113 Q. J. ECON. 653, 655 (1998).

45 Brian J. Hall, *The Six Challenges of Equity-Based Pay Design*, 15 J. APP. CORP. FIN. 21 (2003).

46 Michael C. Jensen & Kevin J. Murphy, *CEO Incentives – It's Not How Much You Pay, but How*, 22 J. APP. FIN. 64 (2010).

47 Patricia M. Dechow, Richard G. Sloan & Amy P. Sweeney, *Causes and Consequences of Earnings Manipulation: An Analysis of Firms Subject to Enforcement Actions by the SEC*, 13 CONTEMP. ACCT. RES. 1 (1996).

48 Patricia M. Dechow and Douglas J. Skinner, *Earnings Management: Reconciling the Views of Accounting Academics, Practitioners, and Regulators*, 14 ACCT. HORIZONS 235, 236–37 (2000).

49 Bengt Holmstron & Steven N. Kaplan, *The State of U.S. Corporate Governance: What's Right and What's Wrong*, 15 J. APP. CORP. FIN. 8 (2003).

50 Natasha Burns and Simi Kedia, *The Impact of Performance-Based Compensation on Misreporting*, 79 J. FIN. ECON. 35 (2006); David J. Denis, Paul Hanouna & Atulya Sarin, *Is There a Dark Side to Incentive Compensation*, 12 J. CORP. FIN. 467 (2006); Jap Efendi, Anup Srivastava, Edward P. Swanson, *Why Do Corporate Managers Misstate*

Financial Statements? The Role of Option Compensation and Other Factors, 85 J. FIN. ECON. 667 (2007).

51 Merle Erickson, Michelle Hanlon & Edward L. Maydew, *Is There a Link between Executive Equity Incentives and Accounting Fraud?*, 44 J. ACCT. RES. 113 (2006).

52 John C. Coffee Jr., *What Caused Enron – A Capsule Social and Economic History of the 1990s*, 89 CORNELL L. REV. 269, 277 (2004).

53 Baruch Lev, *Corporate Earnings: Facts and Fiction*, 17 J. ECON. PERSP., 27, 36 (2003).

54 James C. Spindler, *Vicarious Liability for Bad Corporate Governance: Are We Wrong About 10b-5?*, 13 AM. L. & ECON. REV. 359 (2011).

55 *See* Alexei Barrionuevo, *Enron Chiefs Guilty of Fraud and Conspiracy*, N.Y. TIMES, May 25, 2006. Some of Penn Central's executives were charged with diverting funds from the company but were not convicted.

56 A conviction of Kenneth Lay, another Enron CEO, was vacated after he passed away.

57 Global Crossing, Exchange Act Release No. 51517, 2005 WL 831350, at 2 (Apr. 11, 2005).

58 *See* Greg Hitt & Kathy Chen, *Global Crossing Gets Easier Ride on Capitol Hill Thanks to Enron*, WALL ST. J., Feb. 12, 2002, at A2.

59 Dennis K. Berman, *Global Crossing Board Report Rebukes Counsel*, WALL ST. J., Mar. 11, 2003, at B9.

60 *In re* Global Crossing, Ltd. Sec. Litig., 322 F. Supp.2d 319, 341 (S.D.N.Y. 2004).

61 *In re* Qwest Comm. Inter., Inc., 396 F. Supp.2d 1178, 1184 (D. Colo. 2004).

62 *See* United States v. Nacchio, 573 F.3d 1062 (10th Cir. 2009) (en banc).

63 Notably, this one instance of insider trading occurred after he had resigned from the company. Skilling was acquitted of nine counts of insider trading that allegedly occurred while he was at the company. *See* U.S. v. Skilling, 554 F.3d 529, 542 (5th Cir. 2009).

64 U.S. v. Skilling, 638 F.3d 480, 485–86 (5th Cir. 2011).

65 First Amended Complaint, *In re* WorldCom Sec. Litig. No. 02 Civ. 3288 ¶ 113 (S.D.N.Y. Aug. 1, 2003).

66 Dennis R. Beresford, Nicholas deB. Katzenbach & C.B. Rogers, Jr., Report of the Investigation by the Special Investigative Committee of the Board of Directors of WorldCom, Inc. (Report of the WorldCom Special Investigative Committee) 133 (March 31, 2003).

67 Report of the WorldCom Special Investigative Committee, at 141.

68 Deborah Solomon, *Former WorldCom Exec Pleads Guilty*, WALL ST. J., Sept. 27, 2002.

69 United States v. Ebbers, 458 F.3d 110, 126 (2d Cir. 2006).

70 *See* Jeffrey N. Gordon, *The Rise of Independent Directors in the United States, 1950–2005: Of Shareholder Value and Stock Market Prices*, 59 STAN. L. REV. 1465, 1510–40 (2007).

71 Mark S. Beasley, Joseph V. Carcello & Dana R. Hermanson, Fraudulent Financial Reporting: 1987–1997 An Analysis of U.S. Public Companies 8 (1999).

72 KITTY CALAVITA, HENRY N. PONTELL & ROBERT H. TILLMAN, BIG MONEY CRIME: FRAUD AND POLITICS IN THE SAVINGS AND LOAN CRISIS 20 (1997).

73 Blue Ribbon Committee on Improving the Effectiveness of Corporate Audit Committees, *Report and Recommendations*, 54 BUS. LAW. 1067, 1072-76 (1999).

74 Final Rule: Audit Committee Disclosure, Release No. 34-42266 (Dec. 22, 1999).

75 Arthur Levitt, Speech by SEC Chairman: Renewing the Covenant with Investors (May 10, 2000).

76 Lynn E. Turner, Speech by SEC Staff: Audit Committees: A Call to Action (Oct. 5, 2000).

77 Order Requiring the Filing of Sworn Statements Pursuant to Section 21(a)(1) of the Securities Exchange Act of 1934, OMB Number: 3235-0569 (June 27, 2002).

78 Enron Special Investigative Committee Report, at 148.

79 Report of the WorldCom Special Investigative Committee, at 29.

80 *In re* WorldCom, Inc., First Interim Report of Dick Thornburgh, Case No. 02-15533, at 6 (Bankr. S.D.N.Y. Nov. 4, 2002).

81 *In re* WorldCom, Inc., Second Interim Report of Dick Thornburgh, Case No. 02-15533, at 136 (Bankr. S.D.N.Y. June 9, 2003).

82 *Id.* at 177–82.

83 *Id.* at 11.

84 Jeffrey N. Gordon, *Governance Failures of the Enron Board and the New Information Order of Sarbanes-Oxley*, 35 CONN. L. REV. 1125, 1128 (2003).

85 Permanent Subcommittee on Investigations, Committee on Governmental Affairs United States Senate, The Role of the Board of Directors in Enron's Collapse, 107th Cong., 2d Sess. (July 8, 2002).

86 Urska Velikonja, *The Cost of Securities Fraud*, 54 WM. & MARY L. REV. 1887 (2013).

87 J. Gregory Sidak, *The Failure of Good Intentions: The WorldCom Fraud and the Collapse of American Telecommunications After Deregulation*, 20 YALE J. REG. 207, 242 (2003).

88 Geoffrey Colvin, *The Other Victims of Bernie Ebbers Fraud*, FORTUNE, Aug. 8, 2005, at 32.

89 Sarbanes-Oxley §§ 101, 201–9.

90 *Id.* § 401.

91 *Id.* §§ 304, 402.

92 *Id.* § 406.

93 Corporate and Auditing Accountability, Responsibility, and Transparency Act of 2002, 107th Cong., 2d Sess., H.R. Rep. No. 107-414, at 18 (2002).

94 Public Company Accounting Reform and Investor Protection Act of 2002, 107th Cong., 2d Sess., S. Rep. No. 107-205, at 23 (2002).

95 *Id.* at 24.

96 Sarbanes-Oxley § 301.

97 Standards Relating to Listed Company Audit Committees, Securities Exchange Act Release No. 33-8220 (Apr. 9, 2003).

98 JONATHAN R. MACEY, CORPORATE GOVERNANCE: PROMISES KEPT, PROMISES BROKEN 97 (2008).

99 Sarbanes-Oxley § 407.

100 James D. Cox, *Reforming the Culture of Financial Reporting: The PCAOB and the Metrics for Accounting Measurements*, 81 WASH. U. L. Q. 301, 308 (2003).

101 William H. Beaver, *What Have We Learned from the Recent Corporate Scandals That We Did Not Already Know?*, 8 STAN. J. L. BUS. & FIN. 155, 168 (2002).

102 STEPHEN M. BAINBRIDGE & M. TODD HENDERSON, OUTSOURCING THE BOARD: HOW BOARD SERVICE PROVIDERS CAN IMPROVE CORPORATE GOVERNANCE 27 (2018).

103 Report of the New York Stock Exchange Corporate Accountability and Listing Standards Committee (June 6, 2002).

104 425 F.2d 796 (2d Cir. 1969).

105 Sarbanes-Oxley § 302.

106 *See* Robert B. Thompson & Hillary A. Sale, *Securities Fraud as Corporate Governance: Reflections upon Federalism,* 56 VAND. L. REV. 859, 877 (2003).

107 *See* Lisa M. Fairfax, *Form Over Substance? Officer Certification and the Promise of Enhanced Personal Accountability under the Sarbanes-Oxley Act,* 55 RUTGERS L. REV. 1 (2002).

108 Management's Report on Internal Control Over Financial Reporting and Certification of Disclosure in Exchange Act Periodic Reports, Securities Act Release No. 8238, 68 Fed. Reg. 36,636 (June 18, 2003).

109 Public Company Accounting Oversight Board (PCAOB), Auditing Standard No. 5, PCAOB Release No. 2007-005A, at A1–9 (June 12, 2007).

110 Donald C. Langevoort & Robert B. Thompson, *"Publicness" in Contemporary Securities Regulation after the JOBS Act,* 101 GEO. L. J. 337, 380 (2013).

111 *In re* Caremark Inter. Inc. Deriv. Litig., 698 A.2d 959 (Del. Ch. 1996).

112 911 A.2d 362 (Del. 2006).

CHAPTER 6

1 Sarbanes-Oxley Act of 2002, Pub. L. No. 107–204; 116 Stat. 745.

2 For a discussion of this point, see DONALD C. LANGEVOORT, SELLING HOPE, SELLING RISK: CORPORATIONS, WALL STREET, AND THE DILEMMAS OF INVESTOR PROTECTION 141–52 (2016).

3 Dodd-Frank Wall Street Reform and Consumer Protection Act of 2010, Pub L. No. 111-203, 124 Stat. 1376 [Dodd-Frank].

4 *See, e.g.,* WALTER ADAMS & JAMES BROCK, THE BIGNESS COMPLEX: INDUSTRY, LABOR, AND GOVERNMENT IN THE AMERICAN ECONOMY 41–5 (1986).

5 DAVID ROGERS, THE FUTURE OF AMERICAN BANKING 21 (1993).

6 HAROLD VAN B. CLEVELAND & THOMAS F. HUERTAS, CITIBANK 1812–1970 7–8 (1985).

7 MICHAEL PERINO, THE HELLHOUND OF WALL STREET 135, 150, 179, 181 (2010).

8 JAMES FREEMAN & VERN MCKINLEY, BORROWED TIME: TWO CENTURIES OF BOOMS, BUSTS, AND BAILOUTS AT CITI 188–91 (2018).

9 JEFF MADRICK, AGE OF GREED: THE TRIUMPH OF FINANCE AND THE DECLINE OF AMERICA, 1970 TO THE PRESENT 23 (2011).

10 AMEY STONE & MIKE BREWSTER, KING OF CAPITAL: SANDY WEILL AND THE MAKING OF CITIGROUP 123, 125, 227 (2002).

11 *See, e.g.,* Arthur E. Wilmarth, Jr., *The Road to Repeal of the Glass-Steagall Act,* 17 WAKE FOREST J. BUS. & INTELL. PROP. LAW 441, 513 (2017) (noting that the companies "argued that Citigroup would have a superior ability to withstand financial shocks due to its broadly diversified activities").

12 FREEMAN & MCKINLEY, *supra* note 8, at 236–38, 247–48.

13 Michael Scinolfi, *Travelers and Citicorp to Merge in Megadeal Valued at $83 Billion*, WALL ST. J., Apr. 7, 1998.

14 STONE & BREWSTER, *supra* note 10, at 217–18.

15 *Id.* at 195.

16 FREEMAN & MCKINLEY, *supra* note 8, at 265.

17 Complaint, Sec. & Exch. Comm'n v. Citigroup Inc., No. 1:10-cv-01277 ¶ 1 (July 29, 2010).

18 *Id.* ¶ 22.

19 *Id.* ¶ 24.

20 *Id.* ¶ 19.

21 *Id.* ¶ 32.

22 *Id.* ¶ 36.

23 *Id.* ¶ 45.

24 David Reilly & Robin Sidel, *Shake-Up at Citigroup: Repairing a Citi Machine; Executives Expect Fixing Some Problems to Take until Mid-2008; Skeptical Investors Push the Bank's Shares Down 4.9%*, WALL ST. J., Nov. 6, 2007, at C1.

25 Just two months after its November 2007 disclosure, Citigroup acknowledged it had an additional $10 billion in subprime CDOs on its balance sheet.

26 *In re* Citigroup Inc. Sec. Litig., 753 F. Supp.2d 206, 212 (S.D.N.Y. 2010).

27 Defendants' Memorandum of Law in Support of Their Motion to Dismiss the Amended Consolidated Class Action Complaint [Citigroup Motion to Dismiss], *In re* Citigroup Inc. Sec. Litig., 07 Civ. 9901, at 22 (Mar. 13, 2009).

28 Citigroup Motion to Dismiss, at 24.

29 753 F. Supp.2d 206, 217–18 (2010).

30 *Id.* at 235.

31 Citigroup Motion to Dismiss, at 24

32 Plaintiffs' Memorandum of Law in Opposition to Defendants' Motion to Dismiss the Amended Consolidated Class Action Complaint, *In re* Citigroup Inc. Sec. Litig., 07 Civ. 9901, at 18 (Apr. 24, 2009).

33 753 F. Supp.2d 206, 235–36 (2010).

34 *Id.* at 244–45.

35 *Id.* at 247–78.

36 Denny v. Barber, 576 F.2d 465, 470 (2d Cir. 1978).

37 DiLeo v. Ernst & Young, 901 F.2d 624, 628 (7th Cir. 1990).

38 In the Matter of Continental Illinois Sec. Litig., 962 F.2d 566, 568 (7th Cir. 1992).

39 *See, e.g., In re* Glenfed, Inc. Sec. Litig., 42 F.3d 1541, 1549 (9th Cir. 1994) (en banc); Serabian v. Amoskeag Bank Shares, Inc., 24 F.3d 357, 365 (1st Cir. 1994); *In re* Wells Fargo Sec. Litig., 12 F.3d 922, 930 (9th Cir. 1993).

40 Citigroup Motion to Dismiss, at 39.

41 *In re* Citigroup Inc. Bond Litig., 723 F. Supp.2d 568 (S.D.N.Y. 2010).

42 *See* James J. Park, *Bondholders and Securities Class Actions*, 99 MINN. L. REV. 585 (2014).

43 Specifically, it cited Section 17(a)(2) and 17(a)(3) of the Securities Act of 1933. *See* Aaron v. Sec. & Exch. Comm'n, 446 U.S. 680 (1980).

44 Randall Smith, *Parsing the Settlement at Citi – To Bolster Lawsuits, Stockholders and Bondholders Ask: Was Fraud Involved?*, WALL ST. J., Aug. 2, 2010, at C3.

45 Edward Wyatt, *Judge Accepts Citigroup's Settlement with S.E.C.*, N.Y. TIMES, Sept. 25, 2010, at B2.

46 Complaint, Sec. & Exch. Comm'n v. Daniel H. Mudd, Enrico Dallavecchia & Thomas A. Lund, 11 Civ. 9202 (S.D.N.Y. Dec. 16, 2011).

47 Complaint, Sec. & Exch. Comm'n v. Richard F. Syron, Patricia L. Cook & Donald J. Bisenius, 11 Civ. 9201 (S.D.N.Y. Dec. 14, 2011).

48 Steve Eder, *Lehman Auditor May Bear the Brunt*, WALL ST. J., Mar. 14, 2011, at C1.

49 *See* Report of Anton R. Valukas, *In re* Lehman Brothers Holdings Inc., Ch. 11 Case No. 08-13555, vol. 3 (Bankr. S.D.N.Y. Mar. 11, 2010).

50 Essentially, the argument was that Lehman did not receive sufficient cash from the transaction to guarantee that it could repurchase the asset.

51 Report of Anton R. Valukas, vol. 1, at 7–8.

52 National Commission on the Causes of the Financial and Economic Crisis in the United States, Financial Crisis Inquiry Commission Report 281 (2010).

53 *In re* Lehman Brothers Sec. and ERISA Litig., 799 F. Supp.2d 258, 296 (S.D.N.Y. 2011). Lehman's auditors also paid a significant settlement. *See* Michael Rapoport, *Ernst & Young Agrees to Pay $99 Million in Lehman Settlement; Auditor Was Sued Over Investment Bank's "Repo 105" Transactions*, WALL ST. J., Oct. 18, 2013.

54 *In re* Bear Stearns Co., Inc. Sec., Deriv., and ERISA Litig., 763 F. Supp.2d 423, 461 (S.D.N.Y. 2011).

55 *In re* American Intern. Group, Inc. 2008 Sec. Litig., 741 F. Supp.2d 511 (S.D.N.Y. 2010).

56 The Supreme Court had emphasized the importance of this requirement a few years before the crisis. *See* Dura Pharmaceuticals vs. Broudo, 544 U.S. 336 (2005).

57 Jill E. Fisch, *Cause for Concern: Causation and Federal Securities Fraud*, 94 IOWA L. REV. 811, 871 (2009).

58 Citigroup Motion to Dismiss, at 67.

59 *Id.* at 12.

60 In November 2018, the federal government provided guarantees for $306 billion in Citigroup's assets and provided a $20 billion capital infusion that was in addition to an earlier infusion of $25 billion. Special Inspector General for the Troubled Asset Relief Program, Extraordinary Financial Assistance Provided to Citigroup, Inc. 2–3 (2011).

61 FREEMAN & McKINLEY, *supra* note 8, at 274, 288.

62 *Id.* at 277.

63 National Commission on the Causes of the Financial and Economic Crisis in the United States, Financial Crisis Inquiry Commission Report 307 (2010)

64 *Id.* at 260.

65 *See* Monica Langley, *Behind Citigroup Departures: A Culture Shift by CEO Prince*, WALL ST. J., Aug. 24, 2005.

66 Amended Consolidated Class Action Complaint, *In re* Citigroup Inc. Sec. Litig., Master File No. 07 Civ. 9901 ¶ 493 (Feb. 20, 2009).

67 Santa Fe Industries, Inc. v. Green, 430 U.S. 462, 475 (1977).

68 *In re* Citigroup Inc. Shareholder Deriv. Litig., 964 A.2d 106 (2009).

69 Complaint, Sec. & Exch. Comm'n v. Angela Mozilo, David Sambol & Eric Sieracki, CV 09-03994 (C.D. Cal. June 4, 2009).

70 Complaint, Sec. & Exch. Comm'n v. Brad A. Morrice, Patti M. Dodge & David Kenneally, No. CV 09-01426 (C.D. Cal. Dec. 7, 2009).

71 Henry N. Butler & Larry E. Ribstein, The Sarbanes-Oxley Debacle 75 (2006).

72 *See, e.g.*, Jesse Eisinger, The Chickenshit Club: Why the Justice Department Fails to Prosecute Executives (2017); David Zaring, *Litigating the Financial Crisis*, 100 Va. L. Rev. 1405, 1441 (2014).

73 Amended Consolidated Class Action Complaint, *In re* Citigroup Inc. Sec. Litig., Master File No. 07 Civ. 9901 ¶ 14 (Feb. 20, 2009).

74 National Commission on the Causes of the Financial and Economic Crisis in the United States, *supra* note 63, at 325.

75 In the Matter of Microsoft Corporation, Securities Exchange Act Release No. 46017 (June 3, 2002).

76 Susan Pulliam & Randall Smith, *Citi, SEC Are in Talks to Settle Asset Probe*, Wall St. J., May 28, 2009, at C1.

77 Kitty Calavita, Henry N. Pontell & Robert H. Tillman, Big Money Crime: Fraud and Politics in the Savings and Loan Crisis 130 (1997).

78 *See* People v. Keating, 21 Cal.App.4th 1109 (1993).

79 Calavita et al., *supra* note 77, at 20

80 *Id.* at 130.

81 Jed S. Rakoff, *The Financial Crisis: Why Have No High-Level Executives Been Prosecuted?*, N.Y. Rev. Books (Jan. 9, 2014).

82 Dodd-Frank § 951.

83 *Id.* § 922.

84 Sarbanes-Oxley § 806.

85 Amanda M. Rose, *Better Bounty Hunting: How the SEC's New Whistleblower Program Changes the Securities Fraud Class Action Debate*, 108 Nw. U. L. Rev. 1235, 1275–87 (2014).

86 Securities and Exchange Commission, 2020 Annual Report to Congress: Whistleblower Program (2020).

87 Donald C. Langevoort, *The Social Construction of Sarbanes-Oxley*, 105 Mich. L. Rev. 1817, 1820 (2007) ("[Sarbanes–Oxley's] most important effects may be less about investor protection than about renegotiating the boundary between the public and private spaces in big corporations, a much deeper ideological issue.").

88 U.S. Securities & Exchange Commission, Final Report of the Advisory Committee on Public Companies 59 (2006).

89 Donald C. Langevoort & Robert B. Thompson, *"Publicness" in Contemporary Securities Regulation After the JOBS Act*, 101 Geo. L.J. 337, 340 (2013).

90 *See, e.g.*, Urska Velikonja, *The Cost of Securities Fraud*, 54 Wm. & Mary L. Rev. 1887 (2013).

91 *See* James J. Park, *Two Trends in the Regulation of the Public Corporation*, 7 Ohio State Entrep. Bus. L.J. 429 (2012).

92 *See, e.g.*, Ellen Engel, Rachel M. Hayes & Xue Wang, *The Sarbanes-Oxley Act and Firms' Going-Private Decisions*, 44 J. Acct. & Econ. 116 (2007).

93 Christian Leuz, Alexander Triantis & Tracy Yue Wang, *Why Do Firms Go Dark? Causes and Economic Consequences of Voluntary SEC Deregistrations*, 45 J. Acct. & Econ. 181, 204 (2008).

94 Joseph D. Piotroski & Suraj Srinivasan, *Regulation and Bonding: The Sarbanes-Oxley Act and the Flow of International Listings*, 46 J. ACCT. RES. 383 (2008).

95 ERNST & YOUNG, LOOKING BEHIND THE DECLINING NUMBER OF PUBLIC COMPANIES (May 2017).

96 *Why the Decline in the Number of Listed American Firms Matters*, ECONOMIST, Apr. 22, 2017.

97 Xiaohui Gao, Jay R. Ritter & Zhongyan Zhu, *Where Have All the IPOs Gone?*, 48 J. FIN. & QUAN. ANAL. 1663 (2013).

98 *See, e.g.*, Craig Doidge, G. Andrew Karolyi & René M. Stulz, *The U.S. Left Behind? Financial Globalization and the Rise of IPOs Outside the U.S.*, 110 J. FIN. ECON. 546, 549 (2013) ("Our results make it possible to reject the hypothesis that the regulatory changes of the early 2000s caused the decrease in small-firm IPO activity because it became abnormally low before these changes took place.").

99 *See, e.g.*, Craig Doidge, G. Andrew Karolyi & René M. Stulz, *The U.S. Listing Gap*, 123 J. FIN. ECON. 464 (2017); Andrew Whitten, *Why Are There So Few Public Companies in the US?*, NAT'L BUREAU OF ECON. RESEARCH DIGEST (2015).

100 *The Endangered Public Company*, ECONOMIST, May 19, 2012.

101 IPO TASK FORCE, REBUILDING THE IPO ON-RAMP: PUTTING EMERGING COMPANIES AND THE JOB MARKET BACK ON THE ROAD TO GROWTH (Oct. 20, 2011).

102 *Id.* at 8.

103 *Id.* at 9.

104 Frank Partnoy & Jesse Eisinger, *What's Inside America's Banks?*, THE ATLANTIC (2013).

CHAPTER 7

1 There are still companies that are misstating earnings. More than half of the SEC's accounting enforcement cases in 2019 alleged a misrepresentation with respect to revenue. *See* Cornerstone Research, SEC Enforcement Activity: Public Companies and Subsidiaries (2019).

2 SECURITIES AND EXCHANGE COMMISSION, THE FINANCIAL COLLAPSE OF THE PENN CENTRAL COMPANY: STAFF REPORT TO THE SPECIAL COMMITTEE ON INVESTIGATIONS 4 (1972).

3 Baruch Lev, *Corporate Earnings: Facts and Fiction*, 17 J. ECON. PERSP. 27, 33–4 (2003).

4 THOMAS GRYTA & TED MANN, LIGHTS OUT: PRIDE, DELUSION, AND THE FALL OF GENERAL ELECTRIC 10 (2020).

5 BARUCH LEV, INTANGIBLES: MANAGEMENT, MEASUREMENT, AND REPORTING 101 (2001).

6 *See, e.g.*, Alfred Rappaport, *The Economics of Short-Term Performance Obsession*, 61 FIN. ANAL. J. 65, 77 (2005).

7 *See, e.g.*, Mary M. Bange & Werner F. M. De Bondt, *R&D Budgets and Corporate Earnings Targets*, 4 J. CORP. FIN. 153 (1998) (examining 100 companies from 1977 to 1986); William R. Baber, Patricia M. Fairfield & James A. Haggard, *The Effect of Concern about Reported Income on Discretionary Spending Decisions: The Case of Research and Development*, 66 ACCT. REV. 818 (1991) (examining 438 companies from 1977 to 1987).

8 Eli Bartov, *The Timing of Asset Sales and Earnings Manipulation*, 68 ACCT. REV. 840 (1993).

9 William J. Bruns & Kenneth A. Merchant, *The Dangerous Morality of Managing Earnings*, 72 MGMT. ACCT. 22, 24 (1990).

10 Sugata Roychowdhury, *Earnings Management through Real Activities Manipulation*, 42 J. ACCT. & ECON. 335 (2006).

11 *See, e.g.*, MARGARET M. BLAIR & STEVEN M. H. WALLMAN, UNSEEN WEALTH: REPORT OF THE BROOKINGS TASK FORCE ON INTANGIBLES (2001); Lev, *supra* note 5, at 9.

12 Lev, *supra* note 5, at 99.

13 Cassell Bryan–Low, *Meeting Expectations Used to Draw Favor, Now It Invites Scrutiny*, WALL ST. J., Aug. 5, 2002, at C1.

14 Gerald J. Lobo & Jian Zhou, *Did Conservatism in Financial Reporting Increase After the Sarbanes-Oxley Act? Initial Evidence*, 20 ACCT. HORIZONS 57 (2006).

15 Kevin Koh, Dawn A. Matsumoto & Shivaram Rajgopal, *Meeting or Beating Analyst Expectations in the Post-scandals World: Changes in Stock Market Rewards and Managerial Actions*, 25 CONTEMP. ACCT. RES. 1067 (2008).

16 Dain C. Donelson et al., *Internal Control Weaknesses and Financial Reporting Fraud*, 35 AM. ACCT. ASSOC. 45, 69 (2017); *see also* Gretchen Morgenson, *Sarbanes-Oxley, Bemoaned as a Burden, Is an Investor's Ally*, N.Y. TIMES (Sept. 8, 2017).

17 FINANCIAL EXECUTIVES RESEARCH FOUNDATION, A SURVEY OF INVESTOR RELATIONS AND EARNINGS GUIDANCE 3 (2015).

18 Ken Brown, *Corporate Reform: The First Year: Wall Street Plays Numbers Game with Earnings, Despite Reforms*, WALL ST. J., July 22, 2003, at A1.

19 In the Matter of Hertz Global Holdings, Inc., Accounting and Auditing Enforcement Release No. 4012, Order Instituting Cease-and-Desist Proceedings ¶ 2 (Dec. 31, 2018).

20 Daniel A. Cohen, Aiyesha Day & Thomas Z. Lys, *Real and Accrual-Based Earnings Management in the Pre- and Post-Sarbanes-Oxley Periods*, 83 ACCT. REV. 757 (2008).

21 John R. Graham, Campbell R. Harvey & Shiva Rajgopal, *The Economic Implications of Corporate Financial Reporting*, 40 J. ACCT. & ECON. 3, 5 (2005).

22 *Id.* at 32–5.

23 *Id.* at 35.

24 H. David Sherman & S. David Young, *Where Financial Reporting Still Falls Short*, 94 HARV. BUS. REV. 76 (2016).

25 HALL OF HISTORY FOUNDATION, A CENTURY OF PROGRESS: THE GENERAL ELECTRIC STORY 1876–1978 102 (vol. 4) (1981).

26 JOHN WINTHROP HAMMOND, MEN AND VOLTS: THE STORY OF GENERAL ELECTRIC 180 (1941).

27 JOHN T. BRODERICK, FORTY YEARS WITH GENERAL ELECTRIC 15, 27 (1929); PAUL ISRAEL, EDISON: A LIFE OF INVENTION 336 (1998).

28 THOMAS F. O'BOYLE, AT ANY COST: JACK WELCH, GENERAL ELECTRIC, AND THE PURSUIT OF PROFIT 23 (1998).

29 Hall of History Foundation, *supra* note 25, at 47 (vol. 1).

30 ALFRED D. CHANDLER, THE VISIBLE HAND: THE MANAGERIAL REVOLUTION IN AMERICAN BUSINESS 426 (1977).

31 Tom Nicholas, VC: An American History 59 (2019).

32 Hammond, *supra* note 26, at 389–92.

33 Broderick, *supra* note 27, at 42.

34 Hall of History Foundation, *supra* note 25, at 3 (vol. 4).

35 William E. Rothschild, The Secret to GE's Success 128–29 (2007).

36 Hall of History Foundation, *supra* note 25, at 102 (vol. 4).

37 Broderick, *supra* note 27, at 156–57.

38 Hall of History Foundation, *supra* note 25, at 23 (vol. 4).

39 *Id.* at 28.

40 Elmer C. Bratt, Business Forecasting 280 (1958).

41 *Id.*

42 Bratt, *supra* note 40, at 281.

43 John Thackray, *GE's Planned Prognosis*, Mgmt. Today 66, 66 (Aug. 1978).

44 *Id.* at 67.

45 *Id.* at 69.

46 William E. Rothschild, The Secret to GE's Success 172 (2007).

47 John Herling, The Great Price Conspiracy: The Story of the Antitrust Violations in the Electrical Industry 244 (1962). The company's top management denied knowledge of the conspiracy. *See* Brian Cheffins, The Public Company Transformed 28 (2019).

48 Hammond, *supra* note 26, at 340–43.

49 *Id.* at 383.

50 *Id.* at 387.

51 Thackray, *supra* note 43, at 67.

52 O'Boyle, *supra* note 28, at 68.

53 Noel M. Tichy & Stratford Sherman, Control Your Destiny or Someone Else Will: Lessons in Mastering Change – the Principles Jack Welch Is Using to Revolutionize General Electric 7 (1993).

54 O'Boyle, *supra* note 28, at 33, 121.

55 Randall Smith, Stephen Lipin & Amal Kumar Naj, *Managing Profits: How General Electric Damps Fluctuations in Its Earnings – It Offsets One-Time Gains with Write-Offs, Times Asset Purchases and Sales – Accounting for RCA Deal*, Wall St. J., Nov. 3, 1994, at A1.

56 Complaint, Sec. & Exch. Comm'n v. General Electric Company ¶ 1 (D. Conn. Aug. 4, 2009).

57 Jon Birger, *Glowing Numbers: Investors Know That General Electric Posts Great Earnings. How It Happens Is More of a Mystery – And It Isn't Always Pretty*, Money Mag., Nov. 1, 2000.

58 Smith et al., *supra* note 55.

59 Baruch Lev, *Corporate Earnings: Facts and Fiction*, 17 J. Econ. Persp. 27, 30–1 (2003).

60 Lev, *supra* note 5, at 99.

61 O'Boyle, *supra* note 28, at 40.

62 *See, e.g.*, Birger, *supra* note 57.

63 Chill v. General Electric Co., 101 F.3d 263, 270 (2d Cir. 1996).

64 Jeff Immelt, Hot Seat: What I Learned Leading a Great American Company 229 (2021).

65 William E. Rothschild, The Secret to GE's Success 22–3 (2007).

66 *See, e.g.*, Thomas A. Stewart, *Growth as a Process*, 84 Harv. Bus. Rev. 60, 62 (2006).

67 Cheffins, *supra* note 47, at 30.

68 Gryta & Mann, *supra* note 4, at 54.

69 Geoff Colvin, Katie Benner & Dorie Burke, *GE Under Siege*, Fortune, Oct. 27, 2008, at 84.

70 Consolidated Class Action Complaint, *In re* General Electric Co. Sec. Litig., Complaint, Civ. No. 09-CIV-1951 ¶ 9 (Oct. 2, 2009).

71 *Id.* ¶ 13.

72 *In re* General Electric Co. Sec. Litig., 857 F. Supp.2d 367 (S.D.N.Y. 2012).

73 Broderick, *supra* note 27, at 31.

74 2017 General Electric Annual Report, at 1.

75 Birger, *supra* note 57.

76 *See, e.g.*, Makor Issues & Rights Ltd. v. Tellabs Inc., 513 F.3d 702, 710 (7th Cir. 2008) (noting that if fraud had been revealed, "investors would have discovered that the stock was more volatile than they thought, and risk-averse investors (who predominate) do not like volatility and so, unless it can be diversified away, demand compensation in the form of a lower price; consequently the stock might not recover to its previous level").

77 *See, e.g.*, Mary E. Barth, John A. Elliott & Mark W. Finn, *Market Rewards Associated with Patterns of Increasing Earnings*, 37 J. Acct. Res. 387 (1999).

78 *See, e.g.*, Greebel v. FTP Software, Inc., 194 F.3d 185, 202 (1st Cir. 1999); W. Palm Beach Firefighters' Pension Fund v. Conagra Brands, Inc., 495 F. Supp. 3d 622, 640 (N.D. Ill. 2020).

79 *See, e.g.*, Garfield v. NDC Health Corp., 466 F.3d 1255, 1262 (11th Cir. 2006).

80 Complaint, Sec. & Exch. Comm'n v. Bristol-Myers Squibb Co. ¶ 1 (D. N.J. Aug. 4. 2004). In one such case, a district court dismissed a Rule 10b-5 class action based on the same conduct. *See In re* Bristol-Myers Squibb Sec. Litig., 312 F. Supp.2d 549 (S.D.N.Y. 2004).

81 Gryta & Mann, *supra* note 4, at 52.

82 Complaint, Sec. & Exch. Comm'n v. General Electric Company ¶ 1 (D. Conn. Aug. 4, 2009).

83 Harry Markopolos, General Electric, A Bigger Fraud Than Enron (2019).

84 General Electric Co., Order Instituting Cease-And-Desist Proceedings, Securities Act of 1934 Release No. 90620 (Dec. 9, 2020).

85 *Id.* ¶ 6.

86 *Id.* ¶ 11.

87 This was not the first time the SEC asserted that deferred monetization was deceptive. Indeed, its complaint against Xerox cited a similar practice, though the allegation was not the centerpiece of the SEC's case.

88 Sjunde AP-Fonden v. General Electric Co., No. 17:CV-8457, 2021 WL 311003, at *3 (S.D.N.Y. Jan. 29, 2021).

89 In the Matter of General Electric Company, Order Instituting Cease-And-Desist Proceedings, Securities Act of 1934 Release No. 90620 ¶ 28 (Dec. 9, 2020).

90 In the Matter of Under Armour, Inc., Order Instituting Cease-and-Desist Proceedings Pursuant to Section 8A of the Securities Act of 1933 and Section 21C of the Securities Exchange Act of 1934, Making Findings, and Imposing a Cease-and-Desist Order, at fn.2 (May 3, 2021).

91 *Id.* ¶ 4.

CHAPTER 8

1 134 S. Ct. 2398 (2014).

2 *See* Stuart Banner, Anglo-American Securities Regulation: Cultural and Political Roots, 1690–1860 257 (1998); Paul G. Mahoney, Wasting a Crisis: Why Securities Regulation Fails (2015).

3 Robert Z. Aliber & Charles P. Kindleberger, Manias, Panics, and Crashes (2015) (7th ed.).

4 Roberta Romano, *The Sarbanes–Oxley Act and the Making of Quack Corporate Governance*, 114 Yale L.J. 1521, 1528 (2005).

5 Stephen M. Bainbridge, *Dodd–Frank: Quack Federal Corporate Governance Round II*, 95 Minn. L. Rev. 1779 (2011).
   Much of the resistance to Sarbanes–Oxley and Dodd–Frank reflects a discomfort with regulating corporate governance through federal law. For a view that federalization of corporate governance is desirable, see Marc I. Steinberg, The Federalization of Corporate Governance (2018).

6 Malcolm S. Salter, Innovation Corrupted: The Origins and Legacy of Enron's Collapse 189 (2003).

7 Enron 2000 Annual Report at 29.

8 Dennis R. Beresford, Nicholas deB. Katzenbach & C. B. Rogers, Jr., Report of the Investigation by the Special Investigative Committee of the Board of Directors of WorldCom, Inc. 223 (March 31, 2003).

9 Public Company Accounting Reform and Investor Protection Act of 2002, 107th Cong., 2d Sess., S. Rep. No. 107–205, at 31 (2002).

10 Management's Report on Internal Control Over Financial Reporting and Certification of Disclosure in Exchange Act Periodic Reports, Securities Act Release No. 8238, 68 Fed. Reg. 36,636, 36,657 (June 18, 2003).

11 Peter Iliev, *The Effect of SOX Section 404: Costs, Earnings Quality, and Stock Prices*, 34 J. Fin. 1163, 1166 (2010).

12 Gerald F. Davis, The Vanishing American Corporation: Navigating the Hazards of a New Economy 98 (2016).

13 John C. Coates IV, *The Goals and Promise of the Sarbanes-Oxley Act*, 21 J. Econ. Persp. 91, 107 (2007).

14 Keith Kawashima, *15 Years of SOX: A Look at Compliance Costs and More*, Law360, Aug. 4, 2017, https://www.law360.com/articles/950085/15-years-of-sox-a-look-at-compliance-costs-and-more.

15 Stephen J. Choi, Jessica Erickson & A. C. Pritchard, *Piling On? An Empirical Study of Parallel Derivative Suits*, 14 J. Emp. Legal Stud. 653 (2017).

16 John C. Coffee, Jr., *Reforming the Securities Class Action: An Essay on Deterrence and Its Implementation*, 106 COLUM. L. REV. 1534, 1536 (2006); *but see* James J. Park, *Shareholder Compensation as Dividend*, 108 MICH. L. REV. 323 (2009).

17 *In re* Enron Corp. Sec. Litig., First Amended Consolidated Complaint, Civil Action No. H-01-3624 ¶ 2 (May 14, 2003).

18 511 U.S. 164 (1994).

19 Regents of the University of California v. Credit Suisse First Boston (USA), Inc., 482 F.3d 372, 384 (5th Cir. 2007).

20 Stoneridge Inv. Part., LLC v. Scientific-Atlanta, Inc., 552 U.S. 148 (2008).

21 552 U.S. at 164.

22 133 S. Ct. 1184 (2013).

23 *Id.* at 1208.

24 Halliburton Co. v. Erica John Fund, Inc., 134 S. Ct. 2398 (2014).

25 *Id.* at 2410 (quoting Basic v. Levinson, 485 U.S. 223, 247 (1988)).

26 *See* James J. Park, *Halliburton and the Integrity of the Public Corporation*, 10 DUKE J. CONST. L. & PUB. POL'Y 71 (2015).

27 These statistics are based on my review of case descriptions from the ISS Securities Class Actions Services database.

28 *In re* Ford Motor Co. Sec. Litig., 381 F.3d 563, 570 (6th Cir. 2004).

29 Metzler Invest. GMBH v. Corinthian Colleges, Inc., 540 F.3d 1049, 1070 (9th Cir. 2008).

30 *See* Donald C. Langevoort, *Disasters and Disclosures: Securities Fraud Liability in the Shadow of a Corporate Catastrophe*, 107 GEO. L.J. 967 (2019).

31 Complaint, Sec. & Exch. Comm'n v. BP p.l.c., Case 2:12-cv-02774 (E.D. La. Nov. 15, 2012).

32 *In re* BP p.l.c. Sec. Litig., 843 F. Supp.2d 712, 775 (S.D. Tex. 2012); *see also In re* BHP Billiton Ltd. Sec. Litig., 276 F. Supp.3d 65 (S.D.N.Y. 2017) (finding statements relating to safety of collapsed dam were actionable given company's knowledge of problems with the dam).

33 *See* Complaint, Sec. & Exch. Comm'n v. Volkswagen (N.D. Cal. Mar. 14, 2019).

34 *In re* Volkswagen "Clean Diesel" Marketing, Sales Practices, and Products Liability Litig., MDL No. 2672 CRB, Order Granting in Part and Denying in Part Volkswagen's Motion to Dismiss (Aug. 20, 2020).

35 *See* Complaint, Sec. & Exch. Comm'n v. Facebook, Inc., 3:19-cv-04241 (N.D. Cal. July 19, 2019); *see also In re* Equifax Inc. Sec. Litig., 357 F. Supp.3d 1189 (N.D. Ga. 2019) (denying dismissal of complaint arising out of data breach that alleged credit reporting company touted security system as "advanced" when it was outdated).

36 Facebook won dismissal of a securities class action alleging that the company made misleading statements about its privacy policies for failure to adequately allege loss causation. *In re* Facebook Inc. Sec. Litig., 405 F. Supp.3d 809 (N.D. Cal. 2019).

37 *See, e.g.*, Retail Wholesale & Dept. Store Union Local 338 Retire. Fund v. Hewlett-Packard Co., 845 F.3d 1268 (9th Cir. 2017); Const. Laborers Pension for S. Cal. v. CBS Corp., 433 F. Supp.3d 515 (S.D.N.Y. 2020).

38 *In re* Signet Jewelers Ltd. Sec. Litig., 389 F. Supp.3d 221, 231 (S.D.N.Y. 2019).

39 *See, e.g.*, Amalgamated Clothing and Textile Workers Union v. J. P. Stevens & Co., Inc., 475 F. Supp. 328, 332 (S.D.N.Y. 1979) (observing that "it is simply contrary to human

nature" to make such disclosure); Ralph C. Ferrara, Richard M. Starr & Marc I. Steinberg, *Disclosure of Information Bearing on Management Integrity and Competency*, 76 Nw. U. L. Rev. 555, 590 (1981) ("Although antisocial, unlawful or unethical company policies may have a significant bearing on the integrity and competency of management, courts generally have been reluctant to require disclosure of such practices absent an adjudicated illegality, a pending claim, or an instance of self-dealing").

40 *See* James J. Park, *Reassessing the Distinction between Corporate and Securities Law*, 64 UCLA L. Rev. 116 (2017).

41 Donald Langevoort argues that these cases will often depend on whether there was active as opposed to passive concealment of a serious risk. Langevoort, *supra* note 30, at 971.

42 Homer Kripke, The SEC and Corporate Disclosure: Regulation in Search of Purpose (1979); *see also* Roberta Romano, *Empowering Investors: A Market Approach to Securities Regulation*, 107 Yale L.J. 2359, 2379 (1998).

43 Jamie Dimon & Warren E. Buffett, *Short-Termism Is Harming the Economy: Public Companies Should Reduce or Eliminate the Practice of Estimating Quarterly Earnings*, Wall St. J., June 6, 2018.

44 *See, e.g.*, James J. Park, *Do the Securities Law Promote Short-Termism?*, 10 UC Irvine L. Rev. 991 (2020).

45 This discussion is contained in the Management Discussion & Analysis section. 17 C.F.R. § 229.303(a)(3)(ii)

46 *See* Thomas Gryta et al., *Analysts Steered to "Surprises,"* Wall St. J., Aug. 5, 2016, at A1.

47 *See* 17 C.F.R. § 243.100.

48 Francis A. Lees, Public Disclosure of Corporate Earnings Forecasts vii (1981).

49 Phillis S. McGrath and Francis J. Walsh, Disclosure of Financial Forecasts to Security Analysts and the Public 11 (1973).

50 Henry B. Reiling & John C. Burton, *Financial Statements: Signposts as Well as Milestones*, Harv. Bus. Rev. 45, 53 (1972).

51 William S. Gray III, *Proposal for Systematic Disclosure of Corporate Forecasts*, Fin. Anal. J. 64, 69 (1973).

52 Commission's Findings on Disclosure of Projections of Future Economic Performance by Issuers of Publicly Traded Securities, Securities Act Release No. 33,5362, 1973 WL 149257 (Mar. 19, 1973).

53 The Commission on Auditors' Responsibilities, Report, Conclusions, and Recommendations 32 (1978).

54 *Id.*

55 *See, e.g.*, American Institute of Certified Public Accountants. Financial Forecasts and Projections Task Force, guide for prospective financial information with conforming changes as of May 1, 2006; audit and accounting guide (2006).

56 The SEC has used such a strategy in the past. *See* James J. Park, *Two Trends in the Regulation of the Public Corporation*, 7 Ohio State Entrep. Bus. L. J. 429 (2012).

57 This body of law has been described as "muddled." Donald C. Langevoort & G. Mitu Gulati, *The Muddled Duty to Disclose under Rule 10b-5*, 57 Vand. L. Rev. 1639 (2004).

58 *In re* Burlington Coat Factory Sec. Litig., 114 F.3d 1410, 1432-33 (3d Cir. 1997).

59 Stransky v. Cummins Engine Co., 51 F.3d 1329, 1333 (7th Cir. 1995).

60 *In re* Time Warner Inc. Sec. Litig., 9 F.3d 259, 267 (2d Cir. 1993).

61 The SEC has fewer incentives to over-deter securities fraud. *See, e.g.,* Amanda Rose, *Reforming Securities Litigation Reform: Restructuring the Relationship between Public and Private Enforcement of Rule 10b-5,* 108 COLUM. L. REV. 1301 (2008).

62 The duty to update should extend not only to financial projections but forward-looking statements about significant products. To the extent that companies issue predictions about products that they are developing, they should issue updates if managers have specific knowledge that such predictions have become misleading. *See, e.g., In re* International Business Machines Corp. Sec. Litig., 163 F.3d 102, 110 (2d Cir. 1998) (noting that "there is no duty to update vague statements of optimism or expressions of opinion").

63 *See, e.g.,* James J. Park, *Assessing the Materiality of Financial Misstatements,* 34 J. CORP. L. 513 (2009).

64 SAS No. 99 (Dec. 15, 2002).

65 *See, e.g.,* Amanda Rose, *The Reasonable Investor of Federal Securities Law,* 43 J. CORP. L. 77, 89–93 (2017).

66 *See, e.g.,* David A. Hoffman, *The "Duty" to Be a Rational Shareholder,* 90 MINN. L. REV. 537 (2006); Stefan J. Padfield, *Is Puffery Material to Investors? Maybe We Should Ask Them,* 10 U. PA. J. BUS. & EMPLOY. L. 339 (2008).

67 *See, e.g.,* Zohar Goshen & Gideon Parchomovsky, *The Essential Role of Securities Regulation,* 55 DUKE L.J. 711 (2006).

68 For an example of how state securities regulators have supplemented federal enforcement, see James J. Park & Howard H. Park, *Regulation by Selective Enforcement: The SEC and Initial Coin Offerings,* 61 WASH. U. J. L. & POL'Y 99 (2020).

69 Stephen M. Bainbridge & G. Mitu Gulati, *How Do Judges Maximize? (The Same Way Everybody Else Does – Boundedly): Rules of Thumb in Securities Fraud Opinions,* 51 EMORY L.J. 83 (2002).

70 *See* James J. Park, *Rule 10b-5 and the Rise of the Unjust Enrichment Principle,* 60 DUKE L.J. 345 (2010).

71 *See, e.g.,* United States v. Goyal, 629 F.3d 912, 919 (9th Cir. 2010) (noting "desire to meet ... revenue targets ... is simply evidence of ... doing his job diligently"); *In re* Microstrategy, Inc. Sec. Litig., 115 F. Supp.2d 620, 647 (E.D. Va. 2010) (finding that general motivation "to engage in fraud to meet expectations as to its performance" was "relevant" but "adds little by itself to the scienter calculus"); *In re* Trex Co., Inc. Sec. Litig., 212 F. Supp.2d 596, 607 (W.D. Va. 2002) (observing that "[e]very corporate officer wants to meet analysts' expectations").

Index

CPSIA information can be obtained
at www.ICGtesting.com
Printed in the USA
LVHW051734210722
723953LV00010B/406

9 781108 940412